# Fundamentals of
# Accounting 9E

## Working Papers
## Chapters 17–24

**Claudia Bienias Gilbertson, CPA**
Teaching Professor
North Hennepin Community College
Brooklyn Park, Minnesota

**Mark W. Lehman, CPA**
Associate Professor
School of Accountancy
Mississippi State University
Starkville, Mississippi

SOUTH-WESTERN
CENGAGE Learning

Australia • Brazil • Japan • Korea • Mexico • Singapore • Spain • United Kingdom • United States

# SOUTH-WESTERN
## CENGAGE Learning™

**Fundamentals of Accounting: Working Papers, Chapters 17–24, Ninth Edition**
**Claudia Bienias Gilbertson, Mark W. Lehman**

VP/Editorial Director: Jack W. Calhoun

VP/Editor-in-Chief: Karen Schmohe

VP/Director of Marketing: Bill Hendee

Sr. Marketing Manager: Courtney Schulz

Marketing Coordinator: Gretchen Wildauer

Marketing Communications Manager: Terron Sanders

Production Manager: Patricia Matthews Boies

Content Project Manager: Diane Bowdler

Consulting Editor: Bill Lee

Special Consultants: Sara Wilson, Robert E. First

Manufacturing Buyer: Kevin Kluck

Production Service: LEAP Publishing Services, Inc.

Compositor: GGS Book Services

Cover Designer: Nick & Diane Gliebe, Design Matters

Cover Images: Getty Images, Inc.

For product information and technology assistance, contact us at
**Cengage Learning Customer & Sales Support, 1-800-354-9706**

For permission to use material from this text or product,
submit all requests online at **www.cengage.com/permissions**
Further permissions questions can be emailed to
**permissionrequest@cengage.com**

ISBN-13: 978-0-538-44833-8

ISBN-10: 0-538-44833-4

**South-Western**
5191 Natorp Boulevard
Mason, OH 45040
USA

Cengage Learning is a leading provider of customized learning solutions with office locations around the globe, including Singapore, the United Kingdom, Australia, Mexico, Brazil, and Japan. Locate your local office at **www.cengage.com/global**

Cengage Learning products are represented in Canada by Nelson Education, Ltd.

To learn more about South-Western, visit **www.cengage.com/southwestern**

Purchase any of our products at your local college store or at our preferred online store **www.ichapters.com**

Printed in the United States of America
2 3 4 5 6    14 13 12 11 10

ED046

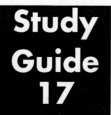

# Study Guide 17

| Name | Perfect Score | Your Score |
|---|---|---|
| Analyzing Uncollectible Accts. Expense and Allowance for Uncollectible Accts. | 20 Pts. | |
| Analyzing Uncollectible Accounts Receivable | 8 Pts. | |
| Journalizing Adjustments for Uncollectible Accounts Expense | 12 Pts. | |
| **Total** | 40 Pts. | |

## Part One—Analyzing Uncollectible Accounts Expense and Allowance for Uncollectible Accounts

**Directions:** Place a *T* for True or an *F* for False in the Answers column to show whether each of the following statements is true or false.

**Answers**

1. A business generally sells on account to encourage sales. (p. 514) — 1. __T__

2. Accounts receivable that cannot be collected are called uncollectible accounts. (p. 514) — 2. __T__

3. Allowing customers to buy now and pay later is an ineffective method for increasing sales. (p. 515) — 3. __F__

4. The amount of accounts receivable that is uncollectible is an expense. (p. 515) — 4. __T__

5. A business usually knows at the end of the fiscal year which customer accounts will become uncollectible. (p. 515) — 5. __F__

6. Allowance for Uncollectible Accounts is a contra account to its related asset account, Accounts Receivable. (p. 515) — 6. __T__

7. Recording an estimate of uncollectible accounts to the contra asset account and the expense account is an application of the Matching Expenses with Revenue accounting concept. (p. 515) — 7. __T__

8. The percentage of total sales on account method of estimating uncollectible accounts expense assumes that a portion of every sales dollar will become uncollectible. (p. 516) — 8. __T__

9. The adjusting entry for Uncollectible Accounts Expense is recorded at the beginning of every accounting period. (p. 516) — 9. __F__ ?

10. The adjustment for uncollectible accounts is planned on the work sheet and then recorded in the general journal. (p. 517) — 10. __T__

11. The adjusting entry for uncollectible accounts does not affect the balance of the accounts receivable account. (p. 517) — 11. __F__

12. When an adjusting entry for uncollectible accounts expense is recorded, Allowance for Uncollectible Accounts is credited. (p. 517) — 12. __T__

13. The debit balance of the Uncollectible Accounts Expense account is the estimated uncollectible accounts from sales on account during the next fiscal year. (p. 517) — 13. __F__

14. When an account is determined to be uncollectible, a journal entry is made to cancel the uncollectible account. (p. 519) — 14. __T__

15. Canceling the balance of a customer account because the customer does not pay is called writing off an account. (p. 519) — 15. __T__

16. Allowance for Uncollectible Accounts is debited to write off a customer account. (p. 519) — 16. __T__

17. Accounts Receivable is debited to write off a customer account. (p. 519) — 17. __F__

18. When a customer account is written off under the allowance method, book value of accounts receivable decreases. (p. 519) — 18. __F__

19. Two journal entries are recorded for the collection of a written-off accounts receivable. (p. 521) — 19. __T__

20. When a previously written-off account is collected, Accounts Receivable is both debited and credited for the amount collected. (p. 523) — 20. __T__

## Part Two—Analyzing Uncollectible Accounts Receivable

**Directions:** For each of the following items, select the choice that best completes the statement. Print the letter identifying your choice in the Answers column.

1.  The loss from an uncollectible account is (A) a liability (B) an expense (C) an asset (D) a reduction in revenue (p. 515)

    1. _B_

2.  When the percentage of total sales on account method is used, the estimated uncollectible accounts expense is calculated by (A) multiplying total sales on account times the percentage (B) dividing total sales on account by the percentage (C) multiplying total sales times the percentage (D) dividing total sales by the percentage (p. 515)

    2. _A_

3.  An Allowance for Uncollectible Accounts balance in the Trial Balance Credit column of a work sheet means (A) there are no uncollectible accounts (B) the estimate has not yet been recorded (C) previous fiscal period estimates have not yet been identified as uncollectible (D) equity has been maintained (p. 516)

    3. _C_

4.  At the end of a fiscal period, the account debited to show the estimated amount of uncollectible accounts is (A) Accounts Receivable (B) Cash (C) Uncollectible Accounts Expense (D) Allowance for Uncollectible Accounts (p. 516)

    4. _C_

5.  At the end of a fiscal period, the account credited to show the estimated amount of uncollectible accounts is (A) Cash (B) Uncollectible Accounts Expense (C) Accounts Receivable (D) Allowance for Uncollectible Accounts (p. 516)

    5. _D_

6.  When the allowance account in the Trial Balance column of a work sheet has a credit balance, the amount of the adjustment is (A) deducted from the trial balance amount (B) not recorded (C) estimated (D) added to the Trial Balance amount (p. 516)

    6. _____

7.  When the account Allowance for Uncollectible Accounts is used, a customer past-due account is written off as uncollectible by (A) debiting Uncollectible Accounts Expense and crediting Accounts Receivable and the customer account (B) debiting Allowance for Uncollectible Accounts and crediting Accounts Receivable and the customer account (C) debiting Accounts Receivable and the customer account and crediting Allowance for Uncollectible Accounts (D) none of these (pp. 519, 520)

    7. _A_

8.  To reopen an account previously written off, (A) one general journal entry is recorded (B) two general journal entries are recorded (C) no journal entries are recorded (D) one general journal entry and one cash receipts journal entry are recorded (p. 521)

    8. _B_

## Part Three—Journalizing Adjustments for Uncollectible Accounts Expense

**Directions:** In Answers Column 1, print the abbreviation for the journal in which each transaction is to be recorded. In Answers Columns 2 and 3, print the letters identifying the accounts to be debited and credited for each transaction.

G—General journal   CR—Cash receipts journal

| Account Titles | Transactions | Answers | | |
|---|---|---|---|---|
| | | Journal | Debit | Credit |
| A. Accounts Receivable | 1–2–3. Recorded adjusting entry for uncollectible accounts expense. (p. 517) | 1. _G_ | 2. _E_ | 3. _B_ |
| B. Allowance for Uncollectible Accounts | 4–5–6. Wrote off Annie's Place past-due account as uncollectible. (pp. 519–520) | 4. _G_ | 5. _B_ | 6. _A_ |
| C. Cash | Received cash in full payment of Annie's Place account, previously written off as uncollectible. | | | |
| D. Annie's Place | 7–8–9. First entry. (p. 521) | 7. _G_ | 8. _A_ | 9. _B_ |
| E. Uncollectible Accounts Expense | 10–11–12. Second entry. (pp. 522, 523) | 10. _CR_ | 11. _C_ | 12. _A_ |

# Participating in Class Discussions

Have you ever been in a class in which one student monopolized the entire class period? Have you ever been in a class in which one student never said a word? Most of us have. Neither the student who speaks too much nor the student who speaks too little is participating in classroom discussion correctly.

## No Time for Shallow Opinions

Some students believe that a class discussion is just a time to express personal opinions. However, class discussions should not be occasions where you speak without thinking. No one is interested in hearing a shallow comment or a long discourse that has not been planned.

## Prepare Properly

If you know that a discussion will be held during a certain class period, do everything possible to prepare yourself properly. Read the text assignment thoroughly first. Then read any related material that you can find, particularly items in current newspapers and magazines.

Organize your thoughts so that you will be able to express your ideas in a logical manner. When you have thought through the topic thoroughly, you should practice what you will say a time or two. You should then be able to make a convincing argument during the discussion.

## Waiting to Speak

In a class discussion, you should spend a great deal more time listening than speaking. If there are 20 students participating in a large discussion group, you probably should speak a total of no more than one or two minutes. If there are only a few students in the group, you may speak a total of five or six minutes.

As you wait your turn to speak, listen carefully to the opinions of others. Many students do not really pay attention to the ideas of others; they simply wait for the other person to stop speaking so that they may begin. If all ideas are not given serious consideration by all participants in the class, little is gained from a class discussion. There is an old saying that bears repeating: "Keep your ears open; you might learn something."

## Presenting Your Ideas

When you have the opportunity to speak in class, present your ideas in a logical order, draw your conclusions, and then stop. You may clarify and illustrate points, but little is gained by simple repetition. Later, if you have other ideas that support your viewpoint, you may express them, following the same guidelines. If you gain the floor just to repeat the points you made previously, you will bore the members of the class, and you will actually hurt your chance of convincing them that you are right.

## A Group Effort

Class discussions are excellent ways to learn material. Everyone can share knowledge, and everyone will profit. Prepare properly, listen attentively, and make your points logically. Your opinion will be valued, and you will learn.

Name _____  Date _____  Class _____

## 17-1 WORK TOGETHER, p. 518

**Estimating and journalizing entries for uncollectible accounts expense**

**1.**

Velson Company

Work Sheet

For Year Ended December 31, 20 – –

| | | | 1 | 2 | 3 | 4 |
|---|---|---|---|---|---|---|
| | ACCOUNT TITLE | | TRIAL BALANCE | | ADJUSTMENTS | |
| | | | DEBIT | CREDIT | DEBIT | CREDIT |
| 6 | Accounts Receivable | | 867 680 00 | | | |
| 7 | Allowance for Uncollectible Accounts | | | 853 00 | | (e) 6 456 — |
| 47 | Uncollectible Accounts Expense | | | | (e) 6 456 — | |

**2., 3.**

GENERAL JOURNAL                                        PAGE 13

| | DATE | ACCOUNT TITLE | DOC. NO. | POST. REF. | DEBIT | CREDIT | |
|---|---|---|---|---|---|---|---|
| | | Adjusting Entries | | | | | |
| 3 | 12/3 31 | Uncollectible Accts Expense | | | 6456 — | | 3 |
| 4 | | Allow. for Uncollectible Accts | | | | 6456 — | 4 |
| 5 | | | | | | | 5 |

**3.**                        **GENERAL LEDGER**

ACCOUNT Accounts Receivable                              ACCOUNT NO. 1130

| DATE | ITEM | POST. REF. | DEBIT | CREDIT | BALANCE | |
|---|---|---|---|---|---|---|
| | | | | | DEBIT | CREDIT |
| 20-- Dec. 31 | Balance | ✔ | | | 867 680 00 | |

ACCOUNT Allowance for Uncollectible Accounts              ACCOUNT NO. 1135

| DATE | ITEM | POST. REF. | DEBIT | CREDIT | BALANCE | |
|---|---|---|---|---|---|---|
| | | | | | DEBIT | CREDIT |
| 20-- Dec. 31 | Balance | ✔ | | | | 853 00 |
| | | G13 | | 6456 | | 7309 — |

ACCOUNT Uncollectible Accounts Expense                    ACCOUNT NO. 6165

| DATE | ITEM | POST. REF. | DEBIT | CREDIT | BALANCE | |
|---|---|---|---|---|---|---|
| | | | | | DEBIT | CREDIT |
| 31 | | G13 | 6456 — | | 6456 — | |

**Estimating and journalizing entries for uncollectible accounts expense**

**1.**

McCaffery Industries

Work Sheet

For Year Ended December 31, 20 – –

| | ACCOUNT TITLE | TRIAL BALANCE | | ADJUSTMENTS | |
|---|---|---|---|---|---|
| | | DEBIT | CREDIT | DEBIT | CREDIT |
| 6 | Accounts Receivable | 131 8 4 8 50 | | | |
| 7 | Allowance for Uncollectible Accounts | | 2 1 6 00 | | (e) 6 1 9 2 20 |
| 47 | Uncollectible Accounts Expense | | | (e) 6 1 9 2 20 | |

**2., 3.**

GENERAL JOURNAL                    PAGE 26

| | DATE | ACCOUNT TITLE | DOC. NO. | POST. REF. | DEBIT | CREDIT | |
|---|---|---|---|---|---|---|---|
| | | Adjusting Entries | | | | | |
| 3 | 31 | Uncollect. Accounts Expense | | | 6 1 9 2 20 | | 3 |
| 4 | | Allowance for Uncollect Accts | | | | 6 1 9 2 20 | 4 |
| 5 | | | | | | | 5 |

**3.**          **GENERAL LEDGER**

ACCOUNT Accounts Receivable                    ACCOUNT NO. 1130

| DATE | ITEM | POST. REF. | DEBIT | CREDIT | BALANCE DEBIT | BALANCE CREDIT |
|---|---|---|---|---|---|---|
| 20-- Dec. 31 | Balance | ✓ | | | 131 8 4 8 50 | |

ACCOUNT Allowance for Uncollectible Accounts                    ACCOUNT NO. 1135

| DATE | ITEM | POST. REF. | DEBIT | CREDIT | BALANCE DEBIT | BALANCE CREDIT |
|---|---|---|---|---|---|---|
| 20-- Dec. 31 | Balance | ✓ | | | | 2 1 6 00 |
| | | | | 6 1 9 2 20 | | 6 4 08 20 |

ACCOUNT Uncollectible Accounts Expense                    ACCOUNT NO. 6165

| DATE | ITEM | POST. REF. | DEBIT | CREDIT | BALANCE DEBIT | BALANCE CREDIT |
|---|---|---|---|---|---|---|
| | | | 6 1 9 2 20 | | 6 1 9 2 20 | |

## 17-2 WORK TOGETHER, p. 524

**Recording entries related to uncollectible accounts receivable**

**1., 2., 3.**

### GENERAL JOURNAL
PAGE 15

| DATE | ACCOUNT TITLE | DOC. NO. | POST. REF. | DEBIT | CREDIT |
|------|---------------|----------|-----------|-------|--------|
| 20-- Nov. 2 | Allowance for Uncollect. Accts. | M345 | 1130 | 849 — | |
| | Accts. Rec./Davidson Corp. | | 1125/110 | | 849 — |
| 3 | Allowance for Uncollect. Accts. | M347 | 1130 | 2488 — | |
| | Acct. Rec./JGF Industries | | 1125/120 | | 2488 — |
| 4 | Allowance for Uncollect. Accts. | M351 | 1130 | 609 — | |
| | Acct. Rec./Sansing Co. | | 1125/140 | | 609 — |
| 14 | Acct. Rec./Lynchburg Co. | M358 | 1125/130 | 1548 — | |
| | Allow. for Uncollect. Accts. | | 1130 | | 1548 — |
| 29 | Acct. Rec./JGF Industries | M361 | 1125/120 | 2488 — | |
| | Allow. for Uncollect. Accts. | | 1130 | | 2488 — |

**1., 2.**

### CASH RECEIPTS JOURNAL
PAGE 24

| DATE | ACCOUNT TITLE | DOC. NO. | POST. REF. | GENERAL DEBIT | GENERAL CREDIT | ACCOUNTS RECEIVABLE CREDIT | SALES CREDIT | SALES TAX PAYABLE CREDIT | SALES DISCOUNT DEBIT | CASH DEBIT |
|------|---------------|----------|-----------|---------------|----------------|----------------------------|--------------|--------------------------|----------------------|------------|
| 14 | Lynchburg Co. | R415 | | | | 1548 — | | | | 1546 — |
| 29 | JGF Industries | R429 | | | | 2488 — | | | | 2488 — |

**2.**

## ACCOUNTS RECEIVABLE LEDGER

CUSTOMER Davidson Corp.                                                                                              CUSTOMER NO. 110

| DATE | | ITEM | POST. REF. | DEBIT | CREDIT | DEBIT BALANCE |
|---|---|---|---|---|---|---|
| 20-- Jan. | 9 | | S1 | 849 00 | | 849 00 |
| Nov | 2 | written off | G15 | | 849 — | — |
| | | | | | | |
| | | | | | | |

CUSTOMER JGF Industries                                                                                              CUSTOMER NO. 120

| DATE | | ITEM | POST. REF. | DEBIT | CREDIT | DEBIT BALANCE |
|---|---|---|---|---|---|---|
| 20-- Mar. | 13 | | S4 | 2488 00 | | 2488 00 |
| Nov | 3 | written off | G15 | | 2488 — | — |
| | 29 | Reopen acct | G15 | 2488 — | | 2488 — |
| | 29 | | CR24 | | 2488 | — |
| | | | | | | |

CUSTOMER Lynchburg Co.                                                                                              CUSTOMER NO. 130

| DATE | | ITEM | POST. REF. | DEBIT | CREDIT | DEBIT BALANCE |
|---|---|---|---|---|---|---|
| 20-- Apr. | 23 | Written off | G5 | | 1548 00 | — |
| Nov | 14 | Reopen acct | G15 | 1548 | | 1548 — |
| | 14 | | CR24 | | 1548 | — |
| | | | | | | |
| | | | | | | |

CUSTOMER Sansing Co.                                                                                              CUSTOMER NO. 140

| DATE | | ITEM | POST. REF. | DEBIT | CREDIT | DEBIT BALANCE |
|---|---|---|---|---|---|---|
| 20-- Jan. | 22 | | S2 | 609 00 | | 609 00 |
| Nov | 4 | written off | G15 | | 609 — | — |
| | | | | | | |
| | | | | | | |

## 17-2 WORK TOGETHER (concluded)

3.

### GENERAL LEDGER

ACCOUNT Accounts Receivable                 ACCOUNT NO. 1125

| DATE | | ITEM | POST. REF. | DEBIT | CREDIT | BALANCE DEBIT | BALANCE CREDIT |
|---|---|---|---|---|---|---|---|
| 20-- Nov. | 1 | Balance | ✔ | | | 50 148 00 | |
| | 2 | | G15 | | 849 — | 49 299 — | |
| | 3 | | G15 | | 2488 — | 46 811 — | |
| | 4 | | G15 | | 609 — | 46 202 — | |
| | 14 | | G15 | 1548 — | | 47 750 — | |
| | 29 | | G15 | 2488 | | 50 238 — | |

ACCOUNT Allowance for Uncollectible Accounts          ACCOUNT NO. 1130

| DATE | | ITEM | POST. REF. | DEBIT | CREDIT | BALANCE DEBIT | BALANCE CREDIT |
|---|---|---|---|---|---|---|---|
| 20-- Nov. | 1 | Balance | ✔ | | | | 4 958 00 |
| | 2 | | G15 | 849 — | | 849 — | 4109 — |
| | 3 | | G15 | 2488 — | | 2488 — | 1621 — |
| | 4 | | G15 | 609 — | | 609 — | 1012 — |
| | 14 | | G15 | | 1548 — | | 2560 — |

**Recording entries related to uncollectible accounts receivable**

**1., 2., 3.**

GENERAL JOURNAL

PAGE 11

| DATE | ACCOUNT TITLE | DOC. NO. | POST. REF. | DEBIT | CREDIT | |
|------|---------------|----------|-----------|-------|--------|---|
| | | | | | | 1 |
| | | | | | | 2 |
| | | | | | | 3 |
| | | | | | | 4 |
| | | | | | | 5 |
| | | | | | | 6 |
| | | | | | | 7 |
| | | | | | | 8 |
| | | | | | | 9 |
| | | | | | | 10 |
| | | | | | | 11 |
| | | | | | | 12 |

**1., 2.**

CASH RECEIPTS JOURNAL

PAGE 15

| | | | | 1 | 2 | 3 | 4 | 5 | 6 | 7 | |
|---|---|---|---|---|---|---|---|---|---|---|---|
| DATE | ACCOUNT TITLE | DOC. NO. | POST. REF. | GENERAL DEBIT | GENERAL CREDIT | ACCOUNTS RECEIVABLE CREDIT | SALES CREDIT | SALES TAX PAYABLE CREDIT | SALES DISCOUNT DEBIT | CASH DEBIT | |
| | | | | | | | | | | | 1 |
| | | | | | | | | | | | 2 |
| | | | | | | | | | | | 3 |
| | | | | | | | | | | | 4 |
| | | | | | | | | | | | 5 |

**17-2** **ON YOUR OWN (continued)**

2.

## ACCOUNTS RECEIVABLE LEDGER

CUSTOMER Peter Ewing                                      CUSTOMER NO. 110

| DATE | ITEM | POST. REF. | DEBIT | CREDIT | DEBIT BALANCE |
|------|------|-----------|-------|--------|---------------|
| 20-- Jan. 9 | | S1 | 6 1 2 00 | | 6 1 2 00 |
| | | | | | |
| | | | | | |

CUSTOMER Tim Haley                                      CUSTOMER NO. 120

| DATE | ITEM | POST. REF. | DEBIT | CREDIT | DEBIT BALANCE |
|------|------|-----------|-------|--------|---------------|
| 20-- Mar. 13 | | S3 | 2 3 8 00 | | 2 3 8 00 |
| | | | | | |
| | | | | | |

CUSTOMER Mike Novak                                      CUSTOMER NO. 130

| DATE | ITEM | POST. REF. | DEBIT | CREDIT | DEBIT BALANCE |
|------|------|-----------|-------|--------|---------------|
| 20-- Apr. 6 | Written off | G4 | | 8 5 3 00 | — |
| | | | | | |
| | | | | | |

CUSTOMER Angela White                                      CUSTOMER NO. 140

| DATE | ITEM | POST. REF | DEBIT | CREDIT | DEBIT BALANCE |
|------|------|-----------|-------|--------|---------------|
| 20-- Feb. 23 | | S2 | 1 5 9 00 | | 1 5 9 00 |
| | | | | | |
| | | | | | |
| | | | | | |

**3.**

**GENERAL LEDGER**

account  Accounts Receivable                                                                                              account no. 1125

| DATE | | ITEM | POST. REF. | DEBIT | CREDIT | BALANCE | |
|---|---|---|---|---|---|---|---|
| | | | | | | DEBIT | CREDIT |
| 20-- Oct. | 1 | Balance | ✔ | | | 50 1 4 8 00 | |
| | | | | | | | |
| | | | | | | | |
| | | | | | | | |
| | | | | | | | |
| | | | | | | | |
| | | | | | | | |

account  Allowance for Uncollectible Accounts                                                                            account no. 1130

| DATE | | ITEM | POST. REF. | DEBIT | CREDIT | BALANCE | |
|---|---|---|---|---|---|---|---|
| | | | | | | DEBIT | CREDIT |
| 20-- Oct. | 1 | Balance | ✔ | | | | 3 4 5 8 00 |
| | | | | | | | |
| | | | | | | | |
| | | | | | | | |
| | | | | | | | |
| | | | | | | | |
| | | | | | | | |

## 17-1 APPLICATION PROBLEM, p. 526

**Estimating and journalizing entries for uncollectible accounts expense**

**1.**

Kellogg, Inc.

Work Sheet

For Year Ended December 31, 20 – –

| | ACCOUNT TITLE | TRIAL BALANCE DEBIT | TRIAL BALANCE CREDIT | ADJUSTMENTS DEBIT | ADJUSTMENTS CREDIT |
|---|---|---|---|---|---|
| | | 1 | 2 | 3 | 4 |
| 6 | Accounts Receivable | 125 84 8 33 | | | |
| 7 | Allowance for Uncollectible Accounts | | 5 3 4 00 | | |
| 47 | Uncollectible Accounts Expense | | | | |

**2., 3.**

GENERAL JOURNAL                                    PAGE 25

| | DATE | ACCOUNT TITLE | DOC. NO. | POST. REF. | DEBIT | CREDIT | |
|---|---|---|---|---|---|---|---|
| 3 | | | | | | | 3 |
| 4 | | | | | | | 4 |
| 5 | | | | | | | 5 |

**3.**                                    **GENERAL LEDGER**

ACCOUNT Accounts Receivable                                    ACCOUNT NO. 1125

| DATE | ITEM | POST. REF. | DEBIT | CREDIT | BALANCE DEBIT | BALANCE CREDIT |
|---|---|---|---|---|---|---|
| 20 – – Dec. 31 | Balance | ✔ | | | 125 84 8 33 | |

ACCOUNT Allowance for Uncollectible Accounts                                    ACCOUNT NO. 1130

| DATE | ITEM | POST. REF. | DEBIT | CREDIT | BALANCE DEBIT | BALANCE CREDIT |
|---|---|---|---|---|---|---|
| 20 – – Dec. 31 | Balance | ✔ | | | | 5 3 4 00 |

ACCOUNT Uncollectible Accounts Expense                                    ACCOUNT NO. 6165

| DATE | ITEM | POST. REF. | DEBIT | CREDIT | BALANCE DEBIT | BALANCE CREDIT |
|---|---|---|---|---|---|---|
| | | | | | | |

**Recording entries related to uncollectible accounts receivable**

**1., 2., 3.**

GENERAL JOURNAL

PAGE 14

| DATE | ACCOUNT TITLE | DOC. NO. | POST. REF. | DEBIT | CREDIT | |
|------|---------------|----------|-----------|-------|--------|---|
| | | | | | | 1 |
| | | | | | | 2 |
| | | | | | | 3 |
| | | | | | | 4 |
| | | | | | | 5 |
| | | | | | | 6 |
| | | | | | | 7 |
| | | | | | | 8 |
| | | | | | | 9 |
| | | | | | | 10 |
| | | | | | | 11 |
| | | | | | | 12 |

**1., 2.**

CASH RECEIPTS JOURNAL

PAGE 19

| | | | | 1 | 2 | 3 | 4 | 5 | 6 | 7 | |
|---|---|---|---|---|---|---|---|---|---|---|---|
| DATE | ACCOUNT TITLE | DOC. NO. | POST. REF. | GENERAL DEBIT | GENERAL CREDIT | ACCOUNTS RECEIVABLE CREDIT | SALES CREDIT | SALES TAX PAYABLE CREDIT | SALES DISCOUNT DEBIT | CASH DEBIT | |
| | | | | | | | | | | | 1 |
| | | | | | | | | | | | 2 |
| | | | | | | | | | | | 3 |
| | | | | | | | | | | | 4 |
| | | | | | | | | | | | 5 |

Name _____  Date _____  Class _____

## 17-2 APPLICATION PROBLEM (continued)

**2.**

### ACCOUNTS RECEIVABLE LEDGER

CUSTOMER Davis Industries     CUSTOMER NO. 110

| DATE | | ITEM | POST. REF. | DEBIT | CREDIT | DEBIT BALANCE |
|---|---|---|---|---|---|---|
| 20-- Feb. | 23 | Written off | G2 | | 1 8 5 00 | — |

CUSTOMER Jackson Company     CUSTOMER NO. 120

| DATE | | ITEM | POST. REF. | DEBIT | CREDIT | DEBIT BALANCE |
|---|---|---|---|---|---|---|
| 20-- Jan. | 4 | | S1 | 1 2 4 00 | | 1 2 4 00 |

CUSTOMER Lancing, Inc.     CUSTOMER NO. 130

| DATE | | ITEM | POST. REF. | DEBIT | CREDIT | DEBIT BALANCE |
|---|---|---|---|---|---|---|
| 20-- Apr. | 2 | | S7 | 2 1 5 00 | | 2 1 5 00 |

CUSTOMER Sanders Mfg.     CUSTOMER NO. 140

| DATE | | ITEM | POST. REF. | DEBIT | CREDIT | DEBIT BALANCE |
|---|---|---|---|---|---|---|
| 20-- Jan. | 23 | | S2 | 8 4 2 00 | | 8 4 2 00 |

3.

**GENERAL LEDGER**

account Accounts Receivable                                                                  account no. 1125

| DATE | | ITEM | POST. REF. | DEBIT | CREDIT | BALANCE | |
|------|--|------|-----------|-------|--------|---------|--|
| | | | | | | DEBIT | CREDIT |
| Sept. | 1 | Balance | ✔ | | | 23 4 8 4 00 | |
| | | | | | | | |
| | | | | | | | |
| | | | | | | | |
| | | | | | | | |
| | | | | | | | |

account Allowance for Uncollectible Accounts                                               account no. 1130

| DATE | | ITEM | POST. REF. | DEBIT | CREDIT | BALANCE | |
|------|--|------|-----------|-------|--------|---------|--|
| | | | | | | DEBIT | CREDIT |
| Sept. | 1 | Balance | ✔ | | | | 2 4 4 8 00 |
| | | | | | | | |
| | | | | | | | |
| | | | | | | | |
| | | | | | | | |
| | | | | | | | |

**17-3** **APPLICATION PROBLEM, p. 527**

**Recording entries related to uncollectible accounts receivable**

**1., 2., 3.**

GENERAL JOURNAL

PAGE 4

| DATE | ACCOUNT TITLE | DOC. NO. | POST. REF. | DEBIT | CREDIT |
|------|---------------|----------|------------|-------|--------|

**1., 2.**

CASH RECEIPTS JOURNAL

PAGE 2

| DATE | ACCOUNT TITLE | DOC. NO. | POST. REF. | GENERAL DEBIT | GENERAL CREDIT | ACCOUNTS RECEIVABLE CREDIT | SALES CREDIT | SALES TAX PAYABLE CREDIT | SALES DISCOUNT DEBIT | CASH DEBIT |
|------|---------------|----------|------------|---------------|----------------|----------------------------|--------------|--------------------------|----------------------|------------|

**2.**

## ACCOUNTS RECEIVABLE LEDGER

CUSTOMER Bearden Co.  CUSTOMER NO. 110

| DATE | | ITEM | POST. REF. | DEBIT | CREDIT | DEBIT BALANCE |
|---|---|---|---|---|---|---|
| 20-- Jan. | 3 | Written off | G1 | | 1 4 5 8 00 | — |
| | | | | | | |
| | | | | | | |

CUSTOMER Camden Enterprises  CUSTOMER NO. 120

| DATE | | ITEM | POST. REF. | DEBIT | CREDIT | DEBIT BALANCE |
|---|---|---|---|---|---|---|
| 20-- Jan. | 3 | Written off | G1 | | 1 7 8 4 00 | — |
| | | | | | | |
| | | | | | | |

CUSTOMER Hampton Industries  CUSTOMER NO. 130

| DATE | | ITEM | POST. REF. | DEBIT | CREDIT | DEBIT BALANCE |
|---|---|---|---|---|---|---|
| 20-- Jan. | 1 | Balance | ✔ | | | 2 5 8 4 00 |
| | | | | | | |
| | | | | | | |

CUSTOMER Rankin Co.  CUSTOMER NO. 140

| DATE | | ITEM | POST. REF. | DEBIT | CREDIT | DEBIT BALANCE |
|---|---|---|---|---|---|---|
| 20-- Jan. | 1 | Balance | ✔ | | | 9 4 8 00 |
| | | | | | | |
| | | | | | | |

CUSTOMER Wilmont Co.  CUSTOMER NO. 150

| DATE | | ITEM | POST. REF. | DEBIT | CREDIT | DEBIT BALANCE |
|---|---|---|---|---|---|---|
| 20-- Jan. | 1 | Balance | ✔ | | | 5 4 8 00 |
| | | | | | | |
| | | | | | | |

## 17-3 APPLICATION PROBLEM (concluded)

**3.**

### GENERAL LEDGER

ACCOUNT Accounts Receivable                                                                ACCOUNT NO. 1130

| DATE | | ITEM | POST. REF. | DEBIT | CREDIT | BALANCE | |
|---|---|---|---|---|---|---|---|
| | | | | | | DEBIT | CREDIT |
| Feb. | 1 | Balance | ✔ | | | 54 15 8 00 | |
| | | | | | | | |
| | | | | | | | |
| | | | | | | | |
| | | | | | | | |
| | | | | | | | |
| | | | | | | | |

ACCOUNT Allowance for Uncollectible Accounts                                              ACCOUNT NO. 1135

| DATE | | ITEM | POST. REF. | DEBIT | CREDIT | BALANCE | |
|---|---|---|---|---|---|---|---|
| | | | | | | DEBIT | CREDIT |
| Feb. | 1 | Balance | ✔ | | | | 2 5 1 4 00 |
| | | | | | | | |
| | | | | | | | |
| | | | | | | | |
| | | | | | | | |
| | | | | | | | |
| | | | | | | | |

**Recording entries for uncollectible accounts**

**1.**

GENERAL JOURNAL

PAGE 20

| | DATE | | ACCOUNT TITLE | DOC. NO. | POST. REF. | DEBIT | CREDIT | |
|---|---|---|---|---|---|---|---|---|
| 1 | | | | | | | | 1 |
| 2 | | | | | | | | 2 |
| 3 | | | | | | | | 3 |
| 4 | | | | | | | | 4 |
| 5 | | | | | | | | 5 |

**2.**

GENERAL JOURNAL

PAGE 22

| | DATE | | ACCOUNT TITLE | DOC. NO. | POST. REF. | DEBIT | CREDIT | |
|---|---|---|---|---|---|---|---|---|
| 1 | | | | | | | | 1 |
| 2 | | | | | | | | 2 |
| 3 | | | | | | | | 3 |
| 4 | | | | | | | | 4 |
| 5 | | | | | | | | 5 |
| 6 | | | | | | | | 6 |

**3.**

GENERAL JOURNAL

PAGE 24

| | DATE | | ACCOUNT TITLE | DOC. NO. | POST. REF. | DEBIT | CREDIT | |
|---|---|---|---|---|---|---|---|---|
| 1 | | | | | | | | 1 |
| 2 | | | | | | | | 2 |
| 3 | | | | | | | | 3 |
| 4 | | | | | | | | 4 |
| 5 | | | | | | | | 5 |
| 6 | | | | | | | | 6 |

**4.**

GENERAL JOURNAL

PAGE 26

| | DATE | | ACCOUNT TITLE | DOC. NO. | POST. REF. | DEBIT | CREDIT | |
|---|---|---|---|---|---|---|---|---|
| 1 | | | | | | | | 1 |
| 2 | | | | | | | | 2 |
| 3 | | | | | | | | 3 |
| 4 | | | | | | | | 4 |
| 5 | | | | | | | | 5 |

**17-4** **MASTERY PROBLEM (continued)**

**2.**

CASH RECEIPTS JOURNAL

PAGE 24

| DATE | ACCOUNT TITLE | DOC. NO. | POST. REF. | GENERAL DEBIT | GENERAL CREDIT | ACCOUNTS RECEIVABLE CREDIT | SALES CREDIT | SALES TAX PAYABLE CREDIT | SALES DISCOUNT DEBIT | CASH DEBIT |
|---|---|---|---|---|---|---|---|---|---|---|
| | | | | | | | | | | |

**3.**

CASH RECEIPTS JOURNAL

PAGE 26

| DATE | ACCOUNT TITLE | DOC. NO. | POST. REF. | GENERAL DEBIT | GENERAL CREDIT | ACCOUNTS RECEIVABLE CREDIT | SALES CREDIT | SALES TAX PAYABLE CREDIT | SALES DISCOUNT DEBIT | CASH DEBIT |
|---|---|---|---|---|---|---|---|---|---|---|
| | | | | | | | | | | |

**1., 2., 3.**

## ACCOUNTS RECEIVABLE LEDGER

CUSTOMER Baker Corp.   CUSTOMER NO. 110

| DATE | ITEM | POST. REF. | DEBIT | CREDIT | DEBIT BALANCE |
|---|---|---|---|---|---|
| 20-- Feb. 11 | | S4 | 8 1 5 00 | | 8 1 5 00 |
| | | | | | |
| | | | | | |

CUSTOMER Franklin, Inc.   CUSTOMER NO. 120

| DATE | ITEM | POST. REF. | DEBIT | CREDIT | DEBIT BALANCE |
|---|---|---|---|---|---|
| 20-- Mar. 15 | | S5 | 1 4 5 8 00 | | 1 4 5 8 00 |
| | | | | | |
| | | | | | |

CUSTOMER Gason Company   CUSTOMER NO. 130

| DATE | ITEM | POST. REF. | DEBIT | CREDIT | DEBIT BALANCE |
|---|---|---|---|---|---|
| 20-- Jan. 1 | Balance | ✔ | | | 9 4 8 00 |
| | | | | | |
| | | | | | |

CUSTOMER Keller Corporation   CUSTOMER NO. 140

| DATE | ITEM | POST. REF. | DEBIT | CREDIT | DEBIT BALANCE |
|---|---|---|---|---|---|
| 20-- Jan. 1 | Balance | ✔ | | | 6 4 8 25 |
| | | | | | |
| | | | | | |

CUSTOMER Pearson Industries   CUSTOMER NO. 150

| DATE | ITEM | POST. REF. | DEBIT | CREDIT | DEBIT BALANCE |
|---|---|---|---|---|---|
| 20-- Apr. 14 | Written off | G8 | | 2 5 1 80 | |
| | | | | | |
| | | | | | |

**17-4** **MASTERY PROBLEM (concluded)**

**1., 2., 3., 4.**

**GENERAL LEDGER**

account **Accounts Receivable**                                                                                        ACCOUNT NO. 1125

| DATE | | ITEM | POST. REF. | DEBIT | CREDIT | BALANCE | |
|---|---|---|---|---|---|---|---|
| | | | | | | DEBIT | CREDIT |
| 20-- Oct. | 1 | Balance | ✔ | | | 68 452 30 | |
| | | | | | | | |
| | | | | | | | |
| | | | | | | | |
| | | | | | | | |
| | | | | | | | |
| | | | | | | | |
| | | | | | | | |
| | | | | | | | |
| | | | | | | | |

account **Allowance for Uncollectible Accounts**                                                     ACCOUNT NO. 1130

| DATE | | ITEM | POST. REF. | DEBIT | CREDIT | BALANCE | |
|---|---|---|---|---|---|---|---|
| | | | | | | DEBIT | CREDIT |
| 20-- Oct. | 1 | Balance | ✔ | | | | 3 210 00 |
| | | | | | | | |
| | | | | | | | |
| | | | | | | | |
| | | | | | | | |
| | | | | | | | |
| | | | | | | | |
| | | | | | | | |
| | | | | | | | |
| | | | | | | | |

account **Uncollectible Accounts Expense**                                                          ACCOUNT NO. 6165

| DATE | ITEM | POST. REF. | DEBIT | CREDIT | BALANCE | |
|---|---|---|---|---|---|---|
| | | | | | DEBIT | CREDIT |
| | | | | | | |
| | | | | | | |

**Recording entries for uncollectible accounts**

| Name | Perfect Score | Your Score |
|---|---|---|
| Identifying Accounting Terms | 7 Pts. | |
| Analyzing Plant Asset Transactions | 14 Pts. | |
| Analyzing Plant Assets and Depreciation | 10 Pts. | |
| **Total** | 31 Pts. | |

## Part One—Identifying Accounting Terms

**Directions:** Select the one term in Column I that best fits each definition in Column II. Print the letter identifying your choice in the Answers column.

| Column I | Column II | Answers |
|---|---|---|
| **A.** assessed value | **1.** Land and anything attached to the land. (p. 536) | 1. _G_ |
| **B.** declining-balance method of depreciation | **2.** All property not classified as real property. (p. 536) | 2. _E_ |
| **C.** gain on plant assets | **3.** The value of an asset determined by tax authorities for the purpose of calculating taxes. (p. 536) | 3. _A_ |
| **D.** loss on plant assets | **4.** An accounting form on which a business records information about each plant asset. (p. 542) | 4. _F_ |
| **E.** personal property | **5.** Revenue that results when a plant asset is sold for more than book value. (p. 548) | 5. _C_ |
| **F.** plant asset record | **6.** The loss that results when a plant asset is sold for less than book value. (p. 549) | 6. _D_ |
| **G.** real property | **7.** Multiplying the book value by a constant depreciation rate at the end of each fiscal period. (p. 551) | 7. _B_ |

## Part Two—Analyzing Plant Asset Transactions

**Directions:** Analyze each of the following transactions into debit and credit parts. Print the letter identifying your choices in the proper Answers column.

### Account Titles

A. Accumulated Depreciation—Office Equipment

B. Accumulated Depreciation—Store Equipment

C. Cash

D. Depreciation Expense—Office Equipment

E. Depreciation Expense—Store Equipment

F. Gain on Plant Assets

G. Office Equipment

H. Loss on Plant Assets

I. Property Tax Expense

J. Store Equipment

### Transactions

**1–2.** Paid cash for new display case. (p. 535)

**3–4.** Paid cash for property taxes. (p. 536)

**5–6.** Recorded annual store equipment depreciation. (p. 543)

**7–8.** Received cash from sale of display case for book value. (p. 546)

**9–10.** Recorded a partial year's depreciation on a cash register to be sold. (p. 547)

**11–12.** Received cash from sale of cash register for more than book value. (p. 548)

**13–14.** Received cash from sale of a computer for less than book value. (p. 549)

### Answers

| | Debit | | Credit |
|---|---|---|---|
| 1. | J | 2. | C |
| 3. | I | 4. | C |
| 5. | E | 6. | B |
| 7. | C | 8. | |
| 9. | | 10. | |
| 11. | C | 12. | |
| 13. | C | 14. | |

## Part Three—Analyzing Plant Assets and Depreciation

**Directions:** For each of the following items, select the choice that best completes the statement. Print the letter identifying your choice in the Answers column.

**Answers**

1. Recording a plant asset at its original cost is an application of the concept (A) Going Concern (B) Matching Expenses with Revenue (C) Objective Evidence (D) Historical Cost (p. 535)

   1. _D_

2. The smallest unit of time used to calculate depreciation is (A) one month (B) half a year (C) one year (D) none of these (p. 539)

   2. _A_

3. The annual depreciation for a plant asset with original cost of $1,000.00, estimated salvage value of $100.00, and estimated useful life of 10 years, using the straight-line method, is (A) $100.00 (B) $1,000.00 (C) $900.00 (D) $90.00 (p. 539)

   3. _D_

4. The accumulated depreciation account should show (A) total depreciation for plant assets since the business was formed (B) total depreciation for plant assets still in use (C) only total depreciation expense for plant assets for the current year (D) next year's estimated depreciation for plant assets (p. 540)

   4. _B_

5. When a plant asset is sold for the asset's book value, (A) cash received plus accumulated depreciation equals original cost (B) cash received plus salvage value equals original cost (C) cash received plus accumulated depreciation plus salvage value equals original cost (D) none of these (p. 546)

   5. _A_

6. When a plant asset is sold for more than the asset's book value, (A) cash received plus accumulated depreciation plus gain on disposal equals original cost plus gain on disposal (B) cash received plus accumulated depreciation equals original cost plus gain on disposal (C) cash received plus accumulated depreciation plus loss on disposal equals original cost (D) cash received plus accumulated depreciation equals original cost plus loss on disposal (p. 548)

   6. _____ B

7. When a plant asset is sold for less than the asset's book value, (A) cash received plus accumulated depreciation plus gain on disposal equals original cost (B) cash received plus accumulated depreciation plus loss on disposal equals original cost (C) cash received plus accumulated depreciation equals original cost plus gain on disposal (D) cash received plus accumulated depreciation equals original cost plus loss on disposal (p. 549)

   7. _____

8. Charging more depreciation expense in the early years is an application of the concept of (A) Matching Expenses with Revenue (B) Realization of Revenue (C) Adequate Disclosure (D) Historical Cost (p. 551)

   8. _A_

9. The declining-balance method of depreciation is calculated by (A) charging an equal amount of depreciation each year (B) subtracting the annual depreciation expense from the book value (C) multiplying the book value by a constant depreciation rate at the end of each fiscal period (D) none of the above (p. 551)

   9. _C_

10. The double declining-balance method of depreciation (A) records a greater depreciation expense in the early years of an asset's useful life (B) records a lesser depreciation expense in the early years of an asset's useful life (C) slows down the recording of depreciation in the early years of an asset's useful life (D) accelerates the recording of depreciation in the later years of an asset's useful life (p. 553)

    10. _A_

# 18-1   WORK TOGETHER, p. 537

## Journalizing buying plant assets and paying property tax

**1., 2.**

### CASH PAYMENTS JOURNAL
PAGE 1

| | DATE 2010 | ACCOUNT TITLE | CK. NO. | POST. REF. | GENERAL DEBIT | GENERAL CREDIT | ACCOUNTS PAYABLE DEBIT | PURCHASES DISCOUNT CREDIT | CASH CREDIT |
|---|---|---|---|---|---|---|---|---|---|
| 1 | Jan. 3 | Store equipment / paint mixer | C142 | | 560 | | | | 560 |
| 2 | 5 | office equipment / office chair | C145 | | 400 | | | | 400 |
| 3 | Feb. 26 | property taxes expense | C182 | | 2400 | | | | 2400 |
| 4 | July 2 | office equipment / filing cabinet | C216 | | 260 | | | | 265 |

*(margin calculations)*
```
 15480          9730
   400           500
 15880         10230
   260
 16140
```

## GENERAL LEDGER

**2.**

ACCOUNT **Office Equipment**     ACCOUNT NO. 1205

| DATE | ITEM | POST. REF. | DEBIT | CREDIT | BALANCE DEBIT | BALANCE CREDIT |
|---|---|---|---|---|---|---|
| 2010 Jan. 1 | Balance | ✓ | | | 1548000 | |
| 5 | | CP1 | 400 | | 15880 | |
| July 2 | | CP1 | 260 | | 16140 | |

ACCOUNT **Store Equipment**     ACCOUNT NO. 1215

| DATE | ITEM | POST. REF. | DEBIT | CREDIT | BALANCE DEBIT | BALANCE CREDIT |
|---|---|---|---|---|---|---|
| 2010 Jan. 1 | Balance | ✓ | | | 973000 | |
| 3 | | CP1 | 500 | | 10230 | |

ACCOUNT **Property Tax Expense**     ACCOUNT NO. 6145

| DATE | ITEM | POST. REF. | DEBIT | CREDIT | BALANCE DEBIT | BALANCE CREDIT |
|---|---|---|---|---|---|---|
| 2010 Feb. 26 | | CP1 | 2400 | | 2400 | |

# Journalizing buying plant assets and paying property tax

## 1., 2.

### CASH PAYMENTS JOURNAL

PAGE 1

| | DATE | ACCOUNT TITLE | CK. NO. | POST. REF. | GENERAL DEBIT | GENERAL CREDIT | ACCOUNTS PAYABLE DEBIT | PURCHASES DISCOUNT CREDIT | CASH CREDIT | |
|---|---|---|---|---|---|---|---|---|---|---|
| 1 | Jan. 2 2010 | office equip / printer | C215 | | 1800 | | | | 1800 | 1 |
| 2 | 5 | stre equip / tile cutter | C216 | | 520 | | | | 520 | 2 |
| 3 | Feb 24 | property tax expense | C232 | | 1800 | | | | 1800 | 3 |
| 4 | Mar 13 | store equip / dolly | C253 | | 325 | | | | 325 | 4 |

## GENERAL LEDGER

### 2.

ACCOUNT Office Equipment   ACCOUNT NO. 1205

| DATE | ITEM | POST. REF. | DEBIT | CREDIT | BALANCE DEBIT | BALANCE CREDIT |
|---|---|---|---|---|---|---|
| Jan. 1 2010 | Balance | ✓ | | | 15 480 00 | |
| 2 | | CP1 | 1800 | | 17280 - | |

15480
1800
17280

ACCOUNT Store Equipment   ACCOUNT NO. 1215

| DATE | ITEM | POST. REF. | DEBIT | CREDIT | BALANCE DEBIT | BALANCE CREDIT |
|---|---|---|---|---|---|---|
| Jan. 1 2010 | Balance | ✓ | | | 9 730 00 | |
| 5 | | CP1 | 520 | | 10250 - | |
| Mar 13 | | CP1 | 325 | | 10 575 - | |

9730
520
10250
325
10575

ACCOUNT Property Tax Expense   ACCOUNT NO. 6145

| DATE | ITEM | POST. REF. | DEBIT | CREDIT | BALANCE DEBIT | BALANCE CREDIT |
|---|---|---|---|---|---|---|
| Feb 24 | | | 1800 | | 1800 | |

**18-2** **WORK TOGETHER, p. 541**

**Calculating depreciation**

Plant asset: _____    Original cost: _____

Depreciation method: _____    Estimated salvage value: _____

Estimated useful life: _____

Date bought: _____

| Year | Beginning Book Value | Annual Depreciation | Accumulated Depreciation | Ending Book Value |
|---|---|---|---|---|
| | | | | |
| | | | | |
| | | | | |
| | | | | |
| | | | | |
| | | | | |
| | | | | |
| | | | | |

Plant asset: _____    Original cost: _____

Depreciation method: _____    Estimated salvage value: _____

Estimated useful life: _____

Date bought: _____

| Year | Beginning Book Value | Annual Depreciation | Accumulated Depreciation | Ending Book Value |
|---|---|---|---|---|
| | | | | |
| | | | | |
| | | | | |
| | | | | |
| | | | | |
| | | | | |
| | | | | |
| | | | | |

**Calculating depreciation**

Plant asset: _____    Original cost: _____
Depreciation method: _____    Estimated salvage value: _____
Estimated useful life: _____
Date bought: _____

| Year | Beginning Book Value | Annual Depreciation | Accumulated Depreciation | Ending Book Value |
|------|---------------------|---------------------|--------------------------|-------------------|
|      |                     |                     |                          |                   |
|      |                     |                     |                          |                   |
|      |                     |                     |                          |                   |
|      |                     |                     |                          |                   |
|      |                     |                     |                          |                   |
|      |                     |                     |                          |                   |
|      |                     |                     |                          |                   |
|      |                     |                     |                          |                   |

Plant asset: _____    Original cost: _____
Depreciation method: _____    Estimated salvage value: _____
Estimated useful life: _____
Date bought: _____

| Year | Beginning Book Value | Annual Depreciation | Accumulated Depreciation | Ending Book Value |
|------|---------------------|---------------------|--------------------------|-------------------|
|      |                     |                     |                          |                   |
|      |                     |                     |                          |                   |
|      |                     |                     |                          |                   |
|      |                     |                     |                          |                   |
|      |                     |                     |                          |                   |
|      |                     |                     |                          |                   |
|      |                     |                     |                          |                   |
|      |                     |                     |                          |                   |

## 18-3 WORK TOGETHER, p. 545

**Journalizing depreciation**

**1.**

PLANT ASSET RECORD No. ____          General Ledger Account No. _____

Description _____          General Ledger Account _____

Date                    Serial
Bought _____    Number _____    Original Cost _____

                        Estimated
Estimated               Salvage                 Depreciation
Useful Life _____   Value _____          Method _____

Disposed of:        Discarded _____    Sold _____    Traded _____
Date _____                Disposal Amount _____

| Year | Annual Depreciation Expense | Accumulated Depreciation | Ending Book Value |
|------|------------------------------|---------------------------|-------------------|
|      |                              |                           |                   |
|      |                              |                           |                   |
|      |                              |                           |                   |
|      |                              |                           |                   |
|      |                              |                           |                   |

PLANT ASSET RECORD No. ____          General Ledger Account No. _____

Description _____          General Ledger Account _____

Date                    Serial
Bought _____    Number _____    Original Cost _____

                        Estimated
Estimated               Salvage                 Depreciation
Useful Life _____   Value _____          Method _____

Disposed of:        Discarded _____    Sold _____    Traded _____
Date _____                Disposal Amount _____

| Year | Annual Depreciation Expense | Accumulated Depreciation | Ending Book Value |
|------|------------------------------|---------------------------|-------------------|
|      |                              |                           |                   |
|      |                              |                           |                   |
|      |                              |                           |                   |
|      |                              |                           |                   |
|      |                              |                           |                   |

**2.**

Fairbrother, Inc.

Work Sheet

For Year Ended December 31, 20 – –

| | ACCOUNT TITLE | TRIAL BALANCE | | ADJUSTMENTS | |
|---|---|---|---|---|---|
| | | DEBIT | CREDIT | DEBIT | CREDIT |
| 10 | Office Equipment | 28 4 8 5 25 | | | |
| 11 | Accumulated Depreciation—Office Equipment | | 14 5 2 2 00 | | |
| 38 | Depreciation Expense—Office Equipment | | | | |

GENERAL JOURNAL

PAGE 20

| | DATE | ACCOUNT TITLE | DOC. NO. | POST. REF. | DEBIT | CREDIT | |
|---|---|---|---|---|---|---|---|
| 1 | | | | | | | 1 |
| 2 | | | | | | | 2 |
| 3 | | | | | | | 3 |
| 4 | | | | | | | 4 |
| 5 | | | | | | | 5 |

**GENERAL LEDGER**

ACCOUNT Office Equipment                                   ACCOUNT NO. 1205

| DATE | ITEM | POST. REF. | DEBIT | CREDIT | BALANCE DEBIT | BALANCE CREDIT |
|---|---|---|---|---|---|---|
| 20 – – Dec. 31 | Balance | ✔ | | | 28 4 8 5 25 | |

ACCOUNT Accumulated Depreciation—Office Equipment          ACCOUNT NO. 1210

| DATE | ITEM | POST. REF. | DEBIT | CREDIT | BALANCE DEBIT | BALANCE CREDIT |
|---|---|---|---|---|---|---|
| 20 – – Dec. 31 | Balance | ✔ | | | | 14 5 2 2 00 |

ACCOUNT Depreciation Expense—Office Equipment              ACCOUNT NO. 6120

| DATE | ITEM | POST. REF. | DEBIT | CREDIT | BALANCE DEBIT | BALANCE CREDIT |
|---|---|---|---|---|---|---|
| | | | | | | |

Name _____ Date _____ Class _____

## 18-3 ON YOUR OWN, p. 545

**Journalizing depreciation**

**1.**

PLANT ASSET RECORD No. ____    General Ledger Account No. _____

Description _____    General Ledger Account _____

Date
Bought _____    Serial Number _____    Original Cost _____

Estimated
Useful Life _____    Estimated Salvage Value _____    Depreciation Method _____

Disposed of:    Discarded _____    Sold _____    Traded _____
Date _____    Disposal Amount _____

| Year | Annual Depreciation Expense | Accumulated Depreciation | Ending Book Value |
|---|---|---|---|
|  |  |  |  |
|  |  |  |  |
|  |  |  |  |
|  |  |  |  |
|  |  |  |  |

PLANT ASSET RECORD No. ____    General Ledger Account No. _____

Description _____    General Ledger Account _____

Date
Bought _____    Serial Number _____    Original Cost _____

Estimated
Useful Life _____    Estimated Salvage Value _____    Depreciation Method _____

Disposed of:    Discarded _____    Sold _____    Traded _____
Date _____    Disposal Amount _____

| Year | Annual Depreciation Expense | Accumulated Depreciation | Ending Book Value |
|---|---|---|---|
|  |  |  |  |
|  |  |  |  |
|  |  |  |  |
|  |  |  |  |
|  |  |  |  |

2.

Wrench Co.

Work Sheet

For Year Ended December 31, 20 – –

| | ACCOUNT TITLE | TRIAL BALANCE | | ADJUSTMENTS | |
|---|---|---|---|---|---|
| | | DEBIT | CREDIT | DEBIT | CREDIT |
| 12 | Store Equipment | 35 8 4 8 22 | | | |
| 13 | Accumulated Depreciation—Store Equipment | | 24 1 1 8 00 | | |
| 39 | Depreciation Expense—Store Equipment | | | | |

GENERAL JOURNAL                                        PAGE 18

| | DATE | ACCOUNT TITLE | DOC. NO. | POST. REF. | DEBIT | CREDIT | |
|---|---|---|---|---|---|---|---|
| 1 | | | | | | | 1 |
| 2 | | | | | | | 2 |
| 3 | | | | | | | 3 |
| 4 | | | | | | | 4 |

**GENERAL LEDGER**

ACCOUNT Store Equipment                                        ACCOUNT NO. 1215

| DATE | ITEM | POST. REF. | DEBIT | CREDIT | BALANCE DEBIT | BALANCE CREDIT |
|---|---|---|---|---|---|---|
| 20– – Dec. 31 | Balance | ✔ | | | 35 8 4 8 22 | |

ACCOUNT Accumulated Depreciation—Store Equipment                ACCOUNT NO. 1220

| DATE | ITEM | POST. REF. | DEBIT | CREDIT | BALANCE DEBIT | BALANCE CREDIT |
|---|---|---|---|---|---|---|
| 20– – Dec. 31 | Balance | ✔ | | | | 24 1 1 8 00 |

ACCOUNT Depreciation Expense—Store Equipment                    ACCOUNT NO. 6125

| DATE | ITEM | POST. REF. | DEBIT | CREDIT | BALANCE DEBIT | BALANCE CREDIT |
|---|---|---|---|---|---|---|
| | | | | | | |

**18-4** **WORK TOGETHER, p. 550**

**Recording the disposal of plant assets**

**1.**

GENERAL JOURNAL

PAGE 11

| DATE | ACCOUNT TITLE | DOC. NO. | POST. REF. | DEBIT | CREDIT | |
|------|---------------|----------|------------|-------|--------|---|
| | | | | | | 1 |
| | | | | | | 2 |
| | | | | | | 3 |
| | | | | | | 4 |
| | | | | | | 5 |

**2.**

CASH RECEIPTS JOURNAL

PAGE 1

| | | | | 1 GENERAL | 2 GENERAL | 3 ACCOUNTS RECEIVABLE CREDIT | 4 SALES CREDIT | 5 SALES TAX PAYABLE CREDIT | 6 SALES DISCOUNT DEBIT | 7 CASH DEBIT | |
|---|---|---|---|---|---|---|---|---|---|---|---|
| DATE | ACCOUNT TITLE | DOC. NO. | POST. REF. | DEBIT | CREDIT | | | | | | |
| | | | | | | | | | | | 1 |
| | | | | | | | | | | | 2 |
| | | | | | | | | | | | 3 |
| | | | | | | | | | | | 4 |
| | | | | | | | | | | | 5 |
| | | | | | | | | | | | 6 |
| | | | | | | | | | | | 7 |

**Recording the disposal of plant assets**

**1.**

GENERAL JOURNAL

PAGE 10

| DATE | ACCOUNT TITLE | DOC. NO. | POST. REF. | DEBIT | CREDIT | |
|------|---------------|----------|-----------|-------|--------|---|
| | | | | | | 1 |
| | | | | | | 2 |
| | | | | | | 3 |
| | | | | | | 4 |
| | | | | | | 5 |

**2.**

CASH RECEIPTS JOURNAL

PAGE 8

| DATE | ACCOUNT TITLE | DOC. NO. | POST. REF. | GENERAL DEBIT | GENERAL CREDIT | ACCOUNTS RECEIVABLE CREDIT | SALES CREDIT | SALES TAX PAYABLE CREDIT | SALES DISCOUNT DEBIT | CASH DEBIT | |
|------|---------------|----------|-----------|---------------|----------------|----------------------------|--------------|--------------------------|----------------------|------------|---|
| | | | | | | | | | | | 1 |
| | | | | | | | | | | | 2 |
| | | | | | | | | | | | 3 |
| | | | | | | | | | | | 4 |
| | | | | | | | | | | | 5 |
| | | | | | | | | | | | 6 |

## 18-5 WORK TOGETHER, p. 554

### Calculating depreciation using the double declining-balance depreciation method

Plant asset: _____          Original cost: _____
Depreciation method: _____   Estimated salvage value: _____
                                             Estimated useful life: _____

| Year | Beginning Book Value | Declining-Balance Rate | Annual Depreciation | Ending Book Value |
|---|---|---|---|---|
| | | | | |
| | | | | |
| | | | | |
| | | | | |
| | | | | |
| | | | | |
| | | | | |
| | | | | |

Plant asset: _____          Original cost: _____
Depreciation method: _____   Estimated salvage value: _____
                                             Estimated useful life: _____

| Year | Beginning Book Value | Declining-Balance Rate | Annual Depreciation | Ending Book Value |
|---|---|---|---|---|
| | | | | |
| | | | | |
| | | | | |
| | | | | |
| | | | | |
| | | | | |
| | | | | |
| | | | | |

Plant asset: _____          Original cost: _____
Depreciation method: _____   Estimated salvage value: _____
                                             Estimated useful life: _____

| Year | Beginning Book Value | Declining-Balance Rate | Annual Depreciation | Ending Book Value |
|---|---|---|---|---|
| | | | | |
| | | | | |
| | | | | |
| | | | | |
| | | | | |
| | | | | |
| | | | | |
| | | | | |

**Calculating depreciation using the double declining-balance depreciation method**

Plant asset: _____    Original cost: _____

Depreciation method: _____    Estimated salvage value _____

                                         Estimated useful life: _____

| Year | Beginning Book Value | Declining-Balance Rate | Annual Depreciation | Ending Book Value |
|------|---------------------|-----------------------|---------------------|-------------------|
|      |                     |                       |                     |                   |
|      |                     |                       |                     |                   |
|      |                     |                       |                     |                   |
|      |                     |                       |                     |                   |
|      |                     |                       |                     |                   |
|      |                     |                       |                     |                   |
|      |                     |                       |                     |                   |
|      |                     |                       |                     |                   |

Plant asset: _____    Original cost: _____

Depreciation method: _____    Estimated salvage value: _____

                                         Estimated useful life: _____

| Year | Beginning Book Value | Declining-Balance Rate | Annual Depreciation | Ending Book Value |
|------|---------------------|-----------------------|---------------------|-------------------|
|      |                     |                       |                     |                   |
|      |                     |                       |                     |                   |
|      |                     |                       |                     |                   |
|      |                     |                       |                     |                   |
|      |                     |                       |                     |                   |
|      |                     |                       |                     |                   |
|      |                     |                       |                     |                   |
|      |                     |                       |                     |                   |

Plant asset: _____    Original cost: _____

Depreciation method: _____    Estimated salvage value: _____

                                         Estimated useful life    _____

| Year | Beginning Book Value | Declining-Balance Rate | Annual Depreciation | Ending Book Value |
|------|---------------------|-----------------------|---------------------|-------------------|
|      |                     |                       |                     |                   |
|      |                     |                       |                     |                   |
|      |                     |                       |                     |                   |
|      |                     |                       |                     |                   |
|      |                     |                       |                     |                   |
|      |                     |                       |                     |                   |
|      |                     |                       |                     |                   |
|      |                     |                       |                     |                   |

          

Name _____ Date _____ Class _____

# 18-1 APPLICATION PROBLEM, p. 556

## Journalizing buying plant assets and paying property tax

### 1., 2.

CASH PAYMENTS JOURNAL

PAGE 1

| DATE | ACCOUNT TITLE | CK. NO. | POST. REF. | GENERAL DEBIT | GENERAL CREDIT | ACCOUNTS PAYABLE DEBIT | PURCHASES DISCOUNT CREDIT | CASH CREDIT |
|------|--------------|---------|-----------|---------------|----------------|------------------------|---------------------------|-------------|
| | | | | | | | | 1 |
| | | | | | | | | 2 |
| | | | | | | | | 3 |
| | | | | | | | | 4 |
| | | | | | | | | 5 |

### 2.

## GENERAL LEDGER

ACCOUNT Office Equipment     ACCOUNT NO. 1205

| DATE | ITEM | POST. REF. | DEBIT | CREDIT | BALANCE DEBIT | BALANCE CREDIT |
|------|------|-----------|-------|--------|---------------|----------------|
| 20-- Jan. 1 | Balance | ✓ | | | 15 848 50 | |

ACCOUNT Store Equipment     ACCOUNT NO. 1215

| DATE | ITEM | POST. REF. | DEBIT | CREDIT | BALANCE DEBIT | BALANCE CREDIT |
|------|------|-----------|-------|--------|---------------|----------------|
| 20-- Jan. 1 | Balance | ✓ | | | 82 483 75 | |

ACCOUNT Property Tax Expense     ACCOUNT NO. 6145

| DATE | ITEM | POST. REF. | DEBIT | CREDIT | BALANCE DEBIT | BALANCE CREDIT |
|------|------|-----------|-------|--------|---------------|----------------|
| | | | | | | |

### Calculating straight-line depreciation

Plant asset: _____      Original cost: _____

Depreciation method: _____      Estimated salvage value: _____

                                                   Estimated useful life: _____

| Year | Beginning Book Value | Annual Depreciation | Accumulated Depreciation | Ending Book Value |
|------|----------------------|---------------------|--------------------------|-------------------|
|      |                      |                     |                          |                   |
|      |                      |                     |                          |                   |
|      |                      |                     |                          |                   |
|      |                      |                     |                          |                   |
|      |                      |                     |                          |                   |
|      |                      |                     |                          |                   |
|      |                      |                     |                          |                   |

Plant asset: _____      Original cost: _____

Depreciation method: _____      Estimated salvage value: _____

                                                   Estimated useful life: _____

| Year | Beginning Book Value | Annual Depreciation | Accumulated Depreciation | Ending Book Value |
|------|----------------------|---------------------|--------------------------|-------------------|
|      |                      |                     |                          |                   |
|      |                      |                     |                          |                   |
|      |                      |                     |                          |                   |
|      |                      |                     |                          |                   |
|      |                      |                     |                          |                   |
|      |                      |                     |                          |                   |
|      |                      |                     |                          |                   |

Plant asset: _____      Original cost: _____

Depreciation method: _____      Estimated salvage value: _____

                                                   Estimated useful life: _____

| Year | Beginning Book Value | Annual Depreciation | Accumulated Depreciation | Ending Book Value |
|------|----------------------|---------------------|--------------------------|-------------------|
|      |                      |                     |                          |                   |
|      |                      |                     |                          |                   |
|      |                      |                     |                          |                   |
|      |                      |                     |                          |                   |
|      |                      |                     |                          |                   |
|      |                      |                     |                          |                   |
|      |                      |                     |                          |                   |

        

## 18-3 APPLICATION PROBLEM, p. 556

**Preparing plant asset records**

**These plant asset records are needed to complete Application Problem 18-5.**

PLANT ASSET RECORD No. _311_     General Ledger Account No. _1215_

Description _____     General Ledger Account _Store Equipment_

| | | |
|---|---|---|
| Date Bought _____ | Serial Number _____ | Original Cost _____ |
| Estimated Useful Life _____ | Estimated Salvage Value _____ | Depreciation Method _____ |

Disposed of:     Discarded _____     Sold _____     Traded _____
Date _____     Disposal Amount _____

| Year | Annual Depreciation Expense | Accumulated Depreciation | Ending Book Value |
|---|---|---|---|
| | | | |
| | | | |
| | | | |
| | | | |
| | | | |
| | | | |
| | | | |
| | | | |
| | | | |
| | | | |
| | | | |
| | | | |
| | | | |

Continue record on back of card

PLANT ASSET RECORD No. 312                    General Ledger Account No. 1205

Description _____            General Ledger Account Office Equipment

Date                    Serial
Bought _____    Number _____    Original Cost _____

                        Estimated
Estimated               Salvage                Depreciation
Useful Life _____  Value _____       Method _____

Disposed of:          Discarded _____    Sold _____    Traded _____
Date _____             Disposal Amount _____

| Year | Annual Depreciation Expense | Accumulated Depreciation | Ending Book Value |
|------|------------------------------|---------------------------|-------------------|
|      |                              |                           |                   |
|      |                              |                           |                   |
|      |                              |                           |                   |
|      |                              |                           |                   |
|      |                              |                           |                   |
|      |                              |                           |                   |
|      |                              |                           |                   |
|      |                              |                           |                   |
|      |                              |                           |                   |
|      |                              |                           |                   |
|      |                              |                           |                   |
|      |                              |                           |                   |

Continue record on back of card

**18-3** **APPLICATION PROBLEM (concluded)**

PLANT ASSET RECORD No.  313                    General Ledger Account No.  1215

Description _____    General Ledger Account  Store Equipment

Date                          Serial
Bought _____    Number _____    Original Cost _____

                              Estimated
Estimated                     Salvage                    Depreciation
Useful Life _____     Value _____        Method _____

Disposed of:          Discarded _____   Sold _____   Traded _____
Date _____        Disposal Amount _____

| Year | Annual Depreciation Expense | Accumulated Depreciation | Ending Book Value |
|---|---|---|---|
|  |  |  |  |
|  |  |  |  |
|  |  |  |  |
|  |  |  |  |
|  |  |  |  |
|  |  |  |  |
|  |  |  |  |
|  |  |  |  |
|  |  |  |  |
|  |  |  |  |
|  |  |  |  |
|  |  |  |  |

Continue record on back of card

**Journalizing annual depreciation expense**

Ester Engineering, Inc.

Work Sheet

For Year Ended December 31, 20 – –

| | | 1 | 2 | 3 | 4 |
|---|---|---|---|---|---|
| | ACCOUNT TITLE | TRIAL BALANCE | | ADJUSTMENTS | |
| | | DEBIT | CREDIT | DEBIT | CREDIT |
| 10 | Office Equipment | 51 2 4 8 25 | | | |
| 11 | Accumulated Depreciation—Office Equipment | | 31 0 0 5 00 | | |
| 38 | Depreciation Expense—Office Equipment | | | | |

## GENERAL LEDGER

ACCOUNT Office Equipment          ACCOUNT NO. 1205

| DATE | ITEM | POST. REF. | DEBIT | CREDIT | BALANCE | |
|---|---|---|---|---|---|---|
| | | | | | DEBIT | CREDIT |
| 20-- Dec. 31 | Balance | ✔ | | | 51 2 4 8 25 | |

ACCOUNT Accumulated Depreciation—Office Equipment          ACCOUNT NO. 1210

| DATE | ITEM | POST. REF. | DEBIT | CREDIT | BALANCE | |
|---|---|---|---|---|---|---|
| | | | | | DEBIT | CREDIT |
| 20-- Dec. 31 | Balance | ✔ | | | | 31 0 0 5 00 |

ACCOUNT Depreciation Expense—Office Equipment          ACCOUNT NO. 6120

| DATE | ITEM | POST. REF. | DEBIT | CREDIT | BALANCE | |
|---|---|---|---|---|---|---|
| | | | | | DEBIT | CREDIT |
| | | | | | | |

## 18-4 APPLICATION PROBLEM (concluded)

GENERAL JOURNAL PAGE 14

| | DATE | | ACCOUNT TITLE | DOC. NO. | POST. REF. | DEBIT | CREDIT | |
|---|---|---|---|---|---|---|---|---|
| 1 | | | | | | | | 1 |
| 2 | | | | | | | | 2 |
| 3 | | | | | | | | 3 |
| 4 | | | | | | | | 4 |
| 5 | | | | | | | | 5 |

**Recording the disposal of plant assets**

**1.**

GENERAL JOURNAL

PAGE 3

| DATE | ACCOUNT TITLE | DOC. NO. | POST. REF. | DEBIT | CREDIT | |
|------|---------------|----------|-----------|-------|--------|---|
| | | | | | | 1 |
| | | | | | | 2 |
| | | | | | | 3 |
| | | | | | | 4 |
| | | | | | | 5 |

**2.**

CASH RECEIPTS JOURNAL

PAGE 3

| | | | | 1 | 2 | 3 | 4 | 5 | 6 | 7 | |
|---|---|---|---|---|---|---|---|---|---|---|---|
| DATE | ACCOUNT TITLE | DOC. NO. | POST. REF. | GENERAL DEBIT | GENERAL CREDIT | ACCOUNTS RECEIVABLE CREDIT | SALES CREDIT | SALES TAX PAYABLE CREDIT | SALES DISCOUNT DEBIT | CASH DEBIT | |
| | | | | | | | | | | | 1 |
| | | | | | | | | | | | 2 |
| | | | | | | | | | | | 3 |
| | | | | | | | | | | | 4 |
| | | | | | | | | | | | 5 |
| | | | | | | | | | | | 6 |
| | | | | | | | | | | | 7 |
| | | | | | | | | | | | 8 |
| | | | | | | | | | | | 9 |
| | | | | | | | | | | | 10 |
| | | | | | | | | | | | 11 |
| | | | | | | | | | | | 12 |
| | | | | | | | | | | | 13 |

## 18-6 APPLICATION PROBLEM, p. 557

**Calculating depreciation using the double declining-balance depreciation method**

| Plant asset: _____ | Original cost: _____ |
|---|---|
| Depreciation method: _____ | Estimated salvage value: _____ |
| | Estimated useful life: _____ |

| Year | Beginning Book Value | Declining-Balance Rate | Annual Depreciation | Ending Book Value |
|---|---|---|---|---|
| | | | | |
| | | | | |
| | | | | |
| | | | | |
| | | | | |
| | | | | |
| | | | | |
| | | | | |

| Plant asset: _____ | Original cost: _____ |
|---|---|
| Depreciation method: _____ | Estimated salvage value: _____ |
| | Estimated useful life: _____ |

| Year | Beginning Book Value | Declining-Balance Rate | Annual Depreciation | Ending Book Value |
|---|---|---|---|---|
| | | | | |
| | | | | |
| | | | | |
| | | | | |
| | | | | |
| | | | | |
| | | | | |
| | | | | |

| Plant asset: _____ | Original cost: _____ |
|---|---|
| Depreciation method: _____ | Estimated salvage value: _____ |
| | Estimated useful life: _____ |

| Year | Beginning Book Value | Declining-Balance Rate | Annual Depreciation | Ending Book Value |
|---|---|---|---|---|
| | | | | |
| | | | | |
| | | | | |
| | | | | |
| | | | | |
| | | | | |
| | | | | |
| | | | | |

**Recording transactions for plant assets**

**1.**

CASH PAYMENTS JOURNAL

PAGE 1

| DATE | ACCOUNT TITLE | CK. NO. | POST. REF. | GENERAL DEBIT | GENERAL CREDIT | ACCOUNTS PAYABLE DEBIT | PURCHASES DISCOUNT CREDIT | CASH CREDIT |
|---|---|---|---|---|---|---|---|---|
| | | | | | | | | |
| | | | | | | | | |
| | | | | | | | | |
| | | | | | | | | |
| | | | | | | | | |
| | | | | | | | | |

## 18-7 MASTERY PROBLEM (continued)

**2., 4., 6.**

PLANT ASSET RECORD No. _____          General Ledger Account No. _____

Description _____          General Ledger Account _____

Date                    Serial
Bought     _____     Number    _____     Original Cost  _____

Estimated                   Estimated
Useful Life _____     Salvage
                            Value     _____     Depreciation
                                                        Method      _____

Disposed of:          Discarded _____     Sold _____     Traded _____
Date _____          Disposal Amount _____

| Year | Annual Depreciation Expense | Accumulated Depreciation | Ending Book Value |
|------|------------------------------|---------------------------|---------------------|
|      |                              |                           |                     |
|      |                              |                           |                     |
|      |                              |                           |                     |
|      |                              |                           |                     |
|      |                              |                           |                     |
|      |                              |                           |                     |

PLANT ASSET RECORD No. _____          General Ledger Account No. _____

Description _____          General Ledger Account _____

Date                    Serial
Bought     _____     Number    _____     Original Cost  _____

Estimated                   Estimated
Useful Life _____     Salvage
                            Value     _____     Depreciation
                                                        Method      _____

Disposed of:          Discarded _____     Sold _____     Traded _____
Date _____          Disposal Amount _____

| Year | Annual Depreciation Expense | Accumulated Depreciation | Ending Book Value |
|------|------------------------------|---------------------------|---------------------|
|      |                              |                           |                     |
|      |                              |                           |                     |
|      |                              |                           |                     |
|      |                              |                           |                     |
|      |                              |                           |                     |
|      |                              |                           |                     |

**3.**

| Plant asset: | Original cost: |
|---|---|
| Depreciation method: | Estimated salvage value: |
| | Estimated useful life: |

| Year | Beginning Book Value | Declining-Balance Rate | Annual Depreciation | Ending Book Value |
|---|---|---|---|---|
| | | | | |
| | | | | |
| | | | | |
| | | | | |
| | | | | |
| | | | | |
| | | | | |
| | | | | |

| Plant asset: | Original cost: |
|---|---|
| Depreciation method: | Estimated salvage value: |
| | Estimated useful life: |

| Year | Beginning Book Value | Annual Depreciation | Accumulated Depreciation | Ending Book Value |
|---|---|---|---|---|
| | | | | |
| | | | | |
| | | | | |
| | | | | |
| | | | | |
| | | | | |
| | | | | |
| | | | | |

# 18-7 MASTERY PROBLEM (concluded)

**5.**

## CASH RECEIPTS JOURNAL
PAGE 2

| DATE | ACCOUNT TITLE | DOC. NO. | POST. REF. | GENERAL DEBIT | GENERAL CREDIT | ACCOUNTS RECEIVABLE CREDIT | SALES CREDIT | SALES TAX PAYABLE CREDIT | SALES DISCOUNT DEBIT | CASH DEBIT |
|------|---------------|----------|------------|---------------|----------------|----------------------------|--------------|--------------------------|----------------------|------------|
| | | | | | | | | | | |

## GENERAL JOURNAL
PAGE 18

| DATE | ACCOUNT TITLE | DOC. NO. | POST. REF. | DEBIT | CREDIT |
|------|---------------|----------|------------|-------|--------|
| | | | | | |

**Calculating a partial year's depreciation using the double declining-balance method**

Plant asset: _____  Original cost: _____

Depreciation method: _____  Estimated salvage value: _____

Estimated useful life: _____

| Year | Beginning Book Value | Declining-Balance Rate | Annual Depreciation | Ending Book Value |
|------|----------------------|------------------------|---------------------|-------------------|
|      |                      |                        |                     |                   |
|      |                      |                        |                     |                   |
|      |                      |                        |                     |                   |
|      |                      |                        |                     |                   |
|      |                      |                        |                     |                   |
|      |                      |                        |                     |                   |
|      |                      |                        |                     |                   |
|      |                      |                        |                     |                   |

Plant asset: _____  Original cost: _____

Depreciation method: _____  Estimated salvage value: _____

Estimated useful life: _____

| Year | Beginning Book Value | Declining-Balance Rate | Annual Depreciation | Ending Book Value |
|------|----------------------|------------------------|---------------------|-------------------|
|      |                      |                        |                     |                   |
|      |                      |                        |                     |                   |
|      |                      |                        |                     |                   |
|      |                      |                        |                     |                   |
|      |                      |                        |                     |                   |
|      |                      |                        |                     |                   |
|      |                      |                        |                     |                   |

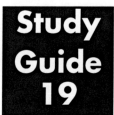

# Study Guide 19

| Name | | Perfect Score | Your Score |
|---|---|---|---|
| | Identifying Accounting Terms | 9 Pts. | |
| | Analyzing Inventory Systems | 10 Pts. | |
| | Analyzing Lifo, Fifo, and Weighted-Average Methods | 12 Pts. | |
| | **Total** | 31 Pts. | |

## Part One—Identifying Accounting Terms

**Directions:** Select the one term in Column I that best fits each definition in Column II. Print the letter identifying your choice in the Answers column.

| Column I | Column II | Answers |
|---|---|---|
| **A.** first-in, first-out inventory costing method | **1.** A merchandise inventory determined by counting, weighing, or measuring items of merchandise on hand. (p. 565) | 1. _____ |
| **B.** gross profit method of estimating inventory | **2.** A merchandise inventory determined by keeping a continuous record of increases, decreases, and balance on hand. (p. 565) | 2. _____ |
| **C.** inventory record | **3.** A form used during a periodic inventory to record information about each item of merchandise on hand. (p. 566) | 3. _____ |
| **D.** last-in, first-out inventory costing method | | |
| **E.** periodic inventory | **4.** A form used to show the kind of merchandise, quantity received, quantity sold, and balance on hand. (p. 567) | 4. _____ |
| **F.** perpetual inventory | **5.** A file of stock records for all merchandise on hand. (p. 567) | 5. _____ |
| **G.** stock ledger | **6.** Using the price of merchandise purchased first to calculate the cost of merchandise sold first. (p. 569) | 6. _____ |
| **H.** stock record | | |
| **I.** weighted-average inventory costing method | **7.** Using the price of merchandise purchased last to calculate the cost of merchandise sold first. (p. 570) | 7. _____ |
| | **8.** Using the average cost of beginning inventory plus merchandise purchased during a fiscal period to calculate the cost of merchandise sold. (p. 571) | 8. _____ |
| | **9.** Estimating inventory by using the previous year's percentage of gross profit on operations. (p. 574) | 9. _____ |

## Part Two—Analyzing Inventory Systems

**Directions:** Place a *T* for True or an *F* for False in the Answers column to show whether each of the following statements is true or false.

1. Merchandise inventory on hand is typically the largest current asset of a merchandising business. (p. 564)    1. _____

2. The only financial statement on which the value of merchandise on hand is reported is the income statement. (p. 564)    2. _____

3. Net income of a business can be decreased by maintaining a merchandise inventory that is larger than needed. (p. 565)    3. _____

4. A perpetual inventory is sometimes known as a physical inventory. (p. 565)    4. _____

5. A minimum inventory balance is the amount of merchandise that will typically last until ordered merchandise can be received from vendors. (p. 565)    5. _____

6. A perpetual inventory system provides day-to-day information about the quality of merchandise on hand. (p. 567)    6. _____

7. A periodic inventory should be taken at least once a month, even when perpetual inventory records are kept. (p. 567)    7. _____

8. Some cash registers use optical scanners to read the UPC codes marked on products. (p. 567)    8. _____

9. First-in, first-out is a method used to determine the quantity of each type of merchandise on hand. (p. 569)    9. _____

10. The gross profit method makes it possible to prepare monthly income statements without taking a periodic inventory. (p. 574)    10. _____

## Part Three—Analyzing Lifo, Fifo, and Weighted-Average Methods

**Directions:** For each of the following items, select the choice that best completes the statement. Print the letter identifying your choice in the Answers column.

**Answers**

1. Calculating an accurate inventory cost to assure that gross profit and net income are reported correctly on the income statement is an application of the accounting concept (A) Consistent Reporting (B) Perpetual Inventory (C) Adequate Disclosure (D) none of these (p. 564)

1. _____

2. When the fifo method is used, cost of merchandise sold is valued at the (A) average price (B) most recent price (C) earliest price (D) none of these (p. 569)

2. _____

3. The fifo method is based on the assumption that the merchandise purchased first is the merchandise (A) sold first (B) sold last (C) in beginning inventory (D) none of these (p. 569)

3. _____

4. When the fifo method is used, ending inventory units are priced at the (A) average price (B) earliest price (C) most recent price (D) none of these (p. 569)

4. _____

5. Using an inventory costing method that charges the most recent costs of merchandise against current revenue is an application of the accounting concept (A) Adequate Disclosure (B) Consistent Reporting (C) Matching Expenses with Revenue (D) none of these (p. 570)

5. _____

6. The lifo method is based on the assumption that the merchandise purchased last is the merchandise (A) sold first (B) sold last (C) in ending inventory (D) none of these (p. 570)

6. _____

7. When the lifo method is used, cost of merchandise sold is priced at the (A) average price (B) earliest price (C) most recent price (D) none of these (p. 570)

7. _____

8. The weighted-average method is based on the assumption that the cost of merchandise sold should be calculated using the (A) average price per unit of beginning inventory (B) average price of ending inventory (C) average price of beginning inventory plus purchases during the fiscal period (D) average price of ending inventory plus purchases during the fiscal period (p. 571)

8. _____

9. When the weighted-average method is used, ending inventory units are priced at the (A) earliest price (B) most recent price (C) average price (D) none of these (p. 571)

9. _____

10. A business that uses the same inventory costing method for all fiscal periods is applying the accounting concept (A) Consistent Reporting (B) Accounting Period Cycle (C) Perpetual Inventory (D) Adequate Disclosure (p. 572)

10. _____

11. In a year of rising prices, the inventory method that gives the lowest possible value for ending inventory is (A) fifo (B) lifo (C) weighted-average (D) gross profit (p. 572)

11. _____

12. In a year of falling prices, the inventory method that gives the lowest possible value for ending inventory is (A) weighted-average (B) lifo (C) fifo (D) gross profit (p. 572)

12. _____

# Using the Library

Being able to use the library properly is an invaluable skill for anyone. You should visit the library in your school or community often and take as much time as necessary to become thoroughly familiar with every section.

Never be afraid to ask for help. Any librarian should be happy to help you locate any information that you need. If you don't know where to look for information, ask someone to help you. If you can't find information, ask for assistance. If you don't know how to use special equipment, ask for a demonstration.

## The Catalog System
Most libraries use either the Library of Congress System or the Dewey Decimal System. Determine which system your library uses and obtain a floor plan of the library to determine where each section is housed. A floor plan is usually available at the main circulation desk, at each entrance to the building, and near the stairs. Take some time to become familiar with every area; it will save you time later when you want to locate a book.

## Texts
If you are preparing to write a paper in a particular subject area, you should become familiar with the texts in that field. You may be able to find a number of books on your topic located in one section of the library.

## Reference Books
Your library probably has many types of reference books. In the reference section of your library, you will find such books as atlases, encyclopedias, dictionaries, and various other sources of information. In reference books, you will be able to find information on people, places, and events that you may need for your paper.

## Periodicals
You will often want to obtain current information on a subject—information that is less than a year old. Current information may be found in the latest issues of periodicals. Your library probably has a collection of newspapers, magazines, and professional journals that you can use when you need current references.

In addition to the latest issues, you may want to read old newspaper and journal articles. Sometimes the library has actual copies of old papers and journals, and sometimes information is available on microfilm.

## Electronic Sources
Your library also subscribes to databases which contain vast amounts of information that is available through a computer terminal. The database may be located in another city or another area of the country; however, you will be able to locate information quickly and easily using a computer. You can even obtain a printed copy by using a printer at your computer terminal.

## Make the Most of Your Library
The information in the library is usually available to anyone who wants to use it. The library is a vast source of information and enjoyment. Use it often and well.

**19-1** WORK TOGETHER, p. 568

**Preparing a stock record**

1.

## STOCK RECORD

Description  16-Gauge Speaker Wire _____          Stock No.  W-394 _____

Reorder  750 _____          Minimum  300 _____          Location  Bin T37 _____

| 1 | 2 | 3 | 4 | 5 | 6 | 7 |
|---|---|---|---|---|---|---|
| INCREASES | | | DECREASES | | | BALANCE |
| DATE | PURCHASE INVOICE NO. | QUANTITY | DATE | SALES INVOICE NO. | QUANTITY | QUANTITY |
| | | | Sept. 15 | 2490 | 150 | 400 |
| | | | | | | |
| | | | | | | |
| | | | | | | |
| | | | | | | |
| | | | | | | |

**19-1** ON YOUR OWN, p. 568

**Preparing a stock record**

1.

## STOCK RECORD

Description  8″ x 10″ white metal frame _____          Stock No.  M-253 _____

Reorder  50 _____          Minimum  20 _____          Location  Bin F45 _____

| 1 | 2 | 3 | 4 | 5 | 6 | 7 |
|---|---|---|---|---|---|---|
| INCREASES | | | DECREASES | | | BALANCE |
| DATE | PURCHASE INVOICE NO. | QUANTITY | DATE | SALES INVOICE NO. | QUANTITY | QUANTITY |
| | | | Oct. 30 | 543 | 20 | 45 |
| | | | | | | |
| | | | | | | |
| | | | | | | |
| | | | | | | |

Determining the cost of inventory using the fifo, lifo, and weighted-average inventory costing methods

**1.**

### FIFO Method

| Purchase Dates | Units Purchased | Unit Price | Total Cost | FIFO Units on Hand | FIFO Cost |
|---|---|---|---|---|---|
| January 1, beginning inventory | 14 | $30.00 | $ 420.00 | | |
| March 29, purchases | 9 | 32.00 | 288.00 | | |
| May 6, purchases | 10 | 34.00 | 340.00 | | |
| August 28, purchases | 8 | 36.00 | 288.00 | | |
| November 8, purchases | 9 | 38.00 | 342.00 | | |
| Totals | 50 | | $1,678.00 | | |

### LIFO Method

| Purchase Dates | Units Purchased | Unit Price | Total Cost | LIFO Units on Hand | LIFO Cost |
|---|---|---|---|---|---|
| January 1, beginning inventory | 14 | $30.00 | $ 420.00 | | |
| March 29, purchases | 9 | 32.00 | 288.00 | | |
| May 6, purchases | 10 | 34.00 | 340.00 | | |
| August 28, purchases | 8 | 36.00 | 288.00 | | |
| November 8, purchases | 9 | 38.00 | 342.00 | | |
| Totals | 50 | | $1,678.00 | | |

### Weighted-Average Method

| Purchases | | | Total Cost |
|---|---|---|---|
| Date | Units | Unit Price | |
| January 1, beginning inventory | 14 | $30.00 | |
| March 29, purchases | 9 | 32.00 | |
| May 6, purchases | 10 | 34.00 | |
| August 28, purchases | 8 | 36.00 | |
| November 8, purchases | 9 | 38.00 | |
| Totals | 50 | | |

## 19-2 ON YOUR OWN, p. 573

**Determining the cost of inventory using the fifo, lifo, and weighted-average inventory costing methods**

1.

### FIFO Method

| Purchase Dates | Units Purchased | Unit Price | Total Cost | FIFO Units on Hand | FIFO Cost |
|---|---|---|---|---|---|
| January 1, beginning inventory | 18 | $4.60 | $ 82.80 | | |
| April 9, purchases | 12 | 4.70 | 56.40 | | |
| June 12, purchases | 14 | 4.80 | 67.20 | | |
| September 22, purchases | 15 | 5.00 | 75.00 | | |
| November 20, purchases | 16 | 5.10 | 81.60 | | |
| Totals | 75 | | $363.00 | | |

### LIFO Method

| Purchase Dates | Units Purchased | Unit Price | Total Cost | LIFO Units on Hand | LIFO Cost |
|---|---|---|---|---|---|
| January 1, beginning inventory | 18 | $4.60 | $ 82.80 | | |
| April 9, purchases | 12 | 4.70 | 56.40 | | |
| June 12, purchases | 14 | 4.80 | 67.20 | | |
| September 22, purchases | 15 | 5.00 | 75.00 | | |
| November 20, purchases | 16 | 5.10 | 81.60 | | |
| Totals | 75 | | $363.00 | | |

### Weighted-Average Method

| Purchases | | | Total Cost |
|---|---|---|---|
| Date | Units | Unit Price | |
| January 1, beginning inventory | 18 | $4.60 | |
| April 9, purchases | 12 | 4.70 | |
| June 12, purchases | 14 | 4.80 | |
| September 22, purchases | 15 | 5.00 | |
| November 20, purchases | 16 | 5.10 | |
| Totals | 75 | | |

**Estimating ending inventory using the gross profit method**

**1.**

STEP 1

Beginning inventory, June 1 ........................................................ _____

*Plus* net purchases for June 1 to June 30 .......................................... _____

*Equals* cost of merchandise available for sale ..................................... _____

STEP 2

Net sales for June 1 to June 30 .................................................... _____

*Times* previous year's gross profit percentage ..................................... _____

*Equals* estimated gross profit on operations ....................................... _____

STEP 3

Net sales for June 1 to June 30 .................................................... _____

*Less* estimated gross profit on operations ......................................... _____

*Equals* estimated cost of merchandise sold ........................................ _____

STEP 4

Cost of merchandise available for sale ............................................. _____

*Less* estimated cost of merchandise sold .......................................... _____

*Equals* estimated ending merchandise inventory ................................... _____

**2.**

Evans Company

Income Statement

For Month Ended June 30, 20 – –

| | | % OF NET SALES |
|---|---|---|
| Operating Revenue: | | |
| Net Sales | | |
| Cost of Merchandise Sold: | | |
| Estimated Beginning Inventory, June 1 | | |
| Net Purchases | | |
| Merchandise Available for Sale | | |
| Less Estimated Ending Inventory, June 30 | | |
| Cost of Merchandise Sold | | |
| Gross Profit on Operations | | |
| Operating Expenses | | |
| Net Income | | |
| | | |

## 19-3 ON YOUR OWN, p. 576

**Estimating ending inventory using the gross profit method**

**1.**

STEP 1
  Beginning inventory, April 1 . . . . . . . . . . . . . . . . . . . . . . . . . . . . . . . . . . . . . . . . . . . . . . .    _____
  *Plus* net purchases for April 1 to April 30 . . . . . . . . . . . . . . . . . . . . . . . . . . . . . . . . . . . . . .    _____
  *Equals* cost of merchandise available for sale . . . . . . . . . . . . . . . . . . . . . . . . . . . . . . . . . .    _____
STEP 2
  Net sales for April 1 to April 30 . . . . . . . . . . . . . . . . . . . . . . . . . . . . . . . . . . . . . . . . . . . . .    _____
  *Times* previous year's gross profit percentage . . . . . . . . . . . . . . . . . . . . . . . . . . . . . . . . . .    _____
  *Equals* estimated gross profit on operations . . . . . . . . . . . . . . . . . . . . . . . . . . . . . . . . . . .    _____
STEP 3
  Net sales for April 1 to April 30 . . . . . . . . . . . . . . . . . . . . . . . . . . . . . . . . . . . . . . . . . . . . .    _____
  *Less* estimated gross profit on operations . . . . . . . . . . . . . . . . . . . . . . . . . . . . . . . . . . . . .    _____
  *Equals* estimated cost of merchandise sold . . . . . . . . . . . . . . . . . . . . . . . . . . . . . . . . . . . .    _____
STEP 4
  Cost of merchandise available for sale . . . . . . . . . . . . . . . . . . . . . . . . . . . . . . . . . . . . . . . .    _____
  *Less* estimated cost of merchandise sold . . . . . . . . . . . . . . . . . . . . . . . . . . . . . . . . . . . . . .    _____
  *Equals* estimated ending merchandise inventory . . . . . . . . . . . . . . . . . . . . . . . . . . . . . . .    _____

**2.**

Luke Enterprises

Income Statement

For Month Ended April 30, 20 – –

| | | | % OF NET SALES |
|---|---|---|---|
| Operating Revenue: | | | |
|   Net Sales | | | |
| Cost of Merchandise Sold: | | | |
|   Estimated Beginning Inventory, April 1 | | | |
|   Net Purchases | | | |
|   Merchandise Available for Sale | | | |
|   Less Estimated Ending Inventory, April 30 | | | |
|   Cost of Merchandise Sold | | | |
| Gross Profit on Operations | | | |
| Operating Expenses | | | |
| Net Income | | | |

**Preparing a stock record**

### STOCK RECORD

Description  450-gallon spa                     Stock No.  HT-450

Reorder  5                     Minimum  2          Location  Area A-4

| 1 | 2 | 3 | 4 | 5 | 6 | 7 |
|---|---|---|---|---|---|---|
| INCREASES | | | DECREASES | | | BALANCE |
| DATE | PURCHASE INVOICE NO. | QUANTITY | DATE | SALES INVOICE NO. | QUANTITY | QUANTITY |
|  |  |  | Jan. 3 | 2399 | 1 | 4 |
|  |  |  |  |  |  |  |
|  |  |  |  |  |  |  |
|  |  |  |  |  |  |  |
|  |  |  |  |  |  |  |
|  |  |  |  |  |  |  |

## 19-2 APPLICATION PROBLEM, p. 578

Determining the cost of inventory using the fifo, lifo, and weighted-average inventory costing methods

### FIFO Method

| Purchase Dates | Units Purchased | Unit Price | Total Cost | FIFO Units on Hand | FIFO Cost |
|---|---|---|---|---|---|
| January 1, beginning inventory | 90 | $2.00 | $180.00 | | |
| March 13, purchases | 78 | 2.10 | 163.80 | | |
| June 8, purchases | 80 | 2.25 | 180.00 | | |
| September 16, purchases | 84 | 2.30 | 193.20 | | |
| December 22, purchases | 88 | 2.40 | 211.20 | | |
| Totals | 420 | | $928.20 | | |

### LIFO Method

| Purchase Dates | Units Purchased | Unit Price | Total Cost | LIFO Units on Hand | LIFO Cost |
|---|---|---|---|---|---|
| January 1, beginning inventory | 90 | $2.00 | $180.00 | | |
| March 13, purchases | 78 | 2.10 | 163.80 | | |
| June 8, purchases | 80 | 2.25 | 180.00 | | |
| September 16, purchases | 84 | 2.30 | 193.20 | | |
| December 22, purchases | 88 | 2.40 | 211.20 | | |
| Totals | 420 | | $928.20 | | |

### Weighted-Average Method

| Purchases | | | Total Cost |
|---|---|---|---|
| Date | Units | Unit Price | |
| January 1, beginning inventory | 90 | $2.00 | |
| March 13, purchases | 78 | 2.10 | |
| June 8, purchases | 80 | 2.25 | |
| September 16, purchases | 84 | 2.30 | |
| December 22, purchases | 88 | 2.40 | |
| Totals | 420 | | |

**Estimating ending inventory using the gross profit method**

**1.**

STEP 1
Beginning inventory, March 1 ....................................................... _____
*Plus* net purchases for March 1 to March 31 ............................... _____
*Equals* cost of merchandise available for sale .......................... _____
STEP 2
Net sales for March 1 to March 31 ............................................. _____
*Times* previous year's gross profit percentage ......................... _____
*Equals* estimated gross profit on operations ............................ _____
STEP 3
Net sales for March 1 to March 31 ............................................. _____
*Less* estimated gross profit on operations ................................ _____
*Equals* estimated cost of merchandise sold ............................... _____
STEP 4
Cost of merchandise available for sale ....................................... _____
*Less* estimated cost of merchandise sold .................................. _____
*Equals* estimated ending merchandise inventory ......................... _____

**2.**

Fultz Industries

Income Statement

For Month Ended March 31, 20 – –

| | | % OF NET SALES |
|---|---|---|
| Operating Revenue: | | |
| Net Sales | | |
| Cost of Merchandise Sold: | | |
| Estimated Beginning Inventory, March 1 | | |
| Net Purchases | | |
| Merchandise Available for Sale | | |
| Less Estimated Ending Inventory, March 31 | | |
| Cost of Merchandise Sold | | |
| Gross Profit on Operations | | |
| Operating Expenses | | |
| Net Income | | |

**19-4** **MASTERY PROBLEM, p. 579**

Determining the cost of inventory using the fifo, lifo, and weighted-average inventory costing methods

1.

| STOCK RECORD | | | | | | |
|---|---|---|---|---|---|---|

Description  Electronic switch                     Stock No.  P-234

Reorder  20                     Minimum  10          Location  Aisle C-2

| 1 | 2 | 3 | 4 | 5 | 6 | 7 |
|---|---|---|---|---|---|---|
| INCREASES | | | DECREASES | | | BALANCE |
| DATE | PURCHASE INVOICE NO. | QUANTITY | DATE | SALES INVOICE NO. | QUANTITY | QUANTITY |
|  |  |  | Jan. 1 |  | 8 | 8 |
|  |  |  |  |  |  |  |
|  |  |  |  |  |  |  |
|  |  |  |  |  |  |  |
|  |  |  |  |  |  |  |
|  |  |  |  |  |  |  |
|  |  |  |  |  |  |  |
|  |  |  |  |  |  |  |

**2.**

### FIFO Method

| Purchase Dates | Units Purchased | Unit Price | Total Cost | FIFO Units on Hand | FIFO Cost |
|---|---|---|---|---|---|
| January 1, beginning inventory | 8 | $4.98 | $ 39.84 | | |
| January 6, purchases | | | | | |
| April 14, purchases | | | | | |
| August 3, purchases | | | | | |
| December 12, purchases | | | | | |
| Totals | | | | | |

### LIFO Method

| Purchase Dates | Units Purchased | Unit Price | Total Cost | LIFO Units on Hand | LIFO Cost |
|---|---|---|---|---|---|
| January 1, beginning inventory | 8 | $4.98 | $ 39.84 | | |
| January 6, purchases | | | | | |
| April 14, purchases | | | | | |
| August 3, purchases | | | | | |
| December 12, purchases | | | | | |
| Totals | | | | | |

### Weighted-Average Method

| Purchases | | | Total Cost |
|---|---|---|---|
| Date | Units | Unit Price | |
| January 1, beginning inventory | 8 | $4.98 | $ 39.84 |
| January 6, purchases | | | |
| April 14, purchases | | | |
| August 3, purchases | | | |
| December 12, purchases | | | |
| Totals | | | |

## 19-4 MASTERY PROBLEM (concluded)

**3.**

|  | Fifo | Lifo | Weighted-Average |
|---|---|---|---|
| Merchandise Available for Sale |  |  |  |
| Ending Inventory |  |  |  |
| Cost of Merchandise Sold |  |  |  |

Highest Cost of Merchandise Sold:

**Determining the cost of merchandise inventory destroyed in a fire**

**1.**

Gross profit on operations . . . . . . . . . . . . . . . . . . . . . . . . . . . . . . . . . . . . . . . . . . . . . . . . . . . . . . _____

*Divided* by net sales . . . . . . . . . . . . . . . . . . . . . . . . . . . . . . . . . . . . . . . . . . . . . . . . . . . . . . . . . _____

*Equals* gross profit percentage of net sales (prior year) . . . . . . . . . . . . . . . . . . . . . . . . . . . . . _____

**2.**

STEP 1

  Beginning inventory, May 1 . . . . . . . . . . . . . . . . . . . . . . . . . . . . . . . . . . . . . . . . . . . . . . . . . . _____

  *Plus* net purchases for May 1 to May 12 . . . . . . . . . . . . . . . . . . . . . . . . . . . . . . . . . . . . . . . _____

  *Equals* cost of merchandise available for sale . . . . . . . . . . . . . . . . . . . . . . . . . . . . . . . . . . _____

STEP 2

  Net sales for May 1 to May 12 . . . . . . . . . . . . . . . . . . . . . . . . . . . . . . . . . . . . . . . . . . . . . . _____

  *Times* previous year's gross profit percentage . . . . . . . . . . . . . . . . . . . . . . . . . . . . . . . . . . _____

  *Equals* estimated gross profit on operations . . . . . . . . . . . . . . . . . . . . . . . . . . . . . . . . . . . . _____

STEP 3

  Net sales for May 1 to May 12 . . . . . . . . . . . . . . . . . . . . . . . . . . . . . . . . . . . . . . . . . . . . . . _____

  *Less* estimated gross profit on operations . . . . . . . . . . . . . . . . . . . . . . . . . . . . . . . . . . . . . . _____

  *Equals* estimated cost of merchandise sold . . . . . . . . . . . . . . . . . . . . . . . . . . . . . . . . . . . . . _____

STEP 4

  Cost of merchandise available for sale . . . . . . . . . . . . . . . . . . . . . . . . . . . . . . . . . . . . . . . . _____

  *Less* estimated cost of merchandise sold . . . . . . . . . . . . . . . . . . . . . . . . . . . . . . . . . . . . . . . _____

  *Equals* estimated ending merchandise inventory . . . . . . . . . . . . . . . . . . . . . . . . . . . . . . . . _____

**3.**

Estimated merchandise inventory, May 12 . . . . . . . . . . . . . . . . . . . . . . . . . . . . . . . . . . . . . . . . . _____

*Less* cost of merchandise inventory not destroyed . . . . . . . . . . . . . . . . . . . . . . . . . . . . . . . . . . _____

*Equals* estimated cost of merchandise inventory destroyed . . . . . . . . . . . . . . . . . . . . . . . . . . . . _____

**4.**

| Murphy Electronics Company | | | |
|---|---|---|---|
| Income Statement | | | |
| For the Period May 1 to May 12, 20 – – | | | |
| | | | % OF NET SALES |
| Operating Revenue: | | | |
|   Net Sales | | | |
| Cost of Merchandise Sold: | | | |
|   Estimated Beginning Inventory, May 1 | | | |
|   Net Purchases | | | |
|   Merchandise Available for Sale | | | |
|   Less Estimated Ending Inventory, May 12 | | | |
|   Cost of Merchandise Sold | | | |
| Gross Profit on Operations | | | |
| Operating Expenses | | | |
| Net Income | | | |

**19-5** **CHALLENGE PROBLEM (concluded)**

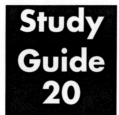

# Study Guide 20

| Name | | Perfect Score | Your Score |
|---|---|---|---|
| | Identifying Accounting Terms | 18 Pts. | |
| | Identifying Accounting Concepts and Practices | 8 Pts. | |
| | Analyzing Notes and Interest | 8 Pts. | |
| | Analyzing Notes Payable and Notes Receivable Transactions | 14 Pts. | |
| | **Total** | 48 Pts. | |

## Part One—Identifying Accounting Terms

**Directions:** Select the one term in Column I that best fits each definition in Column II. Print the letter identifying your choice in the Answers column.

| Column I | Column II | Answers |
|---|---|---|
| **A.** creditor | **1.** The number assigned to identify a specific note. (p. 589) | 1. _____ |
| **B.** current liabilities | **2.** The date a note is signed. (p. 589) | 2. _____ |
| **C.** date of a note | **3.** The person or business to whom the amount of a note is payable. (p. 589) | 3. _____ |
| **D.** dishonored note | **4.** The days, months, or years from the date of signing until a note is to be paid. (p. 589) | 4. _____ |
| **E.** interest | **5.** The original amount of a note. (p. 589) | 5. _____ |
| **F.** interest expense | **6.** The percentage of the principal that is paid for use of the money. (p. 589) | 6. _____ |
| **G.** interest income | **7.** The date a note is due. (p. 589) | 7. _____ |
| **H.** interest rate of a note | **8.** The person or business who signs a note and thus promises to make payment. (p. 589) | 8. _____ |
| **I.** maker of a note | **9.** A written and signed promise to pay a sum of money at a specified time. (p. 589) | 9. _____ |
| **J.** maturity date of a note | **10.** A person or organization to whom a liability is owed. (p. 589) | 10. _____ |
| **K.** maturity value | **11.** Promissory notes signed by a business and given to a creditor. (p. 589) | 11. _____ |
| **L.** notes payable | **12.** An amount paid for the use of money for a period of time. (p. 590) | 12. _____ |
| **M.** notes receivable | **13.** The amount that is due on the maturity date of a note. (p. 590) | 13. _____ |
| **N.** number of a note | **14.** Liabilities due within a short time, usually within a year. (p. 593) | 14. _____ |
| **O.** payee of a note | **15.** The interest accrued on money borrowed. (p. 594) | 15. _____ |
| **P.** principal of a note | **16.** Promissory notes that a business accepts from customers. (p. 598) | 16. _____ |
| **Q.** promissory note | **17.** The interest earned on money loaned. (p. 599) | 17. _____ |
| **R.** time of a note | **18.** A note that is not paid when due. (p. 600) | 18. _____ |

## Part Two—Identifying Accounting Concepts and Practices

**Directions:** Place a *T* for True or an *F* for False in the Answers column to show whether each of the following statements is true or false.

**Answers**

1. When the timing of cash receipts and required cash payments do not match, businesses usually deposit extra cash or borrow cash or make arrangements to delay payments. (p. 588)

1. _____

2. "Interest at 12%" means that 12 cents will be paid for the use of each dollar borrowed for the time of a note. (p. 590)

2. _____

3. An individual with a car loan usually pays the note in partial payments that include part of the principal and part of the interest on the note. (p. 590)

3. _____

4. In interest calculations, time can be expressed in whole years or as a fraction of a year. (p. 590)

4. _____

5. The maturity value of a note is calculated by subtracting the interest rate from the principal. (p. 590)

5. _____

6. The journal entry for signing a note payable includes a debit to Interest Expense. (p. 593)

6. _____

7. The journal entry for paying a note payable includes a debit to Accounts Payable to remove the balance owed. (p. 594)

7. _____

8. When a note receivable is dishonored, the company should immediately write off the account receivable for that customer. (p. 600)

8. _____

## Part Three—Analyzing Notes and Interest

**Directions:** For each of the following items, select the choice that best completes the statement. Print the letter identifying your choice in the Answers column.

**Answers**

1. The most useful evidence of a debt in a court of law is (A) an oral promise to pay (B) an account receivable (C) an account payable (D) a signed note (p. 589)

1. _____

2. The interest on a 180-day, 10% interest-bearing note of $2,000.00 is (A) $20.00 (B) $200.00 (C) $100.00 (D) none of these (p. 590)

2. _____

3. The time of a note issued for less than one year is typically stated in (A) days (B) months (C) a fraction of a year (D) none of these (p. 590)

3. _____

4. The maturity value of a 90-day, 12% interest-bearing note of $600.00 is (A) $582.00 (B) $672.00 (C) $624.00 (D) none of these (p. 590)

4. _____

5. The maturity date of a 90-day note dated August 22 is (A) November 19 (B) November 20 (C) November 21 (D) November 22 (p. 591)

5. _____

6. Notes payable are classified as (A) current assets (B) current liabilities (C) expenses (D) revenue (p. 593)

6. _____

7. The source document for recording cash received from signing a note payable is a (A) receipt (B) check (C) memorandum (D) copy of the note (p. 593)

7. _____

8. Notes receivable are classified as (A) other expense (B) current assets (C) current liabilities (D) other revenue (p. 598)

8. _____

## Part Four—Analyzing Notes Payable and Notes Receivable Transactions

**Directions:** Analyze each of the following transactions into debit and credit parts. Print the letter identifying your choices in the proper Answers column.

| Account Titles | Transactions | Answers Debit | Credit |
|---|---|---|---|
| **A.** Accounts Payable | **1–2.** Signed a 90-day, 10% note. (p. 593) | 1. _____ | 2. _____ |
| **B.** Accounts Receivable | | | |
| **C.** Cash | **3–4.** Paid cash for the maturity value of a note plus interest. (p. 594) | 3. _____ | 4. _____ |
| **D.** Interest Expense | | | |
| **E.** Interest Income | **5–6.** Signed a 60-day, 18% note to Café on the Way for an extension of time on an account payable. (p. 595) | 5. _____ | 6. _____ |
| **F.** Notes Payable | | | |
| **G.** Notes Receivable | **7–8.** Paid cash for the maturity value of the note payable to Café on the Way. (p. 596) | 7. _____ | 8. _____ |
| | **9–10.** Accepted a 90-day, 18% note from Aimee Kane for an extension of time on her account. (p. 598) | 9. _____ | 10. _____ |
| **ACCTS. RECEIVABLE LEDGER** | | | |
| **H.** Aimee Kane | **11–12.** Received cash for the maturity value of the note receivable plus interest from Aimee Kane. (p. 599) | 11. _____ | 12. _____ |
| **I.** Common Grounds Coffee Shop | | | |
| **ACCTS. PAYABLE LEDGER** | **13–14.** Common Grounds Coffee Shop dishonored a note receivable, maturity value due today. (p. 600) | 13. _____ | 14. _____ |
| **J.** Café on the Way | | | |

## 20-1 WORK TOGETHER, p. 592

**Calculating interest, maturity dates, and maturity values for promissory notes**

| Date | Principal | Interest Rate | Time | Interest | Maturity Date | Maturity Value |
|------|-----------|---------------|------|----------|---------------|----------------|
| March 3 | $6,000.00 | 6% | 90 days | | | |
| March 18 | $2,000.00 | 9% | 60 days | | | |

*Calculations:*

**Calculating interest, maturity dates, and maturity values for promissory notes**

| Date | Principal | Interest Rate | Time | Interest | Maturity Date | Maturity Value |
|------|-----------|---------------|------|----------|---------------|----------------|
| June 8 | $20,000.00 | 8% | 180 days | | | |
| June 12 | $10,000.00 | 6% | 90 days | | | |

*Calculations:*

**20-2** **WORK TOGETHER, p. 597**

**Journalizing notes payable transactions**

**1.**

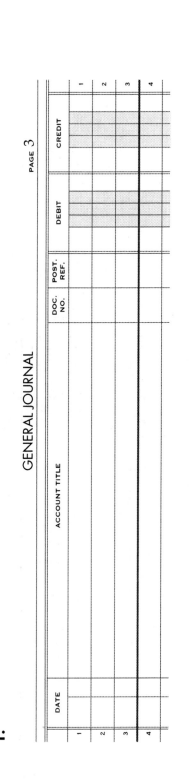

GENERAL JOURNAL                    PAGE 3

| DATE | ACCOUNT TITLE | DOC. NO. | POST. REF. | DEBIT | CREDIT |
|------|---------------|----------|-----------|-------|--------|
| | | | | | |
| | | | | | |
| | | | | | |
| | | | | | |

**1.**

CASH RECEIPTS JOURNAL                    PAGE 5

| DATE | ACCOUNT TITLE | DOC. NO. | POST. REF. | GENERAL DEBIT | GENERAL CREDIT | ACCOUNTS RECEIVABLE CREDIT | SALES CREDIT | SALES TAX PAYABLE CREDIT | SALES DISCOUNT DEBIT | CASH DEBIT |
|------|---------------|----------|-----------|--------|--------|--------|--------|--------|--------|--------|
| | | | | | | | | | | |
| | | | | | | | | | | |
| | | | | | | | | | | |
| | | | | | | | | | | |
| | | | | | | | | | | |

**2.**

CASH PAYMENTS JOURNAL                    PAGE 9

| DATE | ACCOUNT TITLE | CK. NO. | POST. REF. | GENERAL DEBIT | GENERAL CREDIT | ACCOUNTS PAYABLE DEBIT | PURCHASES DISCOUNT CREDIT | CASH CREDIT |
|------|---------------|---------|-----------|--------|--------|--------|--------|--------|
| | | | | | | | | |
| | | | | | | | | |
| | | | | | | | | |
| | | | | | | | | |
| | | | | | | | | |

**Journalizing notes payable transactions**

**1.**

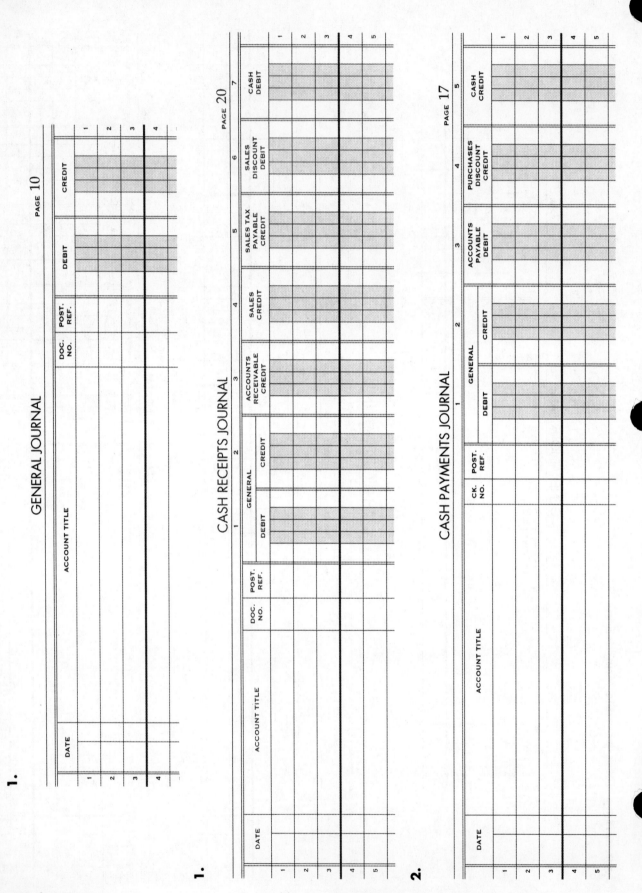

GENERAL JOURNAL — PAGE 10

CASH RECEIPTS JOURNAL — PAGE 20

CASH PAYMENTS JOURNAL — PAGE 17

## 20-3 WORK TOGETHER, p. 602

**Journalizing notes receivable transactions**

### GENERAL JOURNAL

PAGE 2

| DATE | ACCOUNT TITLE | DOC. NO. | POST. REF. | DEBIT | CREDIT | |
|------|---------------|----------|------------|-------|--------|---|
| | | | | | | 1 |
| | | | | | | 2 |
| | | | | | | 3 |
| | | | | | | 4 |
| | | | | | | 5 |
| | | | | | | 6 |

### CASH RECEIPTS JOURNAL

PAGE 3

| | | | | | GENERAL | | ACCOUNTS RECEIVABLE CREDIT | SALES CREDIT | SALES TAX PAYABLE CREDIT | SALES DISCOUNT DEBIT | CASH DEBIT | |
|---|---|---|---|---|---|---|---|---|---|---|---|---|
| DATE | ACCOUNT TITLE | DOC. NO. | POST. REF. | DEBIT | CREDIT | | | | | | | |
| | | | | | | | | | | | | 1 |
| | | | | | | | | | | | | 2 |
| | | | | | | | | | | | | 3 |
| | | | | | | | | | | | | 4 |
| | | | | | | | | | | | | 5 |

**Journalizing notes receivable transactions**

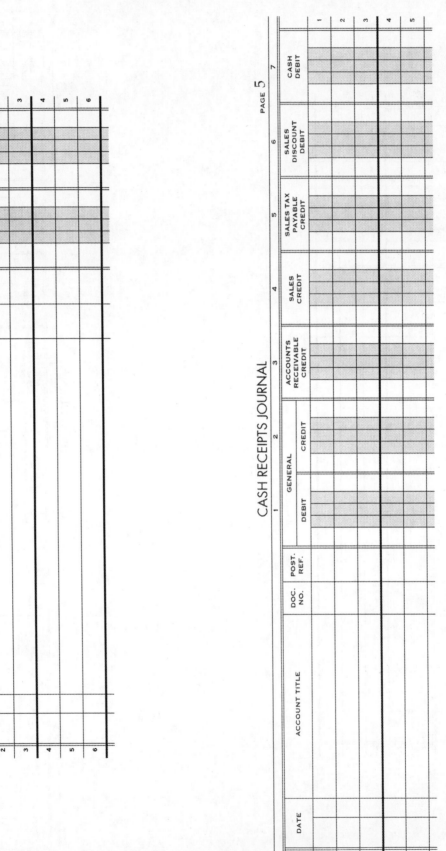

GENERAL JOURNAL

PAGE 3

CASH RECEIPTS JOURNAL

PAGE 5

## 20-1 APPLICATION PROBLEM, p. 604

**Calculating interest, maturity dates, and maturity values for promissory notes**

| Date | Principal | Interest Rate | Time | Interest | Maturity Date | Maturity Value |
|------|-----------|---------------|------|----------|---------------|----------------|
| April 6 | $10,000.00 | 12% | 180 days | | | |
| April 12 | $600.00 | 9% | 60 days | | | |
| April 15 | $5,000.00 | 10% | 90 days | | | |
| April 23 | $3,000.00 | 14% | 60 days | | | |

*Calculations:*

**Journalizing notes payable transactions**

**1.**

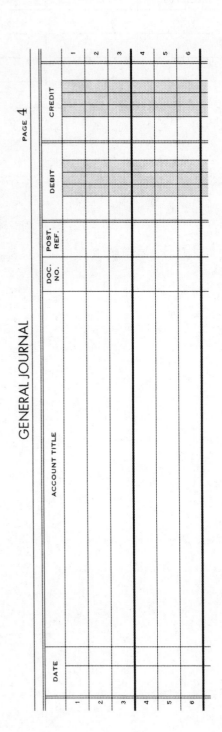

GENERAL JOURNAL PAGE 4

| DATE | ACCOUNT TITLE | DOC. NO. | POST. REF. | DEBIT | CREDIT |
|------|---------------|----------|------------|-------|--------|
| | | | | | |
| | | | | | |
| | | | | | |
| | | | | | |
| | | | | | |
| | | | | | |

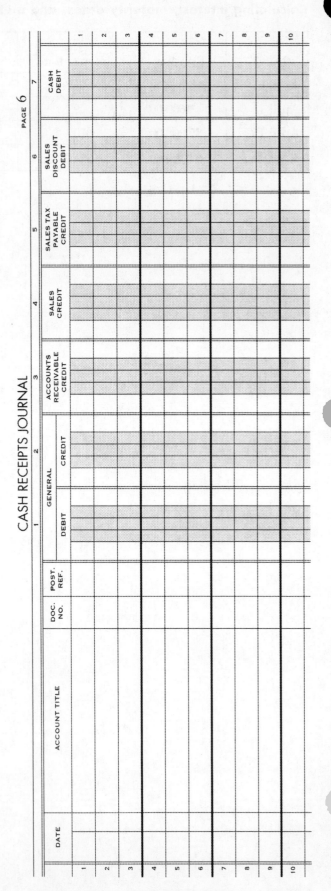

CASH RECEIPTS JOURNAL PAGE 6

| DATE | ACCOUNT TITLE | DOC. NO. | POST. REF. | GENERAL DEBIT | GENERAL CREDIT | ACCOUNTS RECEIVABLE CREDIT | SALES CREDIT | SALES TAX PAYABLE CREDIT | SALES DISCOUNT DEBIT | CASH DEBIT |
|------|---------------|----------|------------|---------------|----------------|----------------------------|--------------|--------------------------|----------------------|------------|
| | | | | | | | | | | |
| | | | | | | | | | | |
| | | | | | | | | | | |
| | | | | | | | | | | |
| | | | | | | | | | | |
| | | | | | | | | | | |
| | | | | | | | | | | |
| | | | | | | | | | | |
| | | | | | | | | | | |
| | | | | | | | | | | |

## 20-2 APPLICATION PROBLEM (concluded)

**CASH PAYMENTS JOURNAL**

**2.**

PAGE 9

| DATE | ACCOUNT TITLE | CK. NO. | POST. REF. | GENERAL DEBIT | GENERAL CREDIT | ACCOUNTS PAYABLE DEBIT | PURCHASES DISCOUNT CREDIT | CASH CREDIT |
|------|---------------|---------|------------|---------------|----------------|------------------------|---------------------------|-------------|
| | | | | | | | | | 1 |
| | | | | | | | | | 2 |
| | | | | | | | | | 3 |
| | | | | | | | | | 4 |
| | | | | | | | | | 5 |
| | | | | | | | | | 6 |
| | | | | | | | | | 7 |
| | | | | | | | | | 8 |
| | | | | | | | | | 9 |
| | | | | | | | | | 10 |
| | | | | | | | | | 11 |
| | | | | | | | | | 12 |
| | | | | | | | | | 13 |
| | | | | | | | | | 14 |
| | | | | | | | | | 15 |
| | | | | | | | | | 16 |
| | | | | | | | | | 17 |
| | | | | | | | | | 18 |
| | | | | | | | | | 19 |
| | | | | | | | | | 20 |
| | | | | | | | | | 21 |
| | | | | | | | | | 22 |
| | | | | | | | | | 23 |
| | | | | | | | | | 24 |

**Journalizing notes receivable transactions**

GENERAL JOURNAL

| | DATE | | ACCOUNT TITLE | DOC. NO. | POST. REF. | DEBIT | CREDIT | |
|---|---|---|---|---|---|---|---|---|
| 1 | | | | | | | | 1 |
| 2 | | | | | | | | 2 |
| 3 | | | | | | | | 3 |
| 4 | | | | | | | | 4 |
| 5 | | | | | | | | 5 |
| 6 | | | | | | | | 6 |
| 7 | | | | | | | | 7 |
| 8 | | | | | | | | 8 |
| 9 | | | | | | | | 9 |
| 10 | | | | | | | | 10 |
| 11 | | | | | | | | 11 |
| 12 | | | | | | | | 12 |
| 13 | | | | | | | | 13 |
| 14 | | | | | | | | 14 |
| 15 | | | | | | | | 15 |
| 16 | | | | | | | | 16 |
| 17 | | | | | | | | 17 |
| 18 | | | | | | | | 18 |
| 19 | | | | | | | | 19 |
| 20 | | | | | | | | 20 |
| 21 | | | | | | | | 21 |
| 22 | | | | | | | | 22 |
| 23 | | | | | | | | 23 |
| 24 | | | | | | | | 24 |
| 25 | | | | | | | | 25 |
| 26 | | | | | | | | 26 |
| 27 | | | | | | | | 27 |
| 28 | | | | | | | | 28 |
| 29 | | | | | | | | 29 |
| 30 | | | | | | | | 30 |
| 31 | | | | | | | | 31 |
| 32 | | | | | | | | 32 |
| 33 | | | | | | | | 33 |

## 20-3 APPLICATION PROBLEM (concluded)

**CASH RECEIPTS JOURNAL**

| | DATE | ACCOUNT TITLE | DOC. NO. | POST. REF. | GENERAL DEBIT (1) | GENERAL CREDIT (2) | ACCOUNTS RECEIVABLE CREDIT (3) | SALES CREDIT (4) | SALES TAX PAYABLE CREDIT (5) | SALES DISCOUNT DEBIT (6) | CASH DEBIT (7) | |
|---|---|---|---|---|---|---|---|---|---|---|---|---|
| 1 | | | | | | | | | | | | 1 |
| 2 | | | | | | | | | | | | 2 |
| 3 | | | | | | | | | | | | 3 |
| 4 | | | | | | | | | | | | 4 |
| 5 | | | | | | | | | | | | 5 |
| 6 | | | | | | | | | | | | 6 |
| 7 | | | | | | | | | | | | 7 |
| 8 | | | | | | | | | | | | 8 |
| 9 | | | | | | | | | | | | 9 |
| 10 | | | | | | | | | | | | 10 |
| 11 | | | | | | | | | | | | 11 |
| 12 | | | | | | | | | | | | 12 |
| 13 | | | | | | | | | | | | 13 |
| 14 | | | | | | | | | | | | 14 |
| 15 | | | | | | | | | | | | 15 |
| 16 | | | | | | | | | | | | 16 |
| 17 | | | | | | | | | | | | 17 |
| 18 | | | | | | | | | | | | 18 |
| 19 | | | | | | | | | | | | 19 |
| 20 | | | | | | | | | | | | 20 |
| 21 | | | | | | | | | | | | 21 |
| 22 | | | | | | | | | | | | 22 |
| 23 | | | | | | | | | | | | 23 |
| 24 | | | | | | | | | | | | 24 |
| 25 | | | | | | | | | | | | 25 |

**Journalizing notes receivable transactions**

GENERAL JOURNAL

PAGE 18

| | DATE | | ACCOUNT TITLE | DOC. NO. | POST. REF. | DEBIT | CREDIT | |
|---|---|---|---|---|---|---|---|---|
| 1 | | | | | | | | 1 |
| 2 | | | | | | | | 2 |
| 3 | | | | | | | | 3 |
| 4 | | | | | | | | 4 |
| 5 | | | | | | | | 5 |
| 6 | | | | | | | | 6 |
| 7 | | | | | | | | 7 |
| 8 | | | | | | | | 8 |
| 9 | | | | | | | | 9 |
| 10 | | | | | | | | 10 |
| 11 | | | | | | | | 11 |
| 12 | | | | | | | | 12 |
| 13 | | | | | | | | 13 |
| 14 | | | | | | | | 14 |
| 15 | | | | | | | | 15 |
| 16 | | | | | | | | 16 |
| 17 | | | | | | | | 17 |
| 18 | | | | | | | | 18 |
| 19 | | | | | | | | 19 |
| 20 | | | | | | | | 20 |
| 21 | | | | | | | | 21 |
| 22 | | | | | | | | 22 |
| 23 | | | | | | | | 23 |
| 24 | | | | | | | | 24 |
| 25 | | | | | | | | 25 |
| 26 | | | | | | | | 26 |
| 27 | | | | | | | | 27 |
| 28 | | | | | | | | 28 |
| 29 | | | | | | | | 29 |
| 30 | | | | | | | | 30 |
| 31 | | | | | | | | 31 |
| 32 | | | | | | | | 32 |
| 33 | | | | | | | | 33 |

## 20-4 APPLICATION PROBLEM (concluded)

CASH RECEIPTS JOURNAL

PAGE 11

| | DATE | ACCOUNT TITLE | DOC. NO. | POST. REF. | GENERAL DEBIT 1 | GENERAL CREDIT 2 | ACCOUNTS RECEIVABLE CREDIT 3 | SALES CREDIT 4 | SALES TAX PAYABLE CREDIT 5 | SALES DISCOUNT DEBIT 6 | CASH DEBIT 7 | |
|---|---|---|---|---|---|---|---|---|---|---|---|---|
| 1 | | | | | | | | | | | | 1 |
| 2 | | | | | | | | | | | | 2 |
| 3 | | | | | | | | | | | | 3 |
| 4 | | | | | | | | | | | | 4 |
| 5 | | | | | | | | | | | | 5 |
| 6 | | | | | | | | | | | | 6 |
| 7 | | | | | | | | | | | | 7 |
| 8 | | | | | | | | | | | | 8 |
| 9 | | | | | | | | | | | | 9 |
| 10 | | | | | | | | | | | | 10 |
| 11 | | | | | | | | | | | | 11 |
| 12 | | | | | | | | | | | | 12 |
| 13 | | | | | | | | | | | | 13 |
| 14 | | | | | | | | | | | | 14 |
| 15 | | | | | | | | | | | | 15 |
| 16 | | | | | | | | | | | | 16 |
| 17 | | | | | | | | | | | | 17 |
| 18 | | | | | | | | | | | | 18 |
| 19 | | | | | | | | | | | | 19 |
| 20 | | | | | | | | | | | | 20 |
| 21 | | | | | | | | | | | | 21 |
| 22 | | | | | | | | | | | | 22 |
| 23 | | | | | | | | | | | | 23 |
| 24 | | | | | | | | | | | | 24 |
| 25 | | | | | | | | | | | | 25 |

**Journalizing notes payable and notes receivable transactions**

**1.**

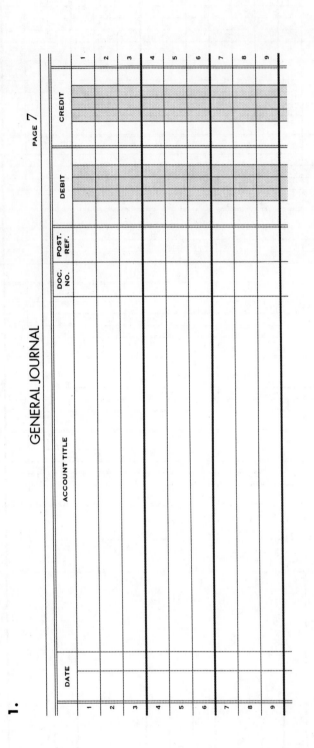

GENERAL JOURNAL PAGE 7

| DATE | ACCOUNT TITLE | DOC. NO. | POST. REF. | DEBIT | CREDIT |
|------|---------------|----------|------------|-------|--------|
| | | | | | |

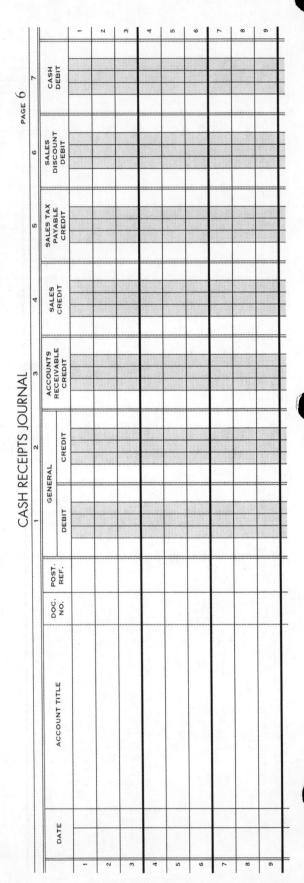

CASH RECEIPTS JOURNAL PAGE 6

## 20-5 MASTERY PROBLEM (continued)

**2.**

CASH PAYMENTS JOURNAL

PAGE 9

3.

| DATE | ACCOUNT TITLE | CK. NO. | POST. REF. | GENERAL DEBIT | GENERAL CREDIT | ACCOUNTS PAYABLE DEBIT | PURCHASES DISCOUNT CREDIT | CASH CREDIT | |
|------|---------------|---------|-----------|---------------|----------------|------------------------|---------------------------|-------------|---|
| | | | | 1 | 2 | 3 | 4 | 5 | |
| | | | | | | | | | 1 |
| | | | | | | | | | 2 |
| | | | | | | | | | 3 |
| | | | | | | | | | 4 |
| | | | | | | | | | 5 |
| | | | | | | | | | 6 |
| | | | | | | | | | 7 |
| | | | | | | | | | 8 |
| | | | | | | | | | 9 |
| | | | | | | | | | 10 |
| | | | | | | | | | 11 |
| | | | | | | | | | 12 |
| | | | | | | | | | 13 |
| | | | | | | | | | 14 |
| | | | | | | | | | 15 |
| | | | | | | | | | 16 |
| | | | | | | | | | 17 |
| | | | | | | | | | 18 |
| | | | | | | | | | 19 |
| | | | | | | | | | 20 |
| | | | | | | | | | 21 |
| | | | | | | | | | 22 |
| | | | | | | | | | 23 |
| | | | | | | | | | 24 |

## 20-6 CHALLENGE PROBLEM, p. 606

**Recording notes receivable stated in months**

**1.**

**2.**

**3.**

**4.**

## REINFORCEMENT ACTIVITY 3 PART A, pp. 610–613

**An accounting cycle for a corporation: journalizing and posting transactions**

**1.**

GENERAL JOURNAL PAGE 12

| | DATE | ACCOUNT TITLE | DOC. NO. | POST. REF. | DEBIT | CREDIT | |
|---|---|---|---|---|---|---|---|
| 1 | | | | | | | 1 |
| 2 | | | | | | | 2 |
| 3 | | | | | | | 3 |
| 4 | | | | | | | 4 |
| 5 | | | | | | | 5 |
| 6 | | | | | | | 6 |
| 7 | | | | | | | 7 |
| 8 | | | | | | | 8 |
| 9 | | | | | | | 9 |
| 10 | | | | | | | 10 |
| 11 | | | | | | | 11 |
| 12 | | | | | | | 12 |
| 13 | | | | | | | 13 |
| 14 | | | | | | | 14 |
| 15 | | | | | | | 15 |
| 16 | | | | | | | 16 |
| 17 | | | | | | | 17 |
| 18 | | | | | | | 18 |
| 19 | | | | | | | 19 |
| 20 | | | | | | | 20 |
| 21 | | | | | | | 21 |
| 22 | | | | | | | 22 |
| 23 | | | | | | | 23 |
| 24 | | | | | | | 24 |
| 25 | | | | | | | 25 |
| 26 | | | | | | | 26 |
| 27 | | | | | | | 27 |
| 28 | | | | | | | 28 |
| 29 | | | | | | | 29 |
| 30 | | | | | | | 30 |
| 31 | | | | | | | 31 |
| 32 | | | | | | | 32 |

# REINFORCEMENT ACTIVITY 3 PART A (continued)

**1., 2.**

SALES JOURNAL

| | DATE | ACCOUNT DEBITED | SALE NO. | POST. REF. | ACCOUNTS RECEIVABLE DEBIT (1) | SALES CREDIT (2) | SALES TAX PAYABLE CREDIT (3) | |
|---|---|---|---|---|---|---|---|---|
| 1 | | | | | | | | 1 |
| 2 | | | | | | | | 2 |
| 3 | | | | | | | | 3 |
| 4 | | | | | | | | 4 |
| 5 | | | | | | | | 5 |
| 6 | | | | | | | | 6 |
| 7 | | | | | | | | 7 |
| 8 | | | | | | | | 8 |
| 9 | | | | | | | | 9 |
| 10 | | | | | | | | 10 |
| 11 | | | | | | | | 11 |
| 12 | | | | | | | | 12 |
| 13 | | | | | | | | 13 |
| 14 | | | | | | | | 14 |
| 15 | | | | | | | | 15 |
| 16 | | | | | | | | 16 |
| 17 | | | | | | | | 17 |
| 18 | | | | | | | | 18 |

# REINFORCEMENT ACTIVITY 3 PART A (continued)

**1., 3.**

PURCHASES JOURNAL

PAGE 12

| | DATE | | ACCOUNT CREDITED | PURCH. NO. | POST. REF. | PURCHASES DR. ACCTS. PAY. CR. | |
|---|---|---|---|---|---|---|---|
| 1 | | | | | | | 1 |
| 2 | | | | | | | 2 |
| 3 | | | | | | | 3 |
| 4 | | | | | | | 4 |
| 5 | | | | | | | 5 |
| 6 | | | | | | | 6 |
| 7 | | | | | | | 7 |
| 8 | | | | | | | 8 |
| 9 | | | | | | | 9 |
| 10 | | | | | | | 10 |
| 11 | | | | | | | 11 |
| 12 | | | | | | | 12 |
| 13 | | | | | | | 13 |
| 14 | | | | | | | 14 |
| 15 | | | | | | | 15 |
| 16 | | | | | | | 16 |
| 17 | | | | | | | 17 |
| 18 | | | | | | | 18 |
| 19 | | | | | | | 19 |
| 20 | | | | | | | 20 |
| 21 | | | | | | | 21 |
| 22 | | | | | | | 22 |
| 23 | | | | | | | 23 |
| 24 | | | | | | | 24 |
| 25 | | | | | | | 25 |

**1., 4., 6.**

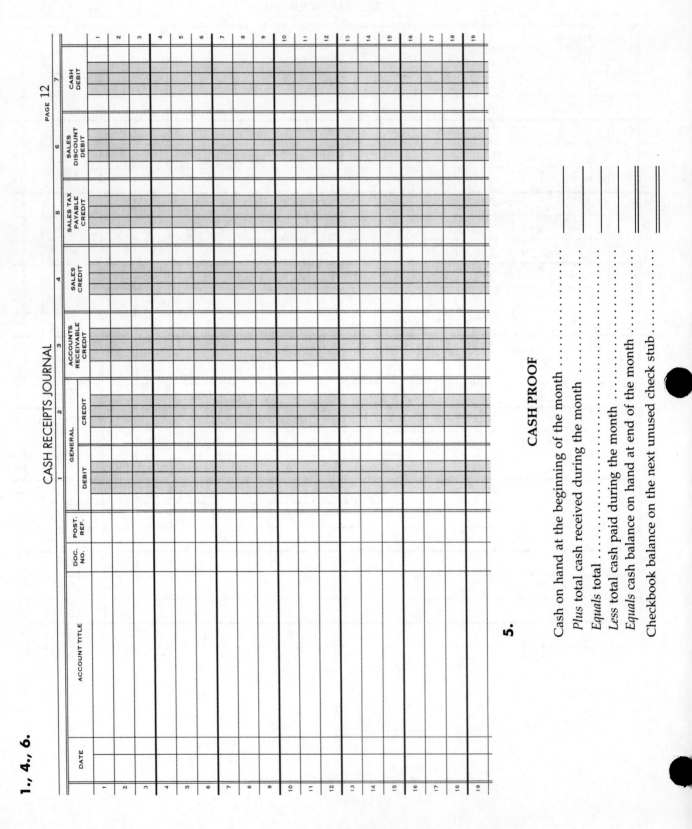

CASH RECEIPTS JOURNAL

PAGE 12

**5.**

## CASH PROOF

Cash on hand at the beginning of the month . . . . . . . . . . . . . . . . . .

*Plus* total cash received during the month . . . . . . . . . . . . . . . . . .

*Equals* total . . . . . . . . . . . . . . . . . .

*Less* total cash paid during the month . . . . . . . . . . . . . . . . . .

*Equals* cash balance on hand at end of the month . . . . . . . . . . . . . . . . . .

Checkbook balance on the next unused check stub . . . . . . . . . . . . . . . . . .

Name _____ Date _____ Class _____

## REINFORCEMENT ACTIVITY 3 PART A (continued)

**1., 4., 7.**

CASH PAYMENTS JOURNAL                                     PAGE 23

| | DATE | ACCOUNT TITLE | CK. NO. | POST. REF. | GENERAL DEBIT | GENERAL CREDIT | ACCOUNTS PAYABLE DEBIT | PURCHASES DISCOUNT CREDIT | CASH CREDIT | |
|---|---|---|---|---|---|---|---|---|---|---|
| 1 | | | | | | | | | | 1 |
| 2 | | | | | | | | | | 2 |
| 3 | | | | | | | | | | 3 |
| 4 | | | | | | | | | | 4 |
| 5 | | | | | | | | | | 5 |
| 6 | | | | | | | | | | 6 |
| 7 | | | | | | | | | | 7 |
| 8 | | | | | | | | | | 8 |
| 9 | | | | | | | | | | 9 |
| 10 | | | | | | | | | | 10 |
| 11 | | | | | | | | | | 11 |
| 12 | | | | | | | | | | 12 |
| 13 | | | | | | | | | | 13 |
| 14 | | | | | | | | | | 14 |
| 15 | | | | | | | | | | 15 |
| 16 | | | | | | | | | | 16 |
| 17 | | | | | | | | | | 17 |
| 18 | | | | | | | | | | 18 |
| 19 | | | | | | | | | | 19 |
| 20 | | | | | | | | | | 20 |
| 21 | | | | | | | | | | 21 |
| 22 | | | | | | | | | | 22 |
| 23 | | | | | | | | | | 23 |
| 24 | | | | | | | | | | 24 |
| 25 | | | | | | | | | | 25 |
| 26 | | | | | | | | | | 26 |
| 27 | | | | | | | | | | 27 |
| 28 | | | | | | | | | | 28 |
| 29 | | | | | | | | | | 29 |
| 30 | | | | | | | | | | 30 |
| 31 | | | | | | | | | | 31 |
| 32 | | | | | | | | | | 32 |

**1., 9.**

PLANT ASSET RECORD No. <u>432</u>  General Ledger Account No. <u>1215</u>

Description <u>Hand Truck</u>  General Ledger Account <u>Warehouse Equip.</u>

Date
Bought <u>January 5, 20X1</u>  Serial Number <u>215-225</u>  Original Cost <u>$2,900.00</u>

Estimated
Useful Life <u>5 years</u>  Estimated Salvage Value <u>$500.00</u>  Depreciation Method <u>Straight-line</u>

Disposed of:  Discarded _____  Sold _____  Traded _____
Date _____  Disposal Amount _____

| Year | Annual Depreciation Expense | Accumulated Depreciation | Ending Book Value |
|------|------|------|------|
| 20X1 | $480.00 | $ 480.00 | $2,420.00 |
| 20X2 | 480.00 | 960.00 | 1,940.00 |
| 20X3 | 480.00 | 1,440.00 | 1,460.00 |
| | | | |
| | | | |

PLANT ASSET RECORD No. <u>667</u>  General Ledger Account No. <u>1205</u>

Description <u>Computer Printer</u>  General Ledger Account <u>Office Equipment</u>

Date
Bought <u>April 5, 20X1</u>  Serial Number <u>BE35CC</u>  Original Cost <u>$850.00</u>

Estimated
Useful Life <u>3 years</u>  Estimated Salvage Value <u>$130.00</u>  Depreciation Method <u>Straight-line</u>

Disposed of:  Discarded _____  Sold _____  Traded _____
Date _____  Disposal Amount _____

| Year | Annual Depreciation Expense | Accumulated Depreciation | Ending Book Value |
|------|------|------|------|
| 20X2 | $180.00 | $180.00 | $670.00 |
| 20X3 | 240.00 | 420.00 | 430.00 |
| | | | |
| | | | |
| | | | |

## REINFORCEMENT ACTIVITY 3 PART A (continued)

| PLANT ASSET RECORD No. _____ | | General Ledger Account No. _____ |
|---|---|---|

Description _____     General Ledger Account _____

| Date Bought _____ | Serial Number _____ | Original Cost _____ |
|---|---|---|

| Estimated Useful Life _____ | Estimated Salvage Value _____ | Depreciation Method _____ |
|---|---|---|

Disposed of:     Discarded _____     Sold _____     Traded _____
Date _____     Disposal Amount _____

| Year | Annual Depreciation Expense | Accumulated Depreciation | Ending Book Value |
|---|---|---|---|
|  |  |  |  |
|  |  |  |  |
|  |  |  |  |
|  |  |  |  |
|  |  |  |  |

# REINFORCEMENT ACTIVITY 3 PART A (continued)

1.

## ACCOUNTS RECEIVABLE LEDGER

CUSTOMER Baker & Associates      CUSTOMER NO. 110

| DATE | ITEM | POST. REF. | DEBIT | CREDIT | DEBIT BALANCE |
|------|------|-----------|-------|--------|---------------|
|      |      |           |       |        |               |
|      |      |           |       |        |               |
|      |      |           |       |        |               |

CUSTOMER Felton Industries      CUSTOMER NO. 120

| DATE | ITEM | POST. REF. | DEBIT | CREDIT | DEBIT BALANCE |
|------|------|-----------|-------|--------|---------------|
| Dec. 1 | Balance | ✔ |  |  | 2 4 6 0 00 |
|      |      |           |       |        |               |
|      |      |           |       |        |               |

CUSTOMER Hilldale School      CUSTOMER NO. 130

| DATE | ITEM | POST. REF. | DEBIT | CREDIT | DEBIT BALANCE |
|------|------|-----------|-------|--------|---------------|
| Dec. 1 | Balance | ✔ |  |  | 2 4 3 00 |
|      |      |           |       |        |               |
|      |      |           |       |        |               |

CUSTOMER Horton Company      CUSTOMER NO. 140

| DATE | ITEM | POST. REF. | DEBIT | CREDIT | DEBIT BALANCE |
|------|------|-----------|-------|--------|---------------|
|      |      |           |       |        |               |
|      |      |           |       |        |               |
|      |      |           |       |        |               |

CUSTOMER Nelson Co.      CUSTOMER NO. 150

| DATE | ITEM | POST. REF. | DEBIT | CREDIT | DEBIT BALANCE |
|------|------|-----------|-------|--------|---------------|
| Dec. 1 | Balance | ✔ |  |  | 3 6 0 0 00 |
|      |      |           |       |        |               |

Name _____ Date _____ Class _____

## REINFORCEMENT ACTIVITY 3 PART A (continued)

| | DATE | | ITEM | POST. REF. | DEBIT | CREDIT | DEBIT BALANCE |
|---|---|---|---|---|---|---|---|
| Dec. | 1 | Balance | | ✔ | | | 3 2 5 0 00 |
| | | | | | | | |
| | | | | | | | |
| | | | | | | | |
| | | | | | | | |
| | | | | | | | |

CUSTOMER Ruocco Plastics    CUSTOMER NO. 160

**8.**

| | | |
|---|---|---|
| | | |
| | | |
| | | |
| | | |
| | | |
| | | |

# REINFORCEMENT ACTIVITY 3 PART A (continued)

**1.**

## ACCOUNTS PAYABLE LEDGER

VENDOR Buntin Supply Company

| DATE | | ITEM | POST. REF. | DEBIT | CREDIT | CREDIT BALANCE |
|---|---|---|---|---|---|---|
| 20-- Dec. | 1 | Balance | ✔ | | | 1 2 7 2 00 |
| | | | | | | |
| | | | | | | |

VENDOR Draper Company

VENDOR NO. 220

| DATE | | ITEM | POST. REF. | DEBIT | CREDIT | CREDIT BALANCE |
|---|---|---|---|---|---|---|
| 20-- Dec. | 1 | Balance | ✔ | | | 1 4 1 7 25 |
| | | | | | | |
| | | | | | | |
| | | | | | | |

VENDOR Glenson Company

VENDOR NO. 230

| DATE | | ITEM | POST. REF. | DEBIT | CREDIT | CREDIT BALANCE |
|---|---|---|---|---|---|---|
| 20-- Dec. | 1 | Balance | ✔ | | | 1 9 8 00 |
| | | | | | | |
| | | | | | | |
| | | | | | | |
| | | | | | | |
| | | | | | | |

VENDOR Hinsdale Supply Co.

VENDOR NO. 240

| DATE | | ITEM | POST. REF. | DEBIT | CREDIT | CREDIT BALANCE |
|---|---|---|---|---|---|---|
| | | | | | | |
| | | | | | | |
| | | | | | | |

VENDOR SHF Corp.

VENDOR NO. 250

| DATE | | ITEM | POST. REF. | DEBIT | CREDIT | CREDIT BALANCE |
|---|---|---|---|---|---|---|
| 20-- Dec. | 1 | Balance | ✔ | | | 5 8 0 00 |
| | | | | | | |
| | | | | | | |

# REINFORCEMENT ACTIVITY 3 PART A (continued)

VENDOR Walbash Manufacturing                                         VENDOR NO. 260

| DATE | | ITEM | POST. REF. | DEBIT | CREDIT | CREDIT BALANCE |
|---|---|---|---|---|---|---|
| Dec. | 1 | Balance | ✔ | | | 6 2 0 00 |
| | | | | | | |
| | | | | | | |

**8.**

| | | | |
|---|---|---|---|
| | | | |
| | | | |
| | | | |
| | | | |
| | | | |
| | | | |
| | | | |
| | | | |
| | | | |
| | | | |

**1., 2., 3., 6., 7., 18., 19., 21.**

## GENERAL LEDGER

ACCOUNT  Cash                                                    ACCOUNT NO. 1105

| DATE | | ITEM | POST. REF. | DEBIT | CREDIT | BALANCE | |
|---|---|---|---|---|---|---|---|
| | | | | | | DEBIT | CREDIT |
| 20-- Dec. | 1 | Balance | ✔ | | | 3 9 5 9 80 | |

ACCOUNT  Petty Cash                                              ACCOUNT NO. 1110

| DATE | | ITEM | POST. REF. | DEBIT | CREDIT | BALANCE | |
|---|---|---|---|---|---|---|---|
| | | | | | | DEBIT | CREDIT |
| 20-- Dec. | 1 | Balance | ✔ | | | 2 0 0 00 | |

ACCOUNT  Notes Receivable                                        ACCOUNT NO. 1115

| DATE | | ITEM | POST. REF. | DEBIT | CREDIT | BALANCE | |
|---|---|---|---|---|---|---|---|
| | | | | | | DEBIT | CREDIT |
| 20-- Dec. | 1 | Balance | ✔ | | | 8 8 0 0 00 | |

ACCOUNT  Interest Receivable                                     ACCOUNT NO. 1120

| DATE | | ITEM | POST. REF. | DEBIT | CREDIT | BALANCE | |
|---|---|---|---|---|---|---|---|
| | | | | | | DEBIT | CREDIT |
| | | | | | | | |

ACCOUNT  Accounts Receivable                                     ACCOUNT NO. 1125

| DATE | | ITEM | POST. REF. | DEBIT | CREDIT | BALANCE | |
|---|---|---|---|---|---|---|---|
| | | | | | | DEBIT | CREDIT |
| 20-- Dec. | 1 | Balance | ✔ | | | 9 5 5 3 00 | |

Name _____ Date _____ Class _____

# REINFORCEMENT ACTIVITY 3 PART A (continued)

ACCOUNT Allowance for Uncollectible Accounts — ACCOUNT NO. 1130

| DATE | ITEM | POST. REF. | DEBIT | CREDIT | BALANCE DEBIT | BALANCE CREDIT |
|------|------|-----------|-------|--------|------|-------|
| Dec. 1 | Balance | ✔ | | | | 4 2 60 |

ACCOUNT Merchandise Inventory — ACCOUNT NO. 1135

| DATE | ITEM | POST. REF. | DEBIT | CREDIT | BALANCE DEBIT | BALANCE CREDIT |
|------|------|-----------|-------|--------|------|-------|
| Dec. 1 | Balance | ✔ | | | 74 1 7 6 95 | |

ACCOUNT Supplies — ACCOUNT NO. 1140

| DATE | ITEM | POST. REF. | DEBIT | CREDIT | BALANCE DEBIT | BALANCE CREDIT |
|------|------|-----------|-------|--------|------|-------|
| Dec. 1 | Balance | ✔ | | | 2 5 0 1 15 | |

ACCOUNT Prepaid Insurance — ACCOUNT NO. 1145

| DATE | ITEM | POST. REF. | DEBIT | CREDIT | BALANCE DEBIT | BALANCE CREDIT |
|------|------|-----------|-------|--------|------|-------|
| Dec. 1 | Balance | ✔ | | | 8 6 0 0 00 | |

ACCOUNT Office Equipment — ACCOUNT NO. 1205

| DATE | ITEM | POST. REF. | DEBIT | CREDIT | BALANCE DEBIT | BALANCE CREDIT |
|------|------|-----------|-------|--------|------|-------|
| Dec. 1 | Balance | ✔ | | | 23 4 8 0 00 | |

# REINFORCEMENT ACTIVITY 3 PART A (continued)

ACCOUNT Accumulated Depreciation—Office Equipment    ACCOUNT NO. 1210

| DATE | ITEM | POST. REF. | DEBIT | CREDIT | BALANCE DEBIT | BALANCE CREDIT |
|---|---|---|---|---|---|---|
| Dec. 1 | Balance | ✔ | | | | 7 5 8 0 00 |

ACCOUNT Warehouse Equipment    ACCOUNT NO. 1215

| DATE | ITEM | POST. REF. | DEBIT | CREDIT | BALANCE DEBIT | BALANCE CREDIT |
|---|---|---|---|---|---|---|
| Dec. 1 | Balance | ✔ | | | 29 0 1 0 00 | |

ACCOUNT Accumulated Depreciation—Warehouse Equipment    ACCOUNT NO. 1220

| DATE | ITEM | POST. REF. | DEBIT | CREDIT | BALANCE DEBIT | BALANCE CREDIT |
|---|---|---|---|---|---|---|
| Dec. 1 | Balance | ✔ | | | | 8 4 8 0 00 |

ACCOUNT Notes Payable    ACCOUNT NO. 2105

| DATE | ITEM | POST. REF. | DEBIT | CREDIT | BALANCE DEBIT | BALANCE CREDIT |
|---|---|---|---|---|---|---|
| Dec. 1 | Balance | ✔ | | | | 20 0 0 0 00 |

ACCOUNT Interest Payable    ACCOUNT NO. 2110

| DATE | ITEM | POST. REF. | DEBIT | CREDIT | BALANCE DEBIT | BALANCE CREDIT |
|---|---|---|---|---|---|---|
| | | | | | | |

## REINFORCEMENT ACTIVITY 3 PART A (continued)

ACCOUNT  Accounts Payable                                    ACCOUNT NO. 2115

| DATE | | ITEM | POST. REF. | DEBIT | CREDIT | BALANCE | |
|---|---|---|---|---|---|---|---|
| | | | | | | DEBIT | CREDIT |
| 20-- Dec. | 1 | Balance | ✔ | | | | 4 0 8 7 25 |
| | | | | | | | |
| | | | | | | | |
| | | | | | | | |
| | | | | | | | |
| | | | | | | | |

ACCOUNT  Federal Income Tax Payable                          ACCOUNT NO. 2120

| DATE | | ITEM | POST. REF. | DEBIT | CREDIT | BALANCE | |
|---|---|---|---|---|---|---|---|
| | | | | | | DEBIT | CREDIT |
| | | | | | | | |
| | | | | | | | |
| | | | | | | | |

ACCOUNT  Employee Income Tax Payable                         ACCOUNT NO. 2125

| DATE | | ITEM | POST. REF. | DEBIT | CREDIT | BALANCE | |
|---|---|---|---|---|---|---|---|
| | | | | | | DEBIT | CREDIT |
| 20-- Dec. | 1 | Balance | ✔ | | | | 3 2 4 00 |
| | | | | | | | |
| | | | | | | | |
| | | | | | | | |
| | | | | | | | |

ACCOUNT  Social Security Tax Payable                         ACCOUNT NO. 2130

| DATE | | ITEM | POST. REF. | DEBIT | CREDIT | BALANCE | |
|---|---|---|---|---|---|---|---|
| | | | | | | DEBIT | CREDIT |
| 20-- Dec. | 1 | Balance | ✔ | | | | 7 4 2 00 |
| | | | | | | | |
| | | | | | | | |
| | | | | | | | |
| | | | | | | | |
| | | | | | | | |

ACCOUNT Medicare Tax Payable                                    ACCOUNT NO. 2135

| DATE | | ITEM | POST. REF. | DEBIT | CREDIT | BALANCE DEBIT | BALANCE CREDIT |
|---|---|---|---|---|---|---|---|
| 20-- Dec. | 1 | Balance | ✔ | | | | 1 6 2 35 |
| | | | | | | | |
| | | | | | | | |
| | | | | | | | |
| | | | | | | | |
| | | | | | | | |

ACCOUNT Sales Tax Payable                                       ACCOUNT NO. 2140

| DATE | | ITEM | POST. REF. | DEBIT | CREDIT | BALANCE DEBIT | BALANCE CREDIT |
|---|---|---|---|---|---|---|---|
| 20-- Dec. | 1 | Balance | ✔ | | | | 4 9 4 2 68 |
| | | | | | | | |
| | | | | | | | |
| | | | | | | | |
| | | | | | | | |

ACCOUNT Unemployment Tax Payable—Federal                        ACCOUNT NO. 2145

| DATE | | ITEM | POST. REF. | DEBIT | CREDIT | BALANCE DEBIT | BALANCE CREDIT |
|---|---|---|---|---|---|---|---|
| 20-- Dec. | 1 | Balance | ✔ | | | | 1 3 05 |
| | | | | | | | |
| | | | | | | | |
| | | | | | | | |

ACCOUNT Unemployment Tax Payable—State                          ACCOUNT NO. 2150

| DATE | | ITEM | POST. REF. | DEBIT | CREDIT | BALANCE DEBIT | BALANCE CREDIT |
|---|---|---|---|---|---|---|---|
| 20-- Dec. | 1 | Balance | ✔ | | | | 8 8 05 |
| | | | | | | | |
| | | | | | | | |
| | | | | | | | |

ACCOUNT Health Insurance Premiums Payable                       ACCOUNT NO. 2155

| DATE | | ITEM | POST. REF. | DEBIT | CREDIT | BALANCE DEBIT | BALANCE CREDIT |
|---|---|---|---|---|---|---|---|
| 20-- Dec. | 1 | Balance | ✔ | | | | 7 2 5 00 |
| | | | | | | | |
| | | | | | | | |

## REINFORCEMENT ACTIVITY 3 PART A (continued)

ACCOUNT Dividends Payable                                ACCOUNT NO. 2160

| DATE | | ITEM | POST. REF. | DEBIT | CREDIT | BALANCE | |
|---|---|---|---|---|---|---|---|
| | | | | | | DEBIT | CREDIT |
| 20-- Dec. | 1 | Balance | ✔ | | | | 5 0 0 0 00 |
| | | | | | | | |

ACCOUNT Capital Stock                                    ACCOUNT NO. 3105

| DATE | | ITEM | POST. REF. | DEBIT | CREDIT | BALANCE | |
|---|---|---|---|---|---|---|---|
| | | | | | | DEBIT | CREDIT |
| 20-- Dec. | 1 | Balance | ✔ | | | | 30 0 0 0 00 |
| | | | | | | | |

ACCOUNT Retained Earnings                                ACCOUNT NO. 3110

| DATE | | ITEM | POST. REF. | DEBIT | CREDIT | BALANCE | |
|---|---|---|---|---|---|---|---|
| | | | | | | DEBIT | CREDIT |
| 20-- Dec. | 1 | Balance | ✔ | | | | 23 8 8 9 20 |
| | | | | | | | |
| | | | | | | | |
| | | | | | | | |

ACCOUNT Dividends                                        ACCOUNT NO. 3115

| DATE | | ITEM | POST. REF. | DEBIT | CREDIT | BALANCE | |
|---|---|---|---|---|---|---|---|
| | | | | | | DEBIT | CREDIT |
| 20-- Dec. | 1 | Balance | ✔ | | | 20 0 0 0 00 | |
| | | | | | | | |
| | | | | | | | |

ACCOUNT Income Summary                                   ACCOUNT NO. 3120

| DATE | | ITEM | POST. REF. | DEBIT | CREDIT | BALANCE | |
|---|---|---|---|---|---|---|---|
| | | | | | | DEBIT | CREDIT |
| | | | | | | | |
| | | | | | | | |
| | | | | | | | |
| | | | | | | | |
| | | | | | | | |

ACCOUNT Sales                                            ACCOUNT NO. 4105

| DATE | | ITEM | POST. REF. | DEBIT | CREDIT | BALANCE | |
|---|---|---|---|---|---|---|---|
| | | | | | | DEBIT | CREDIT |
| 20-- Dec. | 1 | Balance | ✔ | | | | 756 3 9 7 90 |
| | | | | | | | |
| | | | | | | | |
| | | | | | | | |

# REINFORCEMENT ACTIVITY 3 PART A (continued)

ACCOUNT Sales Discount      ACCOUNT NO. 4110

| DATE | ITEM | POST. REF. | DEBIT | CREDIT | BALANCE DEBIT | BALANCE CREDIT |
|---|---|---|---|---|---|---|
| 20-- Dec. 1 | Balance | ✔ | | | 1 8 7 8 60 | |
| | | | | | | |
| | | | | | | |

ACCOUNT Sales Returns and Allowances      ACCOUNT NO. 4115

| DATE | ITEM | POST. REF. | DEBIT | CREDIT | BALANCE DEBIT | BALANCE CREDIT |
|---|---|---|---|---|---|---|
| 20-- Dec. 1 | Balance | ✔ | | | 6 0 5 4 80 | |
| | | | | | | |
| | | | | | | |
| | | | | | | |

ACCOUNT Purchases      ACCOUNT NO. 5105

| DATE | ITEM | POST. REF. | DEBIT | CREDIT | BALANCE DEBIT | BALANCE CREDIT |
|---|---|---|---|---|---|---|
| 20-- Dec. 1 | Balance | ✔ | | | 506 3 5 4 40 | |
| | | | | | | |
| | | | | | | |
| | | | | | | |
| | | | | | | |

ACCOUNT Purchases Discount      ACCOUNT NO. 5110

| DATE | ITEM | POST. REF. | DEBIT | CREDIT | BALANCE DEBIT | BALANCE CREDIT |
|---|---|---|---|---|---|---|
| 20-- Dec. 1 | Balance | ✔ | | | | 3 4 9 3 32 |
| | | | | | | |
| | | | | | | |
| | | | | | | |

ACCOUNT Purchases Returns and Allowances      ACCOUNT NO. 5115

| DATE | ITEM | POST. REF. | DEBIT | CREDIT | BALANCE DEBIT | BALANCE CREDIT |
|---|---|---|---|---|---|---|
| 20-- Dec. 1 | Balance | ✔ | | | | 3 0 3 8 00 |
| | | | | | | |
| | | | | | | |

## REINFORCEMENT ACTIVITY 3 PART A (continued)

ACCOUNT Advertising Expense                                ACCOUNT NO. 6105

| DATE | | ITEM | POST. REF. | DEBIT | CREDIT | BALANCE | |
|---|---|---|---|---|---|---|---|
| | | | | | | DEBIT | CREDIT |
| Dec. | 1 | Balance | ✔ | | | 9 5 5 6 70 | |
| | | | | | | | |
| | | | | | | | |
| | | | | | | | |

ACCOUNT Cash Short and Over                                ACCOUNT NO. 6110

| DATE | | ITEM | POST. REF. | DEBIT | CREDIT | BALANCE | |
|---|---|---|---|---|---|---|---|
| | | | | | | DEBIT | CREDIT |
| Dec. | 1 | Balance | ✔ | | | 2 0 00 | |
| | | | | | | | |
| | | | | | | | |
| | | | | | | | |

ACCOUNT Credit Card Fee Expense                            ACCOUNT NO. 6115

| DATE | | ITEM | POST. REF. | DEBIT | CREDIT | BALANCE | |
|---|---|---|---|---|---|---|---|
| | | | | | | DEBIT | CREDIT |
| Dec. | 1 | Balance | ✔ | | | 14 1 1 1 40 | |
| | | | | | | | |
| | | | | | | | |
| | | | | | | | |

ACCOUNT Depreciation Expense—Office Equipment              ACCOUNT NO. 6120

| DATE | | ITEM | POST. REF. | DEBIT | CREDIT | BALANCE | |
|---|---|---|---|---|---|---|---|
| | | | | | | DEBIT | CREDIT |
| | | | | | | | |
| | | | | | | | |
| | | | | | | | |
| | | | | | | | |

ACCOUNT Depreciation Expense—Warehouse Equipment           ACCOUNT NO. 6125

| DATE | | ITEM | POST. REF. | DEBIT | CREDIT | BALANCE | |
|---|---|---|---|---|---|---|---|
| | | | | | | DEBIT | CREDIT |
| | | | | | | | |
| | | | | | | | |
| | | | | | | | |

# REINFORCEMENT ACTIVITY 3 PART A (continued)

ACCOUNT  Insurance Expense                                              ACCOUNT NO. 6130

| DATE | ITEM | POST. REF. | DEBIT | CREDIT | BALANCE | |
|------|------|-----------|-------|--------|---------|---|
| | | | | | DEBIT | CREDIT |
| | | | | | | |
| | | | | | | |
| | | | | | | |

ACCOUNT  Miscellaneous Expense                                          ACCOUNT NO. 6135

| DATE | ITEM | POST. REF. | DEBIT | CREDIT | BALANCE | |
|------|------|-----------|-------|--------|---------|---|
| | | | | | DEBIT | CREDIT |
| 20-- Dec. | 1 | Balance | ✔ | | | 5 7 3 3 95 | |
| | | | | | | |
| | | | | | | |
| | | | | | | |
| | | | | | | |

ACCOUNT  Payroll Taxes Expense                                          ACCOUNT NO. 6140

| DATE | ITEM | POST. REF. | DEBIT | CREDIT | BALANCE | |
|------|------|-----------|-------|--------|---------|---|
| | | | | | DEBIT | CREDIT |
| 20-- Dec. | 1 | Balance | ✔ | | | 10 1 7 6 85 | |
| | | | | | | |
| | | | | | | |
| | | | | | | |
| | | | | | | |

ACCOUNT  Rent Expense                                                   ACCOUNT NO. 6145

| DATE | ITEM | POST. REF. | DEBIT | CREDIT | BALANCE | |
|------|------|-----------|-------|--------|---------|---|
| | | | | | DEBIT | CREDIT |
| 20-- Dec. | 1 | Balance | ✔ | | | 19 2 5 0 00 | |
| | | | | | | |
| | | | | | | |
| | | | | | | |

ACCOUNT  Repairs Expense                                                ACCOUNT NO. 6150

| DATE | ITEM | POST. REF. | DEBIT | CREDIT | BALANCE | |
|------|------|-----------|-------|--------|---------|---|
| | | | | | DEBIT | CREDIT |
| 20-- Dec. | | Balance | ✔ | | | 1 3 9 4 80 | |
| | | | | | | |

## REINFORCEMENT ACTIVITY 3 PART A (continued)

ACCOUNT Salary Expense                                                          ACCOUNT NO. 6155

| DATE | ITEM | POST. REF. | DEBIT | CREDIT | BALANCE DEBIT | BALANCE CREDIT |
|---|---|---|---|---|---|---|
| 20-- Dec. 1 | Balance | ✔ | | | 99 2 9 8 00 | |
| | | | | | | |
| | | | | | | |
| | | | | | | |
| | | | | | | |

ACCOUNT Supplies Expense                                                        ACCOUNT NO. 6160

| DATE | ITEM | POST. REF. | DEBIT | CREDIT | BALANCE DEBIT | BALANCE CREDIT |
|---|---|---|---|---|---|---|
| | | | | | | |
| | | | | | | |
| | | | | | | |
| | | | | | | |

ACCOUNT Uncollectible Accounts Expense                                          ACCOUNT NO. 6165

| DATE | ITEM | POST. REF. | DEBIT | CREDIT | BALANCE DEBIT | BALANCE CREDIT |
|---|---|---|---|---|---|---|
| | | | | | | |
| | | | | | | |
| | | | | | | |
| | | | | | | |

ACCOUNT Utilities Expense                                                       ACCOUNT NO. 6170

| DATE | ITEM | POST. REF. | DEBIT | CREDIT | BALANCE DEBIT | BALANCE CREDIT |
|---|---|---|---|---|---|---|
| 20-- Dec. 1 | Balance | ✔ | | | 6 8 9 0 00 | |
| | | | | | | |
| | | | | | | |
| | | | | | | |

ACCOUNT Gain on Plant Assets                                                    ACCOUNT NO. 7105

| DATE | ITEM | POST. REF. | DEBIT | CREDIT | BALANCE DEBIT | BALANCE CREDIT |
|---|---|---|---|---|---|---|
| 20-- Dec. 1 | Balance | ✔ | | | | 3 6 5 00 |
| | | | | | | |
| | | | | | | |
| | | | | | | |

ACCOUNT  Interest Income                                      ACCOUNT NO. 7110

| DATE | | ITEM | POST. REF. | DEBIT | CREDIT | BALANCE | |
|---|---|---|---|---|---|---|---|
| | | | | | | DEBIT | CREDIT |
| Dec. 20-- | 1 | Balance | ✔ | | | | 1 8 0 00 |
| | | | | | | | |
| | | | | | | | |
| | | | | | | | |
| | | | | | | | |

ACCOUNT  Interest Expense                                     ACCOUNT NO. 8105

| DATE | | ITEM | POST. REF. | DEBIT | CREDIT | BALANCE | |
|---|---|---|---|---|---|---|---|
| | | | | | | DEBIT | CREDIT |
| Dec. 20-- | 1 | Balance | ✔ | | | 2 3 0 0 00 | |
| | | | | | | | |
| | | | | | | | |
| | | | | | | | |
| | | | | | | | |

ACCOUNT  Loss on Plant Assets                                 ACCOUNT NO. 8110

| DATE | | ITEM | POST. REF. | DEBIT | CREDIT | BALANCE | |
|---|---|---|---|---|---|---|---|
| | | | | | | DEBIT | CREDIT |
| Dec. 20-- | 1 | Balance | ✔ | | | 2 5 0 00 | |
| | | | | | | | |
| | | | | | | | |

ACCOUNT  Federal Income Tax Expense                           ACCOUNT NO. 9105

| DATE | | ITEM | POST. REF. | DEBIT | CREDIT | BALANCE | |
|---|---|---|---|---|---|---|---|
| | | | | | | DEBIT | CREDIT |
| Dec. 20-- | 1 | Balance | ✔ | | | 6 0 0 0 00 | |
| | | | | | | | |
| | | | | | | | |

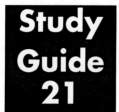

| Name | | Perfect Score | Your Score |
|---|---|---|---|
| | Identifying Accounting Concepts and Practices | 15 Pts. | |
| | Analyzing Accounts Affected by Accrued Revenue and Accrued Expenses | 18 Pts. | |
| | Analyzing Accrued Revenue and Accrued Expenses | 11 Pts. | |
| | **Total** | 44 Pts. | |

## Part One—Identifying Accounting Concepts and Practices

**Directions:** For each of the following items, select the choice that best completes the statement. Print the letter identifying your choice in the Answers column.

**Answers**

1. At the end of a fiscal period, each expense that has been incurred but not paid should be recorded as (A) an adjusting entry (B) a reversing entry (C) a closing entry (D) an opening entry. (p. 616)

1. _____

2. Revenue earned in one fiscal period but not received until a later fiscal period is called (A) accrued expense (B) accrued interest expense (C) accrued revenue (D) deferred interest income. (p. 616)

2. _____

3. Recording adjusting entries for the fiscal period in which the revenue has been earned regardless of when it will be received is an application of the accounting concept (A) Objective Evidence (B) Realization of Revenue (C) Adequate Disclosure (D) Historical Cost. (p. 616)

3. _____

4. At the end of a fiscal period, any revenue that has been earned but not received should be credited to an appropriate (A) revenue account (B) expense account (C) liability account (D) asset account. (p. 616)

4. _____

5. Interest earned but not yet received is called (A) accrued interest income (B) deferred interest income (C) deferred earned income (D) none of these. (p. 617)

5. _____

6. Interest Receivable is (A) an asset (B) a liability (C) revenue (D) an expense. (p. 618)

6. _____

7. An entry made at the beginning of one fiscal period to reverse an adjusting entry made in the previous fiscal period is called (A) a debit entry (B) a credit entry (C) a reversing entry (D) none of these. (p. 619)

7. _____

8. A reversing entry for accrued interest income results in a debit to (A) Interest Receivable (B) Notes Receivable (C) Income Summary (D) Interest Income. (p. 619)

8. _____

9. A reversing entry for accrued interest income will result in an account balance of (A) Interest Receivable debit (B) Interest Income debit (C) Interest Receivable credit (D) Interest Income credit. (p. 619)

9. _____

10. Expenses incurred in one fiscal period but not paid until a later fiscal period are called (A) accrued interest expenses (B) accrued expenses (C) accrued income expenses (D) accrued interest receivable. (p. 622)

10. _____

11. At the end of a fiscal period, each expense that has been incurred but not paid should be debited to an appropriate (A) revenue account (B) expense account (C) asset account (D) liability account. (p. 622)

11. _____

12. Interest incurred but not yet paid is called (A) accrued income expense (B) earned income (C) accrued interest expense (D) deferred interest expense. (p. 622)

12. _____

13. At the end of a fiscal period, each expense that has been incurred but not paid should be credited to an appropriate (A) revenue account (B) expense account (C) asset account (D) liability account. (p. 622)

13. _____

14. A reversing entry for accrued interest expense will result in an account balance of (A) Interest Payable debit (B) Interest Payable credit (C) Interest Expense debit (D) Interest Expense credit. (p. 624)

14. _____

15. An adjusting entry normally is reversed if the adjusting entry creates a balance in (A) a revenue or expense account (B) a revenue and liability account (C) an expense and asset account (D) an asset or liability account. (p. 626)

15. _____

## Part Two—Analyzing Accounts Affected by Accrued Revenue and Accrued Expenses

**Directions:** Analyze each of the following entries into debit and credit parts. Print the letter identifying your choice in the proper Answers columns. Determine in which journal each of the transactions are to be recorded.

G—General journal  CP—Cash payments journal  CR—Cash receipts journal

| Account Titles | Transactions | Journal | Answers Debit | Credit |
|---|---|---|---|---|
| A.  Cash | 1–2–3. Recorded an adjustment for accrued interest income. (p. 617) | 1. _____ | 2. _____ | 3. _____ |
| B.  Interest Expense | 4–5–6. Reversed an adjusting entry for accrued interest income. (p. 619) | 4. _____ | 5. _____ | 6. _____ |
| C.  Interest Income | 7–8–9. Received cash for the maturity value of a 90-day, 12% note. (p. 620) | 7. _____ | 8. _____ | 9. _____ |
| D.  Interest Payable | 10–11–12. Recorded an adjustment for accrued interest expense. (p. 622) | 10. _____ | 11. _____ | 12. _____ |
| E.  Interest Receivable | 13–14–15. Reversed an adjusting entry for accrued interest expense. (p. 624) | 13. _____ | 14. _____ | 15. _____ |
| F.  Notes Payable | 16–17–18. Paid cash for the maturity value of a note payable plus interest. (p. 625) | 16. _____ | 17. _____ | 18. _____ |
| G.  Notes Receivable | | | | |

## Part Three—Analyzing Accrued Revenue and Accrued Expenses

**Directions:** Place a *T* for True or an *F* for False in the Answers column to show whether each of the following statements is true or false.

**Answers**

1. Revenue should be recorded when the revenue is earned. (p. 616)

    1. _____

2. Adjusting entries are made at the beginning of each fiscal period. (p. 616)

    2. _____

3. The adjustment for accrued interest income is planned on a work sheet. (p. 617)

    3. _____

4. Accrued interest income is credited to the interest income account. (p. 617)

    4. _____

5. When an adjusting entry for accrued interest income is made, Interest Receivable is debited. (p. 617)

    5. _____

6. Accrued interest is calculated by multiplying principal times interest rate times time as a fraction of a year. (p. 617)

    6. _____

7. Reversing entries are made on the last day of the fiscal period. (p. 619)

    7. _____

8. A reversing entry for interest income reduces the balance of Interest Receivable. (p. 619)

    8. _____

9. At the end of a fiscal period, the Interest Expense balance after adjustments shows the amount of interest expense that has been incurred in that fiscal period. (p. 622)

    9. _____

10. An Interest Payable credit balance is accrued interest expense incurred in the current year but to be paid in the next year. (p. 622)

    10. _____

11. When a reversing entry is made for accrued interest expense, a debit entry is required to Interest Payable. (p. 624)

    11. _____

# Study Skills

## Following Directions

"I thought you said the paper was due next week."
"Isn't this what I was supposed to do?"
"When did you tell us to do that?"

These are remarks often heard at school. A student has missed a deadline; another has done the wrong assignment; a third did not recall receiving the assignment at all. All three will receive a poor grade when they could easily have made a good grade. Why? The reason is that they did not listen to directions or they did not follow directions.

### Listen Attentively

In order to meet all deadlines, you must listen very carefully when an assignment is made. Your teacher will probably give complete directions, including due date. If any part of the assignment is not clear, you should ask for a clarification when the assignment is made. If you have any doubt about the format, the content, or the due date, you should ask immediately. Do not wait to ask until it is time to turn in the assignment. You may miss the deadline altogether, or you may not allow yourself enough time to complete the assignment properly.

### Follow Directions to the Letter

You must complete each assignment according to the directions your teacher gives. For example, you may be asked to write a major paper. Your teacher will probably give you detailed instructions on how information is to be collected and how it is to be presented in the paper.

If your teacher asks you to obtain references from at least three books, be sure that you do. Four books will be satisfactory, but two will not. If asked to use current references, articles three or four years old will not be satisfactory. If your teacher asks you to use charts and graphs to illustrate your points, be sure that you include them.

### Use the Right Format

There are many formats that are acceptable for preparing most assignments. If your teacher asks you to use a specific format, you must follow it, even if you prefer another. If no format is specified for a writing assignment, you should ask. If there is no preference, you should use a simple format and be completely consistent.

### Right on Schedule

If you have a major assignment given to you at the beginning of the term, begin work early, following all directions. If you leave all the work to do at the last minute, the quality will suffer and so will your grade. It is not usually possible to collect a large amount of information overnight. In addition, if you try to do all your work just before it is due, you will have no time to reflect on the work and change any part that you do not like.

Be absolutely sure to turn your assignment in right on schedule. It should not be necessary for you to ask for extra time to finish it.

### Improve Your Grades

Following directions to the letter is very easy; however, some students never seem to realize this. One of the easiest ways to improve your grades is to prepare every assignment exactly as it is assigned. The result will show in your grades.

Name _____ Date _____ Class _____

## 21-1 WORK TOGETHER, p. 621

**Journalizing and posting entries for accrued revenue**

**1.**

Marris Corporation

Work Sheet

For Year Ended December 31, 20 – –

| | | | 1 | 2 | 3 | 4 |
|---|---|---|---|---|---|---|
| | ACCOUNT TITLE | | TRIAL BALANCE | | ADJUSTMENTS | |
| | | | DEBIT | CREDIT | DEBIT | CREDIT |
| 4 | Interest Receivable | | | | | |
| 50 | Interest Income | | | 1 5 4 5 00 | | |

**2., 3.**

GENERAL JOURNAL                                    PAGE 14

| | DATE | ACCOUNT TITLE | DOC. NO. | POST. REF. | DEBIT | CREDIT | |
|---|---|---|---|---|---|---|---|
| 1 | | | | | | | 1 |
| 2 | | | | | | | 2 |
| 3 | | | | | | | 3 |
| 4 | | | | | | | 4 |
| 5 | | | | | | | 5 |
| 6 | | | | | | | 6 |
| 7 | | | | | | | 7 |
| 8 | | | | | | | 8 |

**4.**

GENERAL JOURNAL                                    PAGE 15

| | DATE | ACCOUNT TITLE | DOC. NO. | POST. REF. | DEBIT | CREDIT | |
|---|---|---|---|---|---|---|---|
| 1 | | | | | | | 1 |
| 2 | | | | | | | 2 |
| 3 | | | | | | | 3 |
| 4 | | | | | | | 4 |

**5.**

CASH RECEIPTS JOURNAL

PAGE 16

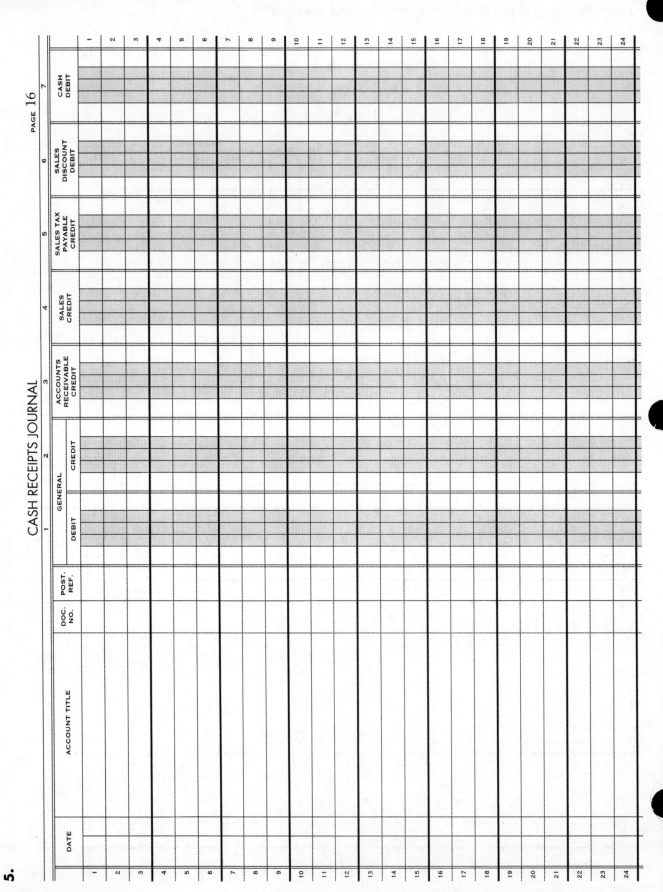

| | | | | 1 GENERAL | 2 | 3 ACCOUNTS RECEIVABLE CREDIT | 4 SALES CREDIT | 5 SALES TAX PAYABLE CREDIT | 6 SALES DISCOUNT DEBIT | 7 CASH DEBIT |
|---|---|---|---|---|---|---|---|---|---|---|
| DATE | ACCOUNT TITLE | DOC. NO. | POST. REF. | DEBIT | CREDIT | | | | | |

## 21-1 WORK TOGETHER (concluded)

**2., 3., 4., 5.**          **GENERAL LEDGER**

ACCOUNT **Notes Receivable**        ACCOUNT NO. **1115**

| DATE | ITEM | POST. REF. | DEBIT | CREDIT | BALANCE DEBIT | BALANCE CREDIT |
|------|------|-----------|-------|--------|-------|--------|
| Nov. 16 | | G11 | 4 000 00 | | 4 000 00 | |
| | | | | | | |
| | | | | | | |

ACCOUNT **Interest Receivable**        ACCOUNT NO. **1120**

| DATE | ITEM | POST. REF. | DEBIT | CREDIT | BALANCE DEBIT | BALANCE CREDIT |
|------|------|-----------|-------|--------|-------|--------|
| | | | | | | |
| | | | | | | |
| | | | | | | |
| | | | | | | |

ACCOUNT **Income Summary**        ACCOUNT NO. **3120**

| DATE | ITEM | POST. REF. | DEBIT | CREDIT | BALANCE DEBIT | BALANCE CREDIT |
|------|------|-----------|-------|--------|-------|--------|
| | | | | | | |
| | | | | | | |
| | | | | | | |
| | | | | | | |

ACCOUNT **Interest Income**        ACCOUNT NO. **7110**

| DATE | ITEM | POST. REF. | DEBIT | CREDIT | BALANCE DEBIT | BALANCE CREDIT |
|------|------|-----------|-------|--------|-------|--------|
| Dec. 31 | | CR15 | | 1 5 00 | | 1 5 45 00 |
| | | | | | | |
| | | | | | | |
| | | | | | | |

**Journalizing and posting entries for accrued revenue**

**1.**

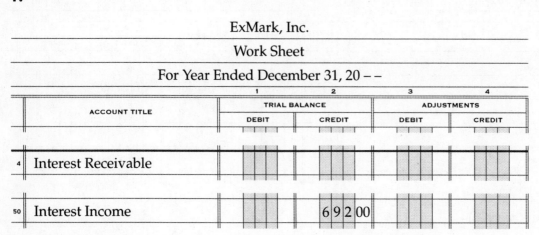

ExMark, Inc.

Work Sheet

For Year Ended December 31, 20 – –

| | | 1 | 2 | 3 | 4 |
|---|---|---|---|---|---|
| | ACCOUNT TITLE | TRIAL BALANCE | | ADJUSTMENTS | |
| | | DEBIT | CREDIT | DEBIT | CREDIT |
| 4 | Interest Receivable | | | | |
| 50 | Interest Income | | 6 9 2 00 | | |

**2., 3.**

GENERAL JOURNAL                                          PAGE 14

| | DATE | ACCOUNT TITLE | DOC. NO. | POST. REF. | DEBIT | CREDIT | |
|---|---|---|---|---|---|---|---|
| 1 | | | | | | | 1 |
| 2 | | | | | | | 2 |
| 3 | | | | | | | 3 |
| 4 | | | | | | | 4 |
| 5 | | | | | | | 5 |
| 6 | | | | | | | 6 |
| 7 | | | | | | | 7 |
| 8 | | | | | | | 8 |

**4.**

GENERAL JOURNAL                                          PAGE 15

| | DATE | ACCOUNT TITLE | DOC. NO. | POST. REF. | DEBIT | CREDIT | |
|---|---|---|---|---|---|---|---|
| 1 | | | | | | | 1 |
| 2 | | | | | | | 2 |
| 3 | | | | | | | 3 |
| 4 | | | | | | | 4 |

Name _____  Date _____  Class _____

## 21-1 ON YOUR OWN (continued)

**5.**

CASH RECEIPTS JOURNAL

PAGE 19

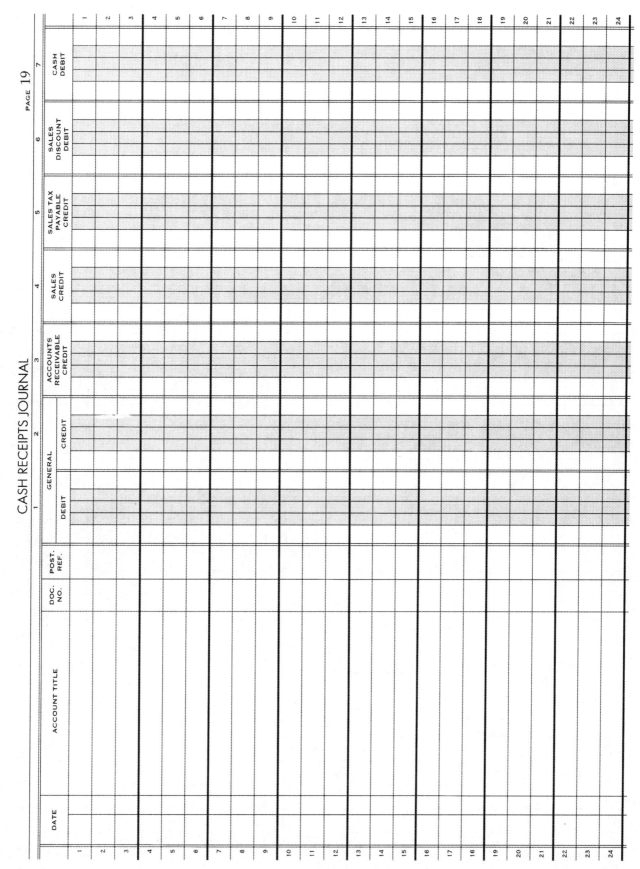

| | | | | GENERAL | | ACCOUNTS RECEIVABLE CREDIT | SALES CREDIT | SALES TAX PAYABLE CREDIT | SALES DISCOUNT DEBIT | CASH DEBIT |
| DATE | ACCOUNT TITLE | DOC. NO. | POST. REF. | DEBIT | CREDIT | | | | | |
|---|---|---|---|---|---|---|---|---|---|---|
| | | | | 1 | 2 | 3 | 4 | 5 | 6 | 7 |
| 1 | | | | | | | | | | |
| 2 | | | | | | | | | | |
| 3 | | | | | | | | | | |
| 4 | | | | | | | | | | |
| 5 | | | | | | | | | | |
| 6 | | | | | | | | | | |
| 7 | | | | | | | | | | |
| 8 | | | | | | | | | | |
| 9 | | | | | | | | | | |
| 10 | | | | | | | | | | |
| 11 | | | | | | | | | | |
| 12 | | | | | | | | | | |
| 13 | | | | | | | | | | |
| 14 | | | | | | | | | | |
| 15 | | | | | | | | | | |
| 16 | | | | | | | | | | |
| 17 | | | | | | | | | | |
| 18 | | | | | | | | | | |
| 19 | | | | | | | | | | |
| 20 | | | | | | | | | | |
| 21 | | | | | | | | | | |
| 22 | | | | | | | | | | |
| 23 | | | | | | | | | | |
| 24 | | | | | | | | | | |

**2., 3., 4., 5.**         **GENERAL LEDGER**

ACCOUNT Notes Receivable         ACCOUNT NO. 1115

| DATE | ITEM | POST. REF. | DEBIT | CREDIT | BALANCE DEBIT | BALANCE CREDIT |
|---|---|---|---|---|---|---|
| Dec. 1 | | G11 | 6 0 0 0 00 | | 6 0 0 0 00 | |
| | | | | | | |
| | | | | | | |
| | | | | | | |

ACCOUNT Interest Receivable         ACCOUNT NO. 1120

| DATE | ITEM | POST. REF. | DEBIT | CREDIT | BALANCE DEBIT | BALANCE CREDIT |
|---|---|---|---|---|---|---|
| | | | | | | |
| | | | | | | |
| | | | | | | |
| | | | | | | |
| | | | | | | |

ACCOUNT Income Summary         ACCOUNT NO. 3120

| DATE | ITEM | POST. REF. | DEBIT | CREDIT | BALANCE DEBIT | BALANCE CREDIT |
|---|---|---|---|---|---|---|
| | | | | | | |
| | | | | | | |
| | | | | | | |
| | | | | | | |
| | | | | | | |

ACCOUNT Interest Income         ACCOUNT NO. 7110

| DATE | ITEM | POST. REF. | DEBIT | CREDIT | BALANCE DEBIT | BALANCE CREDIT |
|---|---|---|---|---|---|---|
| Dec. 31 | | CR15 | | 8 7 50 | | 6 9 2 00 |
| | | | | | | |
| | | | | | | |
| | | | | | | |

Name _____ Date _____ Class _____

## 21-2 WORK TOGETHER, p. 627

**Journalizing and posting entries for accrued expenses**

**1.**

Powers Corporation

Work Sheet

For Year Ended December 31, 20 – –

| | ACCOUNT TITLE | TRIAL BALANCE | | ADJUSTMENTS | |
|---|---|---|---|---|---|
| | | DEBIT | CREDIT | DEBIT | CREDIT |
| 15 | Interest Payable | | | | |
| 51 | Interest Expense | 8 4 7 7 00 | | | |

**2., 3.**

GENERAL JOURNAL                                                PAGE 14

| | DATE | ACCOUNT TITLE | DOC. NO. | POST. REF. | DEBIT | CREDIT | |
|---|---|---|---|---|---|---|---|
| 1 | | | | | | | 1 |
| 2 | | | | | | | 2 |
| 3 | | | | | | | 3 |
| 4 | | | | | | | 4 |
| 5 | | | | | | | 5 |
| 6 | | | | | | | 6 |
| 7 | | | | | | | 7 |
| 8 | | | | | | | 8 |

**4.**

GENERAL JOURNAL                                                PAGE 15

| | DATE | ACCOUNT TITLE | DOC. NO. | POST. REF. | DEBIT | CREDIT | |
|---|---|---|---|---|---|---|---|
| 1 | | | | | | | 1 |
| 2 | | | | | | | 2 |
| 3 | | | | | | | 3 |
| 4 | | | | | | | 4 |

Chapter 21   Accounting for Accrued Revenue and Expenses • **127**

**5.**

CASH PAYMENTS JOURNAL

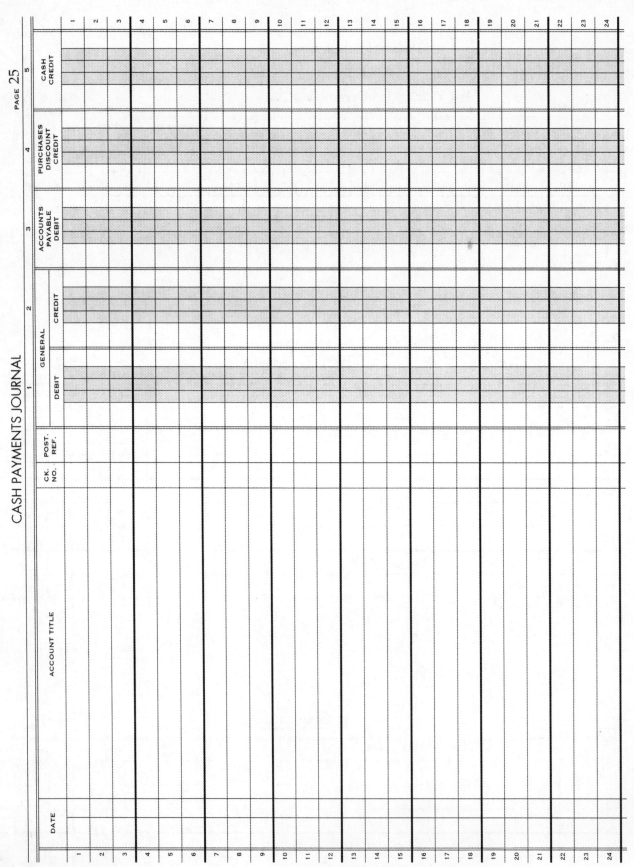

## 21-2 WORK TOGETHER (concluded)

**2., 3., 4., 5.**                    **GENERAL LEDGER**

ACCOUNT Notes Payable                                        ACCOUNT NO. 2105

| DATE | ITEM | POST. REF. | DEBIT | CREDIT | BALANCE DEBIT | BALANCE CREDIT |
|------|------|-----------|-------|--------|--------------|----------------|
| Dec. 1 | | CR13 | | 2 0 0 0 00 | | 2 0 0 0 00 |
| | | | | | | |
| | | | | | | |

ACCOUNT Interest Payable                                     ACCOUNT NO. 2110

| DATE | ITEM | POST. REF. | DEBIT | CREDIT | BALANCE DEBIT | BALANCE CREDIT |
|------|------|-----------|-------|--------|--------------|----------------|
| | | | | | | |
| | | | | | | |
| | | | | | | |
| | | | | | | |

ACCOUNT Income Summary                                       ACCOUNT NO. 3120

| DATE | ITEM | POST. REF. | DEBIT | CREDIT | BALANCE DEBIT | BALANCE CREDIT |
|------|------|-----------|-------|--------|--------------|----------------|
| | | | | | | |
| | | | | | | |
| | | | | | | |
| | | | | | | |

ACCOUNT Interest Expense                                     ACCOUNT NO. 8105

| DATE | ITEM | POST. REF. | DEBIT | CREDIT | BALANCE DEBIT | BALANCE CREDIT |
|------|------|-----------|-------|--------|--------------|----------------|
| Dec. 31 | | CP19 | 1 6 0 00 | | 8 4 7 7 00 | |
| | | | | | | |
| | | | | | | |

**Journalizing and posting entries for accrued expenses**

**1.**

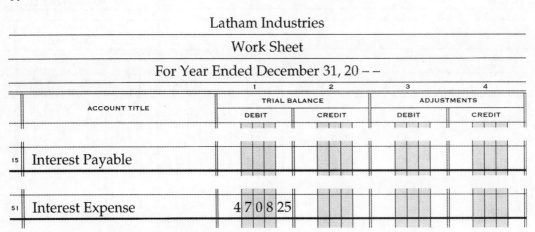

Latham Industries

Work Sheet

For Year Ended December 31, 20 – –

| | | 1 | 2 | 3 | 4 |
|---|---|---|---|---|---|
| | | TRIAL BALANCE | | ADJUSTMENTS | |
| | ACCOUNT TITLE | DEBIT | CREDIT | DEBIT | CREDIT |
| 15 | Interest Payable | | | | |
| 51 | Interest Expense | 4 7 0 8 25 | | | |

**2., 3.**

GENERAL JOURNAL                                                      PAGE 14

| | DATE | ACCOUNT TITLE | DOC. NO. | POST. REF. | DEBIT | CREDIT | |
|---|---|---|---|---|---|---|---|
| 1 | | | | | | | 1 |
| 2 | | | | | | | 2 |
| 3 | | | | | | | 3 |
| 4 | | | | | | | 4 |
| 5 | | | | | | | 5 |
| 6 | | | | | | | 6 |
| 7 | | | | | | | 7 |
| 8 | | | | | | | 8 |

**4.**

GENERAL JOURNAL                                                      PAGE 15

| | DATE | ACCOUNT TITLE | DOC. NO. | POST. REF. | DEBIT | CREDIT | |
|---|---|---|---|---|---|---|---|
| 1 | | | | | | | 1 |
| 2 | | | | | | | 2 |
| 3 | | | | | | | 3 |
| 4 | | | | | | | 4 |

**21-2** **ON YOUR OWN (continued)**

**5.**

CASH PAYMENTS JOURNAL

PAGE 30

| | | | GENERAL | | ACCOUNTS PAYABLE | PURCHASES DISCOUNT | CASH |
|---|---|---|---|---|---|---|---|
| DATE | ACCOUNT TITLE | CK. NO. | POST. REF. | DEBIT | CREDIT | DEBIT | CREDIT | CREDIT |
| | | | | 1 | 2 | 3 | 4 | 5 |

**2., 3., 4., 5.**                     **GENERAL LEDGER**

ACCOUNT Notes Payable                                    ACCOUNT NO. 2105

| DATE | ITEM | POST. REF. | DEBIT | CREDIT | BALANCE DEBIT | BALANCE CREDIT |
|---|---|---|---|---|---|---|
| Oct. 17 | | CR9 | | 5 0 0 0 00 | | 5 0 0 0 00 |
| | | | | | | |
| | | | | | | |

ACCOUNT Interest Payable                                    ACCOUNT NO. 2110

| DATE | ITEM | POST. REF. | DEBIT | CREDIT | BALANCE DEBIT | BALANCE CREDIT |
|---|---|---|---|---|---|---|
| | | | | | | |
| | | | | | | |
| | | | | | | |
| | | | | | | |

ACCOUNT Income Summary                                    ACCOUNT NO. 3120

| DATE | ITEM | POST. REF. | DEBIT | CREDIT | BALANCE DEBIT | BALANCE CREDIT |
|---|---|---|---|---|---|---|
| | | | | | | |
| | | | | | | |
| | | | | | | |
| | | | | | | |

ACCOUNT Interest Expense                                    ACCOUNT NO. 8105

| DATE | ITEM | POST. REF. | DEBIT | CREDIT | BALANCE DEBIT | BALANCE CREDIT |
|---|---|---|---|---|---|---|
| Dec. 31 | | CP24 | 5 0 00 | | 4 7 0 8 25 | |
| | | | | | | |
| | | | | | | |

## 21-1 APPLICATION PROBLEM, p. 629

**Journalizing and posting entries for accrued revenue**

**1.**

Velma Parts Company

Work Sheet

For Year Ended December 31, 20 – –

| | | 1 | 2 | 3 | 4 |
|---|---|---|---|---|---|
| | ACCOUNT TITLE | TRIAL BALANCE | | ADJUSTMENTS | |
| | | DEBIT | CREDIT | DEBIT | CREDIT |
| 4 | Interest Receivable | | | | |
| 50 | Interest Income | | 1 9 6 7 50 | | |

**2., 3.**

GENERAL JOURNAL                                      PAGE 14

| | DATE | ACCOUNT TITLE | DOC. NO. | POST. REF. | DEBIT | CREDIT | |
|---|---|---|---|---|---|---|---|
| 1 | | | | | | | 1 |
| 2 | | | | | | | 2 |
| 3 | | | | | | | 3 |
| 4 | | | | | | | 4 |
| 5 | | | | | | | 5 |
| 6 | | | | | | | 6 |
| 7 | | | | | | | 7 |
| 8 | | | | | | | 8 |

**4.**

GENERAL JOURNAL                                      PAGE 15

| | DATE | ACCOUNT TITLE | DOC. NO. | POST. REF. | DEBIT | CREDIT | |
|---|---|---|---|---|---|---|---|
| 1 | | | | | | | 1 |
| 2 | | | | | | | 2 |
| 3 | | | | | | | 3 |
| 4 | | | | | | | 4 |

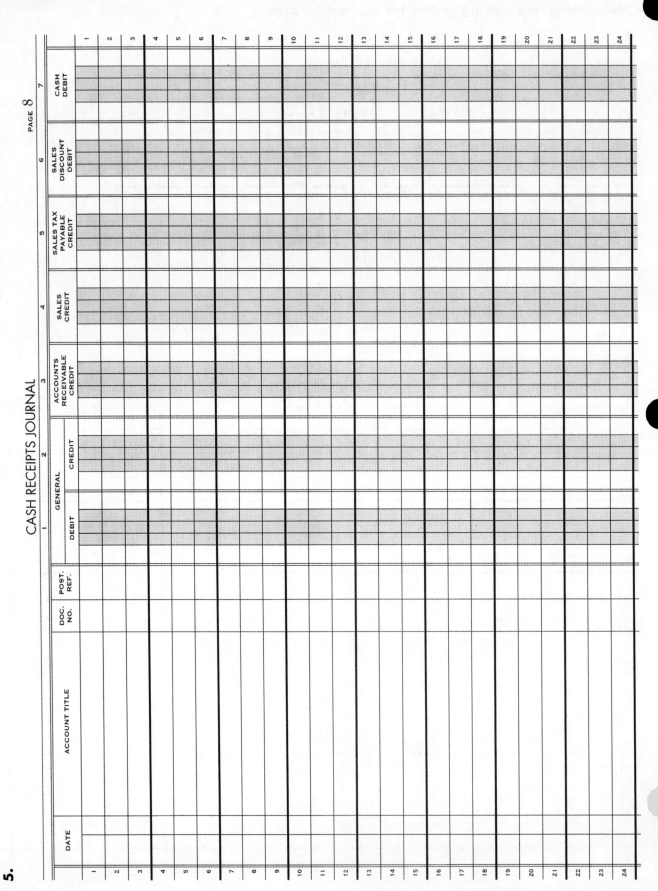

**5.**

## 21-1 APPLICATION PROBLEM (concluded)

**2., 3., 4., 5.**          **GENERAL LEDGER**

ACCOUNT Notes Receivable      ACCOUNT NO. 1115

| DATE | ITEM | POST. REF. | DEBIT | CREDIT | BALANCE DEBIT | BALANCE CREDIT |
|------|------|-----------|-------|--------|-------|--------|
| Nov. 6 | | G11 | 8 1 0 0 00 | | 8 1 0 0 00 | |
| | | | | | | |
| | | | | | | |

ACCOUNT Interest Receivable      ACCOUNT NO. 1120

| DATE | ITEM | POST. REF. | DEBIT | CREDIT | BALANCE DEBIT | BALANCE CREDIT |
|------|------|-----------|-------|--------|-------|--------|
| | | | | | | |
| | | | | | | |
| | | | | | | |
| | | | | | | |
| | | | | | | |

ACCOUNT Income Summary      ACCOUNT NO. 3120

| DATE | ITEM | POST. REF. | DEBIT | CREDIT | BALANCE DEBIT | BALANCE CREDIT |
|------|------|-----------|-------|--------|-------|--------|
| | | | | | | |
| | | | | | | |
| | | | | | | |
| | | | | | | |
| | | | | | | |

ACCOUNT Interest Income      ACCOUNT NO. 7110

| DATE | ITEM | POST. REF. | DEBIT | CREDIT | BALANCE DEBIT | BALANCE CREDIT |
|------|------|-----------|-------|--------|-------|--------|
| Dec. 31 | | CR18 | | 2 5 00 | | 1 9 6 7 50 |
| | | | | | | |
| | | | | | | |

**Journalizing and posting entries for accrued expenses**

**1.**

Delmar Plumbing Supply

Work Sheet

For Year Ended December 31, 20 – –

|  | | | 1 | 2 | 3 | 4 |
|---|---|---|---|---|---|---|
|  | ACCOUNT TITLE | | TRIAL BALANCE | | ADJUSTMENTS | |
|  | | | DEBIT | CREDIT | DEBIT | CREDIT |
| 15 | Interest Payable | | | | | |
| 51 | Interest Expense | | 8 4 8 9 00 | | | |

**2., 3.**

GENERAL JOURNAL

PAGE 14

| | DATE | ACCOUNT TITLE | DOC. NO. | POST. REF. | DEBIT | CREDIT | |
|---|---|---|---|---|---|---|---|
| 1 | | | | | | | 1 |
| 2 | | | | | | | 2 |
| 3 | | | | | | | 3 |
| 4 | | | | | | | 4 |
| 5 | | | | | | | 5 |
| 6 | | | | | | | 6 |
| 7 | | | | | | | 7 |
| 8 | | | | | | | 8 |

**4.**

GENERAL JOURNAL

PAGE 15

| | DATE | ACCOUNT TITLE | DOC. NO. | POST. REF. | DEBIT | CREDIT | |
|---|---|---|---|---|---|---|---|
| 1 | | | | | | | 1 |
| 2 | | | | | | | 2 |
| 3 | | | | | | | 3 |
| 4 | | | | | | | 4 |

## 21-2 APPLICATION PROBLEM (continued)

**5.**

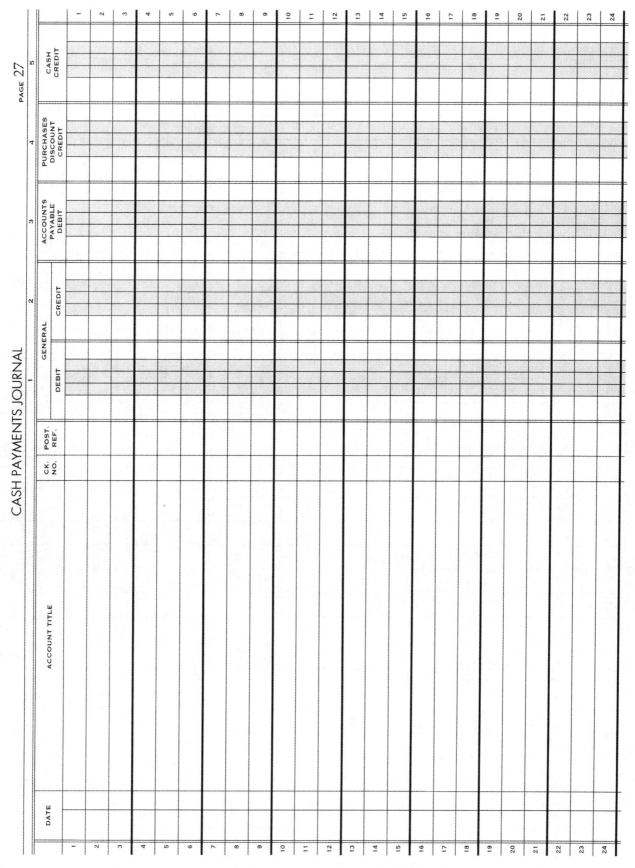

CASH PAYMENTS JOURNAL

PAGE 27

**2., 3., 4., 5.**                                    **GENERAL LEDGER**

ACCOUNT Notes Payable                                          ACCOUNT NO. 2105

| DATE | ITEM | POST. REF. | DEBIT | CREDIT | BALANCE DEBIT | BALANCE CREDIT |
|------|------|-----------|-------|--------|---------------|----------------|
| Dec. 1 | | CR12 | | 12 0 0 0 00 | | 12 0 0 0 00 |
| | | | | | | |
| | | | | | | |

ACCOUNT Interest Payable                                       ACCOUNT NO. 2110

| DATE | ITEM | POST. REF. | DEBIT | CREDIT | BALANCE DEBIT | BALANCE CREDIT |
|------|------|-----------|-------|--------|---------------|----------------|
| | | | | | | |
| | | | | | | |
| | | | | | | |
| | | | | | | |

ACCOUNT Income Summary                                        ACCOUNT NO. 3120

| DATE | ITEM | POST. REF. | DEBIT | CREDIT | BALANCE DEBIT | BALANCE CREDIT |
|------|------|-----------|-------|--------|---------------|----------------|
| | | | | | | |
| | | | | | | |
| | | | | | | |
| | | | | | | |

ACCOUNT Interest Expense                                      ACCOUNT NO. 8105

| DATE | ITEM | POST. REF. | DEBIT | CREDIT | BALANCE DEBIT | BALANCE CREDIT |
|------|------|-----------|-------|--------|---------------|----------------|
| Dec. 31 | | CP21 | 1 6 0 00 | | 8 4 8 9 00 | |
| | | | | | | |
| | | | | | | |

Name _____ Date _____ Class _____

**APPLICATION PROBLEM, pp. 629, 630**

**Journalizing and posting entries for accrued expenses**

**1.**

Patti's Dress Shop

Work Sheet

For Year Ended December 31, 20 – –

|  | ACCOUNT TITLE | TRIAL BALANCE | | ADJUSTMENTS | |
|---|---|---|---|---|---|
|  |  | DEBIT | CREDIT | DEBIT | CREDIT |
| 15 | Interest Payable |  |  |  |  |
| 51 | Interest Expense | 2 8 9 9 00 |  |  |  |

**2.**

GENERAL JOURNAL      PAGE 16

|  | DATE | ACCOUNT TITLE | DOC. NO. | POST. REF. | DEBIT | CREDIT |  |
|---|---|---|---|---|---|---|---|
| 1 |  |  |  |  |  |  | 1 |
| 2 |  |  |  |  |  |  | 2 |
| 3 |  |  |  |  |  |  | 3 |
| 4 |  |  |  |  |  |  | 4 |
| 5 |  |  |  |  |  |  | 5 |
| 6 |  |  |  |  |  |  | 6 |
| 7 |  |  |  |  |  |  | 7 |
| 8 |  |  |  |  |  |  | 8 |

GENERAL JOURNAL      PAGE 17

|  | DATE | ACCOUNT TITLE | DOC. NO. | POST. REF. | DEBIT | CREDIT |  |
|---|---|---|---|---|---|---|---|
| 1 |  |  |  |  |  |  | 1 |
| 2 |  |  |  |  |  |  | 2 |
| 3 |  |  |  |  |  |  | 3 |
| 4 |  |  |  |  |  |  | 4 |

**3.**

CASH PAYMENTS JOURNAL

PAGE 23

| | DATE | ACCOUNT TITLE | CK. NO. | POST. REF. | GENERAL DEBIT | GENERAL CREDIT | ACCOUNTS PAYABLE DEBIT | PURCHASES DISCOUNT CREDIT | CASH CREDIT | |
|---|---|---|---|---|---|---|---|---|---|---|
| 1 | | | | | | | | | | 1 |
| 2 | | | | | | | | | | 2 |
| 3 | | | | | | | | | | 3 |
| 4 | | | | | | | | | | 4 |
| 5 | | | | | | | | | | 5 |
| 6 | | | | | | | | | | 6 |
| 7 | | | | | | | | | | 7 |
| 8 | | | | | | | | | | 8 |
| 9 | | | | | | | | | | 9 |
| 10 | | | | | | | | | | 10 |
| 11 | | | | | | | | | | 11 |
| 12 | | | | | | | | | | 12 |
| 13 | | | | | | | | | | 13 |
| 14 | | | | | | | | | | 14 |
| 15 | | | | | | | | | | 15 |
| 16 | | | | | | | | | | 16 |
| 17 | | | | | | | | | | 17 |
| 18 | | | | | | | | | | 18 |
| 19 | | | | | | | | | | 19 |
| 20 | | | | | | | | | | 20 |
| 21 | | | | | | | | | | 21 |
| 22 | | | | | | | | | | 22 |
| 23 | | | | | | | | | | 23 |
| 24 | | | | | | | | | | 24 |

**21-3** **APPLICATION PROBLEM (concluded)**

**2., 3.**                          **GENERAL LEDGER**

ACCOUNT Notes Payable                                    ACCOUNT NO. 2105

| DATE | ITEM | POST. REF. | DEBIT | CREDIT | BALANCE DEBIT | BALANCE CREDIT |
|------|------|------------|-------|--------|---------------|----------------|
| Oct. 14 | | CR11 | | 10 0 0 0 00 | | 10 0 0 0 00 |
| | | | | | | |
| | | | | | | |

ACCOUNT Interest Payable                                 ACCOUNT NO. 2110

| DATE | ITEM | POST. REF. | DEBIT | CREDIT | BALANCE DEBIT | BALANCE CREDIT |
|------|------|------------|-------|--------|---------------|----------------|
| | | | | | | |
| | | | | | | |
| | | | | | | |
| | | | | | | |

ACCOUNT Income Summary                                   ACCOUNT NO. 3120

| DATE | ITEM | POST. REF. | DEBIT | CREDIT | BALANCE DEBIT | BALANCE CREDIT |
|------|------|------------|-------|--------|---------------|----------------|
| | | | | | | |
| | | | | | | |
| | | | | | | |
| | | | | | | |

ACCOUNT Interest Expense                                 ACCOUNT NO. 8105

| DATE | ITEM | POST. REF. | DEBIT | CREDIT | BALANCE DEBIT | BALANCE CREDIT |
|------|------|------------|-------|--------|---------------|----------------|
| Dec. 31 | | CP19 | 8 0 00 | | 2 8 9 9 00 | |
| | | | | | | |
| | | | | | | |

**Journalizing and posting entries for accrued interest revenue and expenses**

**1.**

Youngblood, Inc.

Work Sheet

For Year Ended December 31, 20X1

| | ACCOUNT TITLE | TRIAL BALANCE | | ADJUSTMENTS | |
|---|---|---|---|---|---|
| | | DEBIT | CREDIT | DEBIT | CREDIT |
| 4 | Interest Receivable | | | | |
| 15 | Interest Payable | | | | |
| 50 | Interest Income | | 1 6 6 7 00 | | |
| 51 | Interest Expense | 2 7 3 2 00 | | | |

**2., 3.**

GENERAL JOURNAL                                    PAGE 15

| | DATE | ACCOUNT TITLE | DOC. NO. | POST. REF. | DEBIT | CREDIT | |
|---|---|---|---|---|---|---|---|
| 1 | | | | | | | 1 |
| 2 | | | | | | | 2 |
| 3 | | | | | | | 3 |
| 4 | | | | | | | 4 |
| 5 | | | | | | | 5 |
| 6 | | | | | | | 6 |
| 7 | | | | | | | 7 |
| 8 | | | | | | | 8 |
| 9 | | | | | | | 9 |
| 10 | | | | | | | 10 |
| 11 | | | | | | | 11 |

**4.**

GENERAL JOURNAL                                    PAGE 16

| | DATE | ACCOUNT TITLE | DOC. NO. | POST. REF. | DEBIT | CREDIT | |
|---|---|---|---|---|---|---|---|
| 1 | | | | | | | 1 |
| 2 | | | | | | | 2 |
| 3 | | | | | | | 3 |
| 4 | | | | | | | 4 |
| 5 | | | | | | | 5 |

**21-4** **MASTERY PROBLEM (continued)**

**5.**

CASH RECEIPTS JOURNAL

PAGE 16

| | | | GENERAL | | ACCOUNTS RECEIVABLE CREDIT | SALES CREDIT | SALES TAX PAYABLE CREDIT | SALES DISCOUNT DEBIT | CASH DEBIT |
|---|---|---|---|---|---|---|---|---|---|
| DATE | ACCOUNT TITLE | DOC. NO. | POST. REF. | DEBIT | CREDIT | | | | | |
| | | | | 1 | 2 | 3 | 4 | 5 | 6 | 7 |

**6.**

CASH PAYMENTS JOURNAL

PAGE 28

| | | | | GENERAL | | ACCOUNTS PAYABLE DEBIT | PURCHASES DISCOUNT CREDIT | CASH CREDIT |
|---|---|---|---|---|---|---|---|---|
| DATE | ACCOUNT TITLE | CK. NO. | POST. REF. | DEBIT | CREDIT | | | |
| | | | | 1 | 2 | 3 | 4 | 5 |

**2., 3., 4., 5., 6.**      **GENERAL LEDGER**

ACCOUNT Notes Receivable    ACCOUNT NO. 1115

| DATE | ITEM | POST. REF. | DEBIT | CREDIT | BALANCE DEBIT | BALANCE CREDIT |
|---|---|---|---|---|---|---|
| Nov. 11 | | G12 | 9 0 0 00 | | 9 0 0 00 | |

ACCOUNT Interest Receivable    ACCOUNT NO. 1120

| DATE | ITEM | POST. REF. | DEBIT | CREDIT | BALANCE DEBIT | BALANCE CREDIT |
|---|---|---|---|---|---|---|
| | | | | | | |

ACCOUNT Notes Payable    ACCOUNT NO. 2105

| DATE | ITEM | POST. REF. | DEBIT | CREDIT | BALANCE DEBIT | BALANCE CREDIT |
|---|---|---|---|---|---|---|
| Dec. 6 | | CR12 | | 7 2 0 0 00 | | 7 2 0 0 00 |

ACCOUNT Interest Payable    ACCOUNT NO. 2110

| DATE | ITEM | POST. REF. | DEBIT | CREDIT | BALANCE DEBIT | BALANCE CREDIT |
|---|---|---|---|---|---|---|
| | | | | | | |

## 21-4 MASTERY PROBLEM (concluded)

**2., 3., 4., 5., 6.**                    **GENERAL LEDGER**

ACCOUNT Income Summary                                    ACCOUNT NO. 3120

| DATE | ITEM | POST. REF. | DEBIT | CREDIT | BALANCE DEBIT | BALANCE CREDIT |
|------|------|-----------|-------|--------|------|--------|
|      |      |           |       |        |      |        |
|      |      |           |       |        |      |        |
|      |      |           |       |        |      |        |
|      |      |           |       |        |      |        |
|      |      |           |       |        |      |        |

ACCOUNT Interest Income                                   ACCOUNT NO. 7110

| DATE | ITEM | POST. REF. | DEBIT | CREDIT | BALANCE DEBIT | BALANCE CREDIT |
|------|------|-----------|-------|--------|------|--------|
| Dec. 31 |   | CR14      |       | 3 2 00 |      | 1 6 6 7 00 |
|      |      |           |       |        |      |        |
|      |      |           |       |        |      |        |
|      |      |           |       |        |      |        |

ACCOUNT Interest Expense                                  ACCOUNT NO. 8105

| DATE | ITEM | POST. REF. | DEBIT | CREDIT | BALANCE DEBIT | BALANCE CREDIT |
|------|------|-----------|-------|--------|------|--------|
| Dec. 31 |   | CP21      | 8 7 50 |       | 2 7 3 2 00 |        |
|      |      |           |       |        |      |        |
|      |      |           |       |        |      |        |
|      |      |           |       |        |      |        |
|      |      |           |       |        |      |        |

**Journalizing and posting entries for accrued interest revenue and expenses**

**1.**

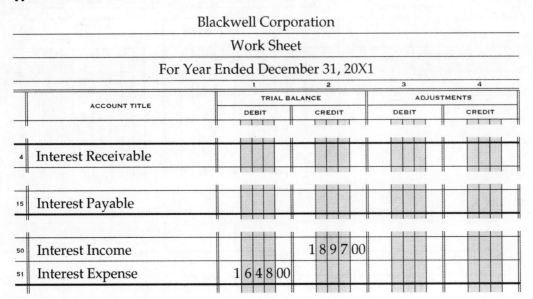

Blackwell Corporation

Work Sheet

For Year Ended December 31, 20X1

| | | | 1 | 2 | 3 | 4 |
|---|---|---|---|---|---|---|
| | ACCOUNT TITLE | | TRIAL BALANCE | | ADJUSTMENTS | |
| | | | DEBIT | CREDIT | DEBIT | CREDIT |
| 4 | Interest Receivable | | | | | |
| 15 | Interest Payable | | | | | |
| 50 | Interest Income | | | 1 8 9 7 00 | | |
| 51 | Interest Expense | | 1 6 4 8 00 | | | |

**2.**

GENERAL JOURNAL                                          PAGE 16

| | DATE | ACCOUNT TITLE | DOC. NO. | POST. REF. | DEBIT | CREDIT | |
|---|---|---|---|---|---|---|---|
| 1 | | | | | | | 1 |
| 2 | | | | | | | 2 |
| 3 | | | | | | | 3 |
| 4 | | | | | | | 4 |
| 5 | | | | | | | 5 |
| 6 | | | | | | | 6 |
| 7 | | | | | | | 7 |
| 8 | | | | | | | 8 |
| 9 | | | | | | | 9 |
| 10 | | | | | | | 10 |
| 11 | | | | | | | 11 |

GENERAL JOURNAL                                          PAGE 17

| | DATE | ACCOUNT TITLE | DOC. NO. | POST. REF. | DEBIT | CREDIT | |
|---|---|---|---|---|---|---|---|
| 1 | | | | | | | 1 |
| 2 | | | | | | | 2 |
| 3 | | | | | | | 3 |
| 4 | | | | | | | 4 |
| 5 | | | | | | | 5 |

**21-5** **CHALLENGE PROBLEM (continued)**

**3.**

## GENERAL JOURNAL

PAGE 18

| DATE | ACCOUNT TITLE | DOC. NO. | POST. REF. | DEBIT | CREDIT | |
|------|---------------|----------|------------|-------|--------|---|
| | | | | | | 1 |
| | | | | | | 2 |
| | | | | | | 3 |
| | | | | | | 4 |
| | | | | | | 5 |

## CASH PAYMENTS JOURNAL

PAGE 15

| DATE | ACCOUNT TITLE | CK. NO. | POST. REF. | GENERAL DEBIT | GENERAL CREDIT | ACCOUNTS PAYABLE DEBIT | PURCHASES DISCOUNT CREDIT | CASH CREDIT | |
|------|---------------|---------|------------|-------|--------|-------|-------|------|---|
| | | | | | | | | | 1 |
| | | | | | | | | | 2 |
| | | | | | | | | | 3 |
| | | | | | | | | | 4 |
| | | | | | | | | | 5 |
| | | | | | | | | | 6 |
| | | | | | | | | | 7 |
| | | | | | | | | | 8 |
| | | | | | | | | | 9 |
| | | | | | | | | | 10 |
| | | | | | | | | | 11 |
| | | | | | | | | | 12 |

**2., 3.**                                    **GENERAL LEDGER**

ACCOUNT Notes Receivable                                                         ACCOUNT NO. 1115

| DATE | | ITEM | POST. REF. | DEBIT | CREDIT | BALANCE | |
|---|---|---|---|---|---|---|---|
| | | | | | | DEBIT | CREDIT |
| Dec. | 8 | | G14 | 9 0 0 00 | | 9 0 0 00 | |
| | | | | | | | |
| | | | | | | | |

ACCOUNT Interest Receivable                                                      ACCOUNT NO. 1120

| DATE | | ITEM | POST. REF. | DEBIT | CREDIT | BALANCE | |
|---|---|---|---|---|---|---|---|
| | | | | | | DEBIT | CREDIT |
| | | | | | | | |
| | | | | | | | |
| | | | | | | | |
| | | | | | | | |
| | | | | | | | |

ACCOUNT Notes Payable                                                            ACCOUNT NO. 2105

| DATE | | ITEM | POST. REF. | DEBIT | CREDIT | BALANCE | |
|---|---|---|---|---|---|---|---|
| | | | | | | DEBIT | CREDIT |
| Dec. | 15 | | CR12 | | 10 0 0 0 00 | | 10 0 0 0 00 |
| | | | | | | | |
| | | | | | | | |

ACCOUNT Interest Payable                                                         ACCOUNT NO. 2110

| DATE | | ITEM | POST. REF. | DEBIT | CREDIT | BALANCE | |
|---|---|---|---|---|---|---|---|
| | | | | | | DEBIT | CREDIT |
| | | | | | | | |
| | | | | | | | |
| | | | | | | | |
| | | | | | | | |

## 21-5 CHALLENGE PROBLEM (concluded)

**2., 3.**                    **GENERAL LEDGER**

ACCOUNT Income Summary                                      ACCOUNT NO. 3120

| DATE | ITEM | POST. REF. | DEBIT | CREDIT | BALANCE DEBIT | BALANCE CREDIT |
|------|------|------------|-------|--------|---------------|----------------|
|      |      |            |       |        |               |                |
|      |      |            |       |        |               |                |
|      |      |            |       |        |               |                |
|      |      |            |       |        |               |                |

ACCOUNT Interest Income                                     ACCOUNT NO. 7110

| DATE | ITEM | POST. REF. | DEBIT | CREDIT | BALANCE DEBIT | BALANCE CREDIT |
|------|------|------------|-------|--------|---------------|----------------|
| Dec. 31 |   | CR12       |       | 85 00  |               | 1 8 9 7 00     |
|      |      |            |       |        |               |                |
|      |      |            |       |        |               |                |
|      |      |            |       |        |               |                |

ACCOUNT Interest Expense                                    ACCOUNT NO. 8105

| DATE | ITEM | POST. REF. | DEBIT | CREDIT | BALANCE DEBIT | BALANCE CREDIT |
|------|------|------------|-------|--------|---------------|----------------|
| Dec. 31 |   | CP12       | 1 0 0 00 |     | 1 6 4 8 00    |                |
|      |      |            |       |        |               |                |
|      |      |            |       |        |               |                |
|      |      |            |       |        |               |                |

# Study Guide 22

| Name | Perfect Score | Your Score |
|---|---|---|
| Identifying Accounting Concepts and Practices for End-of-Fiscal-Period Work | 20 Pts. | |
| Analyzing End-of-Fiscal-Period Entries for a Corporation | 34 Pts. | |
| **Total** | 54 Pts. | |

## Part One—Identifying Accounting Concepts and Practices for End-of-Fiscal-Period Work

**Directions:** Place a *T* for True or an *F* for False in the Answers column to show whether each of the following statements is true or false.

**Answers**

1. Financial statements are prepared using a completed work sheet. (p. 636)

1. _____

2. Businesses use work sheets to plan adjustments and provide information needed to prepare financial statements. (p. 636)

2. _____

3. All accounts that need to be brought up to date are adjusted after financial statements are prepared. (p. 637)

3. _____

4. To adjust the interest income earned during the current fiscal period but not yet received, the Interest Receivable account is debited. (p. 638)

4. _____

5. To bring the Supplies account up to date, the balance of supplies needs to be decreased by the cost of supplies used during the year. (p. 638)

5. _____

6. Federal income tax is an expense of a corporation. (p. 639)

6. _____

7. The tax rate for federal income tax varies depending on the amount of net income earned. (p. 639)

7. _____

8. Corporations with less than $50,000 net income pay smaller tax rates than corporations with larger net incomes. (p. 640)

8. _____

9. When the total of a work sheet's Income Statement Credit column is larger than the total of the Income Statement Debit column, the difference represents net loss of the business. (p. 641)

9. _____

10. A work sheet's Balance Sheet columns are used to calculate net income after federal income tax. (p. 641)

10. _____

11. The balance of Capital Stock is recorded in the Income Statement columns of a work sheet. (p. 642)

11. _____

12. A corporation's preparation of financial statements to report the financial progress during a fiscal period is an application of the Accounting Period Cycle concept. (p. 646)

12. _____

13. To calculate the component percentage of cost of merchandise sold, divide net sales by cost of merchandise sold. (p. 647)

13. _____

14. A statement of stockholders' equity contains two major sections: capital stock and retained earnings. (p. 649)

14. _____

15. The book value of an asset is reported on a balance sheet by listing two amounts: the balance of the asset account and the balance of the asset's contra account. (p. 651)

15. _____

16. An example of a long-term liability is Mortgage Payable. (p. 651)

16. _____

17. A business can use the amount of working capital to provide a convenient relative measurement from year to year. (p. 652)

17. _____

18. Closing entries for a corporation are made from information in a balance sheet. (p. 655)

19. Dividends increase the earnings retained by a corporation. (p. 657)

20. A reversing entry is desirable if an adjusting entry creates a balance in an asset or a liability account. (p. 658)

## Part Two—Analyzing End-of-Fiscal-Period Entries for a Corporation

**Directions:** For each closing or reversing entry described, decide which accounts are debited and credited. Print the letter identifying your choice in the proper Answers columns. (Accounts are listed in alphabetical order.)

| Account Titles | Transactions | Answers Debit | Credit |
|---|---|---|---|
| A. Cash Short and Over | 1–2. Closing entry for the sales account. (p. 655) | 1. _____ | 2. _____ |
| B. Depreciation Expense —Store Equipment | 3–4. Closing entry for purchases discount. (p. 655) | 3. _____ | 4. _____ |
| C. Dividends | 5–6. Closing entry for the purchases returns and allowances account. (p. 655) | 5. _____ | 6. _____ |
| D. Dividends Payable | | | |
| E. Federal Income Tax Expense | 7–8. Closing entry for the gain on plant assets account. (p. 655) | 7. _____ | 8. _____ |
| F. Federal Income Tax Payable | 9–10. Closing entry for the interest income account. (p. 655) | 9. _____ | 10. _____ |
| G. Gain on Plant Assets | | | |
| H. Income Summary | 11–12. Closing entry for the sales discount account. (p. 656) | 11. _____ | 12. _____ |
| I. Insurance Expense | 13–14. Closing entry for the purchases account. (p. 656) | 13. _____ | 14. _____ |
| J. Interest Expense | | | |
| K. Interest Income | 15–16. Closing entry for the cash short and over account (cash is short). (p. 656) | 15. _____ | 16. _____ |
| L. Interest Payable | 17–18. Closing entry for the cash short and over account (cash is over). (p. 656) | 17. _____ | 18. _____ |
| M. Interest Receivable | | | |
| N. Loss on Plant Assets | 19–20. Closing entry for the depreciation expense—store equipment account. (p. 656) | 19. _____ | 20. _____ |
| O. Purchases | 21–22. Closing entry for the federal income tax expense account. (p. 656) | 21. _____ | 22. _____ |
| P. Purchases Discount | | | |
| Q. Purchases Returns and Allowances | 23–24. Closing entry for the income summary account (net income). (p. 657) | 23. _____ | 24. _____ |
| R. Retained Earnings | 25–26. Closing entry for the income summary account (net loss). (p. 657) | 25. _____ | 26. _____ |
| S. Sales | 27–28. Closing entry for the dividends account. (p. 657) | 27. _____ | 28. _____ |
| T. Sales Discount | 29–30. Reversing entry for the accrued interest income account. (p. 658) | 29. _____ | 30. _____ |
| | 31–32. Reversing entry for the accrued interest expense. (p. 658) | 31. _____ | 32. _____ |
| | 33–34. Reversing entry for the federal income tax payable account. (p. 658) | 33. _____ | 34. _____ |

## Estimating Math Answers

Being able to estimate math answers quickly is advantageous for everyone. When you go shopping, do you know approximately how much your bill is going to be before you check out? Before you work out a math problem at school, do you know about what the answer should be?

### Make a Good Guess
Being able to estimate answers will help you at school. Suppose you want to average 10 grades ranging from 90 to 100. You should be able to estimate that the total of the 10 grades should be about 950, and the average should be about 95. If your answer is 70 when you calculate the average, you know immediately that the answer is not sensible.

### Avoid Errors Using Decimal Places
Students sometimes place a decimal in the wrong place in the answer to a math problem. This is an error that you will not make if you know approximately how much the answer should be before you begin figuring.

This may sound surprising, but students sometimes make an error similar to the following. The teacher asks what is 10 percent of $100, and the student answers $1,000.

Any student who takes a few seconds to think about the problem will know immediately that the answer is smaller, not larger, than the original $100. By estimating the answer first, you can avoid making what appears to be a ridiculous error.

### Dependence on the Calculator
The pocket calculator is a wonderful device. It can save you a great amount of time when you must do a math problem. However, you must not let yourself become so dependent on a calculator that you make errors simply because you do not estimate answers.

### A Sensible Approach
Being able to estimate math answers can help you every day. Before you begin calculating, ask yourself what a sensible answer would be. If the final answer is not reasonably close to your estimate, you have very likely made an error. A little practice can save you money when you shop and improve your grades at school.

[This page left blank intentionally.]

**Preparing a work sheet for a corporation**

**1., 2.**

Webster Corporation

Work Sheet

For Year Ended December 31, 20 - -

| | | ACCOUNT TITLE | TRIAL BALANCE DEBIT | TRIAL BALANCE CREDIT | ADJUSTMENTS DEBIT | ADJUSTMENTS CREDIT | INCOME STATEMENT DEBIT | INCOME STATEMENT CREDIT | BALANCE SHEET DEBIT | BALANCE SHEET CREDIT | |
|---|---|---|---|---|---|---|---|---|---|---|---|
| 1 | | Cash | 90 05 22 3 | | | | | | | | 1 |
| 2 | | Petty Cash | 3 0 0 00 | | | | | | | | 2 |
| 3 | | Notes Receivable | 10 9 5 2 00 | | | | | | | | 3 |
| 4 | | Interest Receivable | | | | | | | | | 4 |
| 5 | | Accounts Receivable | 70 0 9 4 10 | | | | | | | | 5 |
| 6 | | Allowance for Uncoll. Accts. | | 4 4 64 | | | | | | | 6 |
| 7 | | Merchandise Inventory | 64 3 1 6 30 | | | | | | | | 7 |
| 8 | | Supplies | 2 5 5 2 08 | | | | | | | | 8 |
| 9 | | Prepaid Insurance | 9 0 7 1 60 | | | | | | | | 9 |
| 10 | | Office Equipment | 27 9 4 0 00 | | | | | | | | 10 |
| 11 | | Accum. Depr.—Office Equip. | | 6 7 3 5 00 | | | | | | | 11 |
| 12 | | Store Equipment | 22 1 9 9 20 | | | | | | | | 12 |
| 13 | | Accum. Depr.—Store Equip. | | 6 3 5 7 40 | | | | | | | 13 |
| 14 | | Notes Payable | | 14 4 0 0 00 | | | | | | | 14 |
| 15 | | Interest Payable | | | | | | | | | 15 |
| 16 | | Accounts Payable | | 60 1 1 6 18 | | | | | | | 16 |
| 17 | | Employee Inc. Tax Payable | | 1 6 5 2 40 | | | | | | | 17 |
| 18 | | Federal Inc. Tax Payable | | | | | | | | | 18 |
| 19 | | Social Security Tax Payable | | 1 5 4 9 19 | | | | | | | 19 |
| 20 | | Medicare Tax Payable | | 3 5 7 51 | | | | | | | 20 |
| 21 | | Sales Tax Payable | | 6 6 5 2 60 | | | | | | | 21 |
| 22 | | Unemploy. Tax Pay.—Fed. | | 3 3 44 | | | | | | | 22 |
| 23 | | Unemploy. Tax Pay.—State | | 2 2 5 72 | | | | | | | 23 |
| 24 | | Health Ins. Premiums Pay. | | 7 0 2 60 | | | | | | | 24 |
| 25 | | Dividends Payable | | 10 8 0 0 00 | | | | | | | 25 |
| 26 | | Capital Stock | | 100 0 0 0 00 | | | | | | | 26 |
| 27 | | Retained Earnings | | 59 2 4 1 54 | | | | | | | 27 |
| 28 | | Dividends | 43 2 0 0 00 | | | | | | | | 28 |
| 29 | | Income Summary | | | | | | | | | 29 |
| 30 | | Sales | | 1075 8 6 8 30 | | | | | | | 30 |
| 31 | | Sales Discount | 2 0 2 0 80 | | | | | | | | 31 |
| 32 | | Sales Ret. and Allowances | 8 3 4 7 20 | | | | | | | | 32 |

Total of Income Statement Credit column  _____

*Less* total of Income Statement Debit column
before federal income tax  _____

*Equals* Net Income before Federal Income Tax  ══════════════

## 22-1 WORK TOGETHER (concluded)

**Webster Corporation**

**Work Sheet (continued)**

**For Year Ended December 31, 20 --**

| | TRIAL BALANCE | | ADJUSTMENTS | | INCOME STATEMENT | | BALANCE SHEET | |
| ACCOUNT TITLE | DEBIT | CREDIT | DEBIT | CREDIT | DEBIT | CREDIT | DEBIT | CREDIT |
|---|---|---|---|---|---|---|---|---|
| 33 Purchases | 737 4 6 4 80 | | | | | | | |
| 34 Purchases Discount | | 5 4 8 3 60 | | | | | | |
| 35 Purchases Ret. and Allow. | | 2 7 1 6 14 | | | | | | |
| 36 Advertising Expense | 15 9 4 7 00 | | | | | | | |
| 37 Cash Short and Over | 9 15 | | | | | | | |
| 38 Credit Card Fee Expense | 10 0 6 6 94 | | | | | | | |
| 39 Depr. Exp.—Office Equip. | | | | | | | | |
| 40 Depr. Exp.—Store Equip. | | | | | | | | |
| 41 Insurance Expense | | | | | | | | |
| 42 Miscellaneous Expense | 8 6 8 2 20 | | | | | | | |
| 43 Payroll Taxes Expense | 14 9 6 6 00 | | | | | | | |
| 44 Rent Expense | 28 9 1 5 00 | | | | | | | |
| 45 Repair Expense | 3 4 8 5 00 | | | | | | | |
| 46 Salary Expense | 158 9 6 4 00 | | | | | | | |
| 47 Supplies Expense | | | | | | | | |
| 48 Uncollectible Accounts Exp. | | | | | | | | |
| 49 Utilities Expense | 2 6 6 1 00 | | | | | | | |
| 50 Gain on Plant Assets | | 1 1 0 00 | | | | | | |
| 51 Interest Income | | 8 9 4 48 | | | | | | |
| 52 Interest Expense | 2 1 8 6 14 | | | | | | | |
| 53 Loss on Plant Assets | 2 4 8 00 | | | | | | | |
| 54 Federal Income Tax Expense | 19 3 0 0 00 | | | | | | | |
| 55 | 1353 9 4 0 74 | 1353 9 4 0 74 | | | | | | |
| 56 Net Inc. after Fed. Inc. Tax | | | | | | | | |
| 57 | | | | | | | | |
| 58 | | | | | | | | |
| 59 | | | | | | | | |
| 60 | | | | | | | | |
| 61 | | | | | | | | |
| 62 | | | | | | | | |

| Net Income before Taxes | × | Tax Rate | = | Federal Income Tax Amount |
|---|---|---|---|---|
| $50,000.00 | × | 15% | = | |
| Plus    25,000.00 | × | 25% | = | |
| Plus | × | 34% | = | |
| Plus | × | 39% | = | |
| Total | | | | |

## Preparing a work sheet for a corporation

**1., 2.**

Osborn Corporation

Work Sheet

For Year Ended December 31, 20 --

| | ACCOUNT TITLE | TRIAL BALANCE DEBIT | TRIAL BALANCE CREDIT | ADJUSTMENTS DEBIT | ADJUSTMENTS CREDIT | INCOME STATEMENT DEBIT | INCOME STATEMENT CREDIT | BALANCE SHEET DEBIT | BALANCE SHEET CREDIT |
|---|---|---|---|---|---|---|---|---|---|
| 1 | Cash | 68 4 8 8 00 | | | | | | | |
| 2 | Petty Cash | 3 0 0 00 | | | | | | | |
| 3 | Notes Receivable | 8 0 0 0 00 | | | | | | | |
| 4 | Interest Receivable | | | | | | | | |
| 5 | Accounts Receivable | 82 4 8 3 22 | | | | | | | |
| 6 | Allowance for Uncoll. Accts. | | 2 8 0 00 | | | | | | |
| 7 | Merchandise Inventory | 195 8 8 4 25 | | | | | | | |
| 8 | Supplies | 9 2 1 8 25 | | | | | | | |
| 9 | Prepaid Insurance | 15 8 0 0 00 | | | | | | | |
| 10 | Office Equipment | 35 1 8 8 50 | | | | | | | |
| 11 | Accum. Depr.—Office Equip. | | 22 1 8 8 50 | | | | | | |
| 12 | Store Equipment | 43 8 8 4 25 | | | | | | | |
| 13 | Accum. Depr.—Store Equip. | | 28 1 7 8 00 | | | | | | |
| 14 | Notes Payable | | 9 0 0 0 00 | | | | | | |
| 15 | Interest Payable | | | | | | | | |
| 16 | Accounts Payable | | 18 4 8 9 25 | | | | | | |
| 17 | Employee Inc. Tax Payable | | 2 2 5 6 00 | | | | | | |
| 18 | Federal Inc. Tax Payable | | | | | | | | |
| 19 | Social Security Tax Payable | | 2 1 2 1 34 | | | | | | |
| 20 | Medicare Tax Payable | | 5 1 2 66 | | | | | | |
| 21 | Sales Tax Payable | | 5 9 7 6 00 | | | | | | |
| 22 | Unemploy. Tax Pay.—Fed. | | 4 5 60 | | | | | | |
| 23 | Unemploy. Tax Pay.—State | | 2 9 2 80 | | | | | | |
| 24 | Health Ins. Premiums Pay. | | 6 7 2 00 | | | | | | |
| 25 | Dividends Payable | | 5 0 0 0 00 | | | | | | |
| 26 | Capital Stock | | 50 0 0 0 00 | | | | | | |
| 27 | Retained Earnings | | 54 1 4 2 16 | | | | | | |
| 28 | Dividends | 20 0 0 0 00 | | | | | | | |

Total of Income Statement Credit column    _____

*Less* total of Income Statement Debit column
    before federal income tax    _____

*Equals* Net Income before Federal Income Tax    _____

## 22-1 ON YOUR OWN (concluded)

Osborn Corporation
Work Sheet (continued)
For Year Ended December 31, 20 --

| # | Account Title | Trial Balance Debit | Trial Balance Credit | Adjustments Debit | Adjustments Credit | Income Statement Debit | Income Statement Credit | Balance Sheet Debit | Balance Sheet Credit |
|---|---|---|---|---|---|---|---|---|---|
| 29 | Income Summary | | | | | | | | |
| 30 | Sales | | 2584 48 3 25 | | | | | | |
| 31 | Sales Discount | 12 4 85 28 | | | | | | | |
| 32 | Sales Returns and Allow. | 22 8 94 10 | | | | | | | |
| 33 | Purchases | 1638 8 17 14 | | | | | | | |
| 34 | Purchases Discount | | 7 8 91 17 | | | | | | |
| 35 | Purchases Ret. and Allow. | | 6 1 48 20 | | | | | | |
| 36 | Advertising Expense | 38 1 14 20 | | | | | | | |
| 37 | Cash Short and Over | 15 33 | | | | | | | |
| 38 | Credit Card Fee Expense | 18 1 22 10 | | | | | | | |
| 39 | Depr. Exp.—Office Equip. | | | | | | | | |
| 40 | Depr. Exp.—Store Equip. | | | | | | | | |
| 41 | Insurance Expense | | | | | | | | |
| 42 | Miscellaneous Expense | 29 4 85 25 | | | | | | | |
| 43 | Payroll Taxes Expense | 32 1 48 24 | | | | | | | |
| 44 | Rent Expense | 54 0 0 0 00 | | | | | | | |
| 45 | Repair Expense | 12 4 87 93 | | | | | | | |
| 46 | Salary Expense | 421 5 84 99 | | | | | | | |
| 47 | Supplies Expense | | | | | | | | |
| 48 | Uncollectible Accounts Exp. | | | | | | | | |
| 49 | Utilities Expense | 23 1 99 90 | | | | | | | |
| 50 | Gain on Plant Assets | | 24 5 80 00 | | | | | | |
| 51 | Interest Income | | 6 2 5 0 0 | | | | | | |
| 52 | Interest Expense | 17 8 0 0 00 | | | | | | | |
| 53 | Loss on Plant Assets | 20 1 9 00 | | | | | | | |
| 54 | Federal Income Tax Expense | 76 0 0 0 00 | | | | | | | |
| 55 | | 2800 7 5 9 93 | 2800 7 5 9 93 | | | | | | |
| 56 | Net Inc. after Fed. Inc. Tax | | | | | | | | |
| 57 | | | | | | | | | |

| Net Income before Taxes | × | Tax Rate | = | Federal Income Tax Amount |
|---|---|---|---|---|
| $ 50,000.00 | × | 15% | = | |
| Plus     25,000.00 | × | 25% | = | |
| Plus     25,000.00 | × | 34% | = | |
| Plus | × | 39% | = | |
| Total | | | | |

**WORK TOGETHER, p. 648**

**Preparing an income statement for a corporation**

1.

| | | | | | | % OF NET SALES |
|---|---|---|---|---|---|---|
| | | | | | | |

## 22-2 WORK TOGETHER (concluded)

**1.**

| | | | % OF NET SALES |
|---|---|---|---|
| | | | |
| | | | |
| | | | |
| | | | |
| | | | |
| | | | |
| | | | |
| | | | |
| | | | |
| | | | |
| | | | |
| | | | |

**2.**

| | Acceptable % | Actual % | Positive Result Yes | Positive Result No | Recommended Action If Needed |
|---|---|---|---|---|---|
| Cost of merchandise sold | Not more than 68.0% | | | | |
| Gross profit on operations | Not less than 32.0% | | | | |
| Total operating expenses | Not more than 22.0% | | | | |
| Income from operations | Not less than 10.0% | | | | |
| Net deduction from other revenue and expenses | Not more than 0.1% | | | | |
| Net income before federal income tax | Not less than 9.8% | | | | |

**ON YOUR OWN, p. 648**

**Preparing an income statement for a corporation**

**1.**

| | | | | | % OF NET SALES |
|---|---|---|---|---|---|
| | | | | | |
| | | | | | |
| | | | | | |
| | | | | | |
| | | | | | |
| | | | | | |
| | | | | | |
| | | | | | |
| | | | | | |
| | | | | | |
| | | | | | |
| | | | | | |
| | | | | | |
| | | | | | |
| | | | | | |
| | | | | | |
| | | | | | |
| | | | | | |
| | | | | | |
| | | | | | |
| | | | | | |
| | | | | | |
| | | | | | |
| | | | | | |
| | | | | | |
| | | | | | |
| | | | | | |
| | | | | | |
| | | | | | |
| | | | | | |
| | | | | | |
| | | | | | |
| | | | | | |
| | | | | | |

## 22-2 ON YOUR OWN (concluded)

**1.**

| | | | |
|---|---|---|---|
| | | | % OF NET SALES |

| | Acceptable % | Actual % | Positive Result | | Recommended Action If Needed |
|---|---|---|---|---|---|
| | | | Yes | No | |
| Cost of merchandise sold | Not more than 60.0% | | | | |
| Gross profit on operations | Not less than 40.0% | | | | |
| Total operating expenses | Not more than 28.0% | | | | |
| Income from operations | Not less than 12.0% | | | | |
| Net deduction from other revenue and expenses | Not more than 0.1% | | | | |
| Net income before federal income tax | Not less than 11.9% | | | | |

**22-3** WORK TOGETHER, p. 653

Preparing a statement of stockholders' equity and balance sheet for a corporation

1.

## 22-3 WORK TOGETHER (continued)

**2.**

**2.**

**3., 4.**

| | Acceptable | Actual | Positive Result | | Recommended Action If Needed |
|---|---|---|---|---|---|
| | | | Yes | No | |
| Working capital | Not less than $150,000 | | | | |
| Current ratio | Between 2.0 to 1 and 3.0 to 1 | | | | |

## 22-3 ON YOUR OWN, p. 653

**Preparing a statement of stockholders' equity and balance sheet for a corporation**

1.

2.

## 22-3 ON YOUR OWN (concluded)

**3., 4.**

| | Acceptable | Actual | Positive Result | | Recommended Action If Needed |
|---|---|---|---|---|---|
| | | | Yes | No | |
| Working capital | Not less than $100,000 | | | | |
| Current ratio | Between 5.0 to 1 and 6.0 to 1 | | | | |

**Journalizing adjusting, closing, and reversing entries for a corporation**

1.

GENERAL JOURNAL

PAGE 15

| | DATE | | ACCOUNT TITLE | DOC. NO. | POST. REF. | DEBIT | CREDIT | |
|---|---|---|---|---|---|---|---|---|
| 1 | | | | | | | | 1 |
| 2 | | | | | | | | 2 |
| 3 | | | | | | | | 3 |
| 4 | | | | | | | | 4 |
| 5 | | | | | | | | 5 |
| 6 | | | | | | | | 6 |
| 7 | | | | | | | | 7 |
| 8 | | | | | | | | 8 |
| 9 | | | | | | | | 9 |
| 10 | | | | | | | | 10 |
| 11 | | | | | | | | 11 |
| 12 | | | | | | | | 12 |
| 13 | | | | | | | | 13 |
| 14 | | | | | | | | 14 |
| 15 | | | | | | | | 15 |
| 16 | | | | | | | | 16 |
| 17 | | | | | | | | 17 |
| 18 | | | | | | | | 18 |
| 19 | | | | | | | | 19 |
| 20 | | | | | | | | 20 |
| 21 | | | | | | | | 21 |
| 22 | | | | | | | | 22 |
| 23 | | | | | | | | 23 |
| 24 | | | | | | | | 24 |
| 25 | | | | | | | | 25 |
| 26 | | | | | | | | 26 |
| 27 | | | | | | | | 27 |
| 28 | | | | | | | | 28 |
| 29 | | | | | | | | 29 |
| 30 | | | | | | | | 30 |
| 31 | | | | | | | | 31 |
| 32 | | | | | | | | 32 |

**22-4** **WORK TOGETHER (continued)**

2.

GENERAL JOURNAL

| | DATE | ACCOUNT TITLE | DOC. NO. | POST. REF. | DEBIT | CREDIT | |
|---|---|---|---|---|---|---|---|
| 1 | | | | | | | 1 |
| 2 | | | | | | | 2 |
| 3 | | | | | | | 3 |
| 4 | | | | | | | 4 |
| 5 | | | | | | | 5 |
| 6 | | | | | | | 6 |
| 7 | | | | | | | 7 |
| 8 | | | | | | | 8 |
| 9 | | | | | | | 9 |
| 10 | | | | | | | 10 |
| 11 | | | | | | | 11 |
| 12 | | | | | | | 12 |
| 13 | | | | | | | 13 |
| 14 | | | | | | | 14 |
| 15 | | | | | | | 15 |
| 16 | | | | | | | 16 |
| 17 | | | | | | | 17 |
| 18 | | | | | | | 18 |
| 19 | | | | | | | 19 |
| 20 | | | | | | | 20 |
| 21 | | | | | | | 21 |
| 22 | | | | | | | 22 |
| 23 | | | | | | | 23 |
| 24 | | | | | | | 24 |
| 25 | | | | | | | 25 |
| 26 | | | | | | | 26 |
| 27 | | | | | | | 27 |
| 28 | | | | | | | 28 |
| 29 | | | | | | | 29 |
| 30 | | | | | | | 30 |
| 31 | | | | | | | 31 |
| 32 | | | | | | | 32 |
| 33 | | | | | | | 33 |

**3.**

GENERAL JOURNAL

| | DATE | | ACCOUNT TITLE | DOC. NO. | POST. REF. | DEBIT | CREDIT | |
|---|---|---|---|---|---|---|---|---|
| 1 | | | | | | | | 1 |
| 2 | | | | | | | | 2 |
| 3 | | | | | | | | 3 |
| 4 | | | | | | | | 4 |
| 5 | | | | | | | | 5 |
| 6 | | | | | | | | 6 |
| 7 | | | | | | | | 7 |
| 8 | | | | | | | | 8 |
| 9 | | | | | | | | 9 |
| 10 | | | | | | | | 10 |
| 11 | | | | | | | | 11 |
| 12 | | | | | | | | 12 |
| 13 | | | | | | | | 13 |
| 14 | | | | | | | | 14 |
| 15 | | | | | | | | 15 |
| 16 | | | | | | | | 16 |
| 17 | | | | | | | | 17 |
| 18 | | | | | | | | 18 |
| 19 | | | | | | | | 19 |
| 20 | | | | | | | | 20 |
| 21 | | | | | | | | 21 |
| 22 | | | | | | | | 22 |
| 23 | | | | | | | | 23 |
| 24 | | | | | | | | 24 |
| 25 | | | | | | | | 25 |
| 26 | | | | | | | | 26 |
| 27 | | | | | | | | 27 |
| 28 | | | | | | | | 28 |
| 29 | | | | | | | | 29 |
| 30 | | | | | | | | 30 |
| 31 | | | | | | | | 31 |
| 32 | | | | | | | | 32 |
| 33 | | | | | | | | 33 |

## 22-4  ON YOUR OWN, p. 660

**Journalizing adjusting, closing, and reversing entries for a corporation**

**1.**

GENERAL JOURNAL

| | DATE | ACCOUNT TITLE | DOC. NO. | POST. REF. | DEBIT | CREDIT | |
|---|---|---|---|---|---|---|---|
| 1 | | | | | | | 1 |
| 2 | | | | | | | 2 |
| 3 | | | | | | | 3 |
| 4 | | | | | | | 4 |
| 5 | | | | | | | 5 |
| 6 | | | | | | | 6 |
| 7 | | | | | | | 7 |
| 8 | | | | | | | 8 |
| 9 | | | | | | | 9 |
| 10 | | | | | | | 10 |
| 11 | | | | | | | 11 |
| 12 | | | | | | | 12 |
| 13 | | | | | | | 13 |
| 14 | | | | | | | 14 |
| 15 | | | | | | | 15 |
| 16 | | | | | | | 16 |
| 17 | | | | | | | 17 |
| 18 | | | | | | | 18 |
| 19 | | | | | | | 19 |
| 20 | | | | | | | 20 |
| 21 | | | | | | | 21 |
| 22 | | | | | | | 22 |
| 23 | | | | | | | 23 |
| 24 | | | | | | | 24 |
| 25 | | | | | | | 25 |
| 26 | | | | | | | 26 |
| 27 | | | | | | | 27 |
| 28 | | | | | | | 28 |
| 29 | | | | | | | 29 |
| 30 | | | | | | | 30 |
| 31 | | | | | | | 31 |
| 32 | | | | | | | 32 |

**2.**

GENERAL JOURNAL PAGE 19

| | DATE | | ACCOUNT TITLE | DOC. NO. | POST. REF. | DEBIT | CREDIT | |
|---|---|---|---|---|---|---|---|---|
| 1 | | | | | | | | 1 |
| 2 | | | | | | | | 2 |
| 3 | | | | | | | | 3 |
| 4 | | | | | | | | 4 |
| 5 | | | | | | | | 5 |
| 6 | | | | | | | | 6 |
| 7 | | | | | | | | 7 |
| 8 | | | | | | | | 8 |
| 9 | | | | | | | | 9 |
| 10 | | | | | | | | 10 |
| 11 | | | | | | | | 11 |
| 12 | | | | | | | | 12 |
| 13 | | | | | | | | 13 |
| 14 | | | | | | | | 14 |
| 15 | | | | | | | | 15 |
| 16 | | | | | | | | 16 |
| 17 | | | | | | | | 17 |
| 18 | | | | | | | | 18 |
| 19 | | | | | | | | 19 |
| 20 | | | | | | | | 20 |
| 21 | | | | | | | | 21 |
| 22 | | | | | | | | 22 |
| 23 | | | | | | | | 23 |
| 24 | | | | | | | | 24 |
| 25 | | | | | | | | 25 |
| 26 | | | | | | | | 26 |
| 27 | | | | | | | | 27 |
| 28 | | | | | | | | 28 |
| 29 | | | | | | | | 29 |
| 30 | | | | | | | | 30 |
| 31 | | | | | | | | 31 |
| 32 | | | | | | | | 32 |
| 33 | | | | | | | | 33 |

**22-4** **ON YOUR OWN (concluded)**

**3.**

GENERAL JOURNAL                                                          PAGE 20

| | DATE | | ACCOUNT TITLE | DOC. NO. | POST. REF. | DEBIT | CREDIT | |
|---|---|---|---|---|---|---|---|---|
| 1 | | | | | | | | 1 |
| 2 | | | | | | | | 2 |
| 3 | | | | | | | | 3 |
| 4 | | | | | | | | 4 |
| 5 | | | | | | | | 5 |
| 6 | | | | | | | | 6 |
| 7 | | | | | | | | 7 |
| 8 | | | | | | | | 8 |
| 9 | | | | | | | | 9 |
| 10 | | | | | | | | 10 |
| 11 | | | | | | | | 11 |
| 12 | | | | | | | | 12 |
| 13 | | | | | | | | 13 |
| 14 | | | | | | | | 14 |
| 15 | | | | | | | | 15 |
| 16 | | | | | | | | 16 |
| 17 | | | | | | | | 17 |
| 18 | | | | | | | | 18 |
| 19 | | | | | | | | 19 |
| 20 | | | | | | | | 20 |
| 21 | | | | | | | | 21 |
| 22 | | | | | | | | 22 |
| 23 | | | | | | | | 23 |
| 24 | | | | | | | | 24 |
| 25 | | | | | | | | 25 |
| 26 | | | | | | | | 26 |
| 27 | | | | | | | | 27 |
| 28 | | | | | | | | 28 |
| 29 | | | | | | | | 29 |
| 30 | | | | | | | | 30 |
| 31 | | | | | | | | 31 |
| 32 | | | | | | | | 32 |
| 33 | | | | | | | | 33 |

**APPLICATION PROBLEM, p. 662**

**Preparing a work sheet for a corporation**

**1., 2.**

Donovan Lumber Corporation

Work Sheet

For Year Ended December 31, 20 – –

| | ACCOUNT TITLE | TRIAL BALANCE DEBIT | TRIAL BALANCE CREDIT | ADJUSTMENTS DEBIT | ADJUSTMENTS CREDIT | INCOME STATEMENT DEBIT | INCOME STATEMENT CREDIT | BALANCE SHEET DEBIT | BALANCE SHEET CREDIT | |
|---|---|---|---|---|---|---|---|---|---|---|
| 1 | Cash | 3 8 4 8 58 | | | | | | | | 1 |
| 2 | Petty Cash | 3 0 0 00 | | | | | | | | 2 |
| 3 | Notes Receivable | 5 8 4 8 80 | | | | | | | | 3 |
| 4 | Interest Receivable | | | | | | | | | 4 |
| 5 | Accounts Receivable | 57 1 8 7 80 | | | | | | | | 5 |
| 6 | Allowance for Uncoll. Accts. | | 6 6 48 | | | | | | | 6 |
| 7 | Merchandise Inventory | 78 8 5 8 00 | | | | | | | | 7 |
| 8 | Supplies | 4 9 8 7 70 | | | | | | | | 8 |
| 9 | Prepaid Insurance | 8 9 4 8 00 | | | | | | | | 9 |
| 10 | Office Equipment | 26 4 8 8 00 | | | | | | | | 10 |
| 11 | Accum. Depr.—Office Equip. | | 8 4 8 8 00 | | | | | | | 11 |
| 12 | Store Equipment | 17 4 9 8 00 | | | | | | | | 12 |
| 13 | Accum. Depr.—Store Equip. | | 4 8 7 1 40 | | | | | | | 13 |
| 14 | Notes Payable | | 30 0 0 0 00 | | | | | | | 14 |
| 15 | Interest Payable | | | | | | | | | 15 |
| 16 | Accounts Payable | | 8 3 7 2 80 | | | | | | | 16 |
| 17 | Employee Inc. Tax Payable | | 1 4 8 6 30 | | | | | | | 17 |
| 18 | Federal Inc. Tax Payable | | | | | | | | | 18 |
| 19 | Social Security Tax Payable | | 1 2 0 9 81 | | | | | | | 19 |
| 20 | Medicare Tax Payable | | 2 7 9 19 | | | | | | | 20 |
| 21 | Sales Tax Payable | | 2 8 4 7 00 | | | | | | | 21 |
| 22 | Unemploy. Tax Pay.—Fed. | | 2 9 25 | | | | | | | 22 |
| 23 | Unemploy. Tax Pay.—State | | 1 9 5 00 | | | | | | | 23 |
| 24 | Health Ins. Premiums Pay. | | 3 4 8 80 | | | | | | | 24 |
| 25 | Dividends Payable | | 5 0 0 0 00 | | | | | | | 25 |
| 26 | Capital Stock | | 50 0 0 0 00 | | | | | | | 26 |
| 27 | Retained Earnings | | 30 8 2 3 18 | | | | | | | 27 |
| 28 | Dividends | 20 0 0 0 00 | | | | | | | | 28 |
| 29 | Income Summary | | | | | | | | | 29 |
| 30 | Sales | | 983 8 3 7 20 | | | | | | | 30 |
| 31 | Sales Discount | 1 8 9 4 50 | | | | | | | | 31 |
| 32 | Sales Ret. and Allowances | 4 5 8 3 50 | | | | | | | | 32 |

**2.** Total of Income Statement Credit column  _____

   *Less* total of Income Statement Debit column

      before federal income tax  _____

   *Equals* Net Income before Federal Income Tax  _____

## 22-1 APPLICATION PROBLEM (concluded)

Donovan Lumber Corporation

Work Sheet (continued)

For Year Ended December 31, 20--

| | ACCOUNT TITLE | TRIAL BALANCE DEBIT | TRIAL BALANCE CREDIT | ADJUSTMENTS DEBIT | ADJUSTMENTS CREDIT | INCOME STATEMENT DEBIT | INCOME STATEMENT CREDIT | BALANCE SHEET DEBIT | BALANCE SHEET CREDIT |
|---|---|---|---|---|---|---|---|---|---|
| 33 | Purchases | 697 3 1 8 50 | | | | | | | |
| 34 | Purchases Discount | | 4 2 1 5 50 | | | | | | |
| 35 | Purchases Ret. and Allow. | | 1 8 4 8 47 | | | | | | |
| 36 | Advertising Expense | 9 4 8 3 80 | | | | | | | |
| 37 | Cash Short and Over | 1 0 20 | | | | | | | |
| 38 | Credit Card Fee Expense | 8 4 8 2 90 | | | | | | | |
| 39 | Depr. Exp.—Office Equip. | | | | | | | | |
| 40 | Depr. Exp.—Store Equip. | | | | | | | | |
| 41 | Insurance Expense | | | | | | | | |
| 42 | Miscellaneous Expense | 9 1 8 4 80 | | | | | | | |
| 43 | Payroll Taxes Expense | 12 8 4 8 00 | | | | | | | |
| 44 | Rent Expense | 15 0 0 0 00 | | | | | | | |
| 45 | Repair Expense | 4 1 0 4 80 | | | | | | | |
| 46 | Salary Expense | 125 4 8 3 20 | | | | | | | |
| 47 | Supplies Expense | | | | | | | | |
| 48 | Uncollectible Accounts Exp. | | | | | | | | |
| 49 | Utilities Expense | 7 1 5 8 90 | | | | | | | |
| 50 | Gain on Plant Assets | | 7 15 00 | | | | | | |
| 51 | Interest Income | | 2 27 00 | | | | | | |
| 52 | Interest Expense | 3 1 5 8 40 | | | | | | | |
| 53 | Loss on Plant Assets | 1 84 00 | | | | | | | |
| 54 | Federal Income Tax Expense | 120 0 0 0 00 | | | | | | | |
| 55 | | 1134 8 6 0 38 | 1134 8 6 0 38 | | | | | | |
| 56 | Net Inc. after Fed. Inc. Tax | | | | | | | | |
| 57 | | | | | | | | | |
| 58 | | | | | | | | | |
| 59 | | | | | | | | | |
| 60 | | | | | | | | | |
| 61 | | | | | | | | | |
| 62 | | | | | | | | | |
| 63 | | | | | | | | | |
| 64 | | | | | | | | | |

**2.**

| Net Income before Taxes | × | Tax Rate | = | Federal Income Tax Amount |
|---|---|---|---|---|
| $50,000.00 | × | 15% | = | |
| Plus | × | 25% | = | |
| Plus | × | 34% | = | |
| Plus | × | 39% | = | |
| Total | | | | |

**Preparing an income statement for a corporation**

1., 2.

| | | | | | % OF NET SALES |
|---|---|---|---|---|---|
| | | | | | |
| | | | | | |
| | | | | | |
| | | | | | |
| | | | | | |
| | | | | | |
| | | | | | |
| | | | | | |
| | | | | | |
| | | | | | |
| | | | | | |
| | | | | | |
| | | | | | |
| | | | | | |
| | | | | | |
| | | | | | |
| | | | | | |
| | | | | | |
| | | | | | |
| | | | | | |
| | | | | | |
| | | | | | |
| | | | | | |
| | | | | | |
| | | | | | |
| | | | | | |
| | | | | | |
| | | | | | |
| | | | | | |
| | | | | | |
| | | | | | |

**22-2** **APPLICATION PROBLEM (concluded)**

**1., 2.**

| | | | % OF NET SALES |
|---|---|---|---|
| | | | |
| | | | |
| | | | |
| | | | |
| | | | |
| | | | |
| | | | |
| | | | |
| | | | |
| | | | |
| | | | |

**3.**

| | Acceptable % | Actual % | Positive Result | | Recommended Action If Needed |
|---|---|---|---|---|---|
| | | | Yes | No | |
| Cost of merchandise sold | Not more than 70.0% | | | | |
| Gross profit on operations | Not less than 30.0% | | | | |
| Total operating expenses | Not more than 25.0% | | | | |
| Income from operations | Not less than 5.0% | | | | |
| Net deduction from other revenue and expenses | Not more than 0.1% | | | | |
| Net income before federal income tax | Not less than 4.9% | | | | |

**Preparing a statement of stockholders' equity and balance sheet for a corporation**

**1.**

## 22-3 APPLICATION PROBLEM (continued)

**2.**

**2.**

|  |  |  |  |  |  |
|--|--|--|--|--|--|
|  |  |  |  |  |  |
|  |  |  |  |  |  |
|  |  |  |  |  |  |
|  |  |  |  |  |  |
|  |  |  |  |  |  |
|  |  |  |  |  |  |
|  |  |  |  |  |  |
|  |  |  |  |  |  |
|  |  |  |  |  |  |
|  |  |  |  |  |  |
|  |  |  |  |  |  |
|  |  |  |  |  |  |
|  |  |  |  |  |  |
|  |  |  |  |  |  |
|  |  |  |  |  |  |
|  |  |  |  |  |  |
|  |  |  |  |  |  |
|  |  |  |  |  |  |

**3., 4.**

|  | Acceptable | Actual | Positive Result | | Recommended Action If Needed |
|--|--|--|--|--|--|
|  |  |  | Yes | No |  |
| Working capital | Not less than $100,000 |  |  |  |  |
| Current ratio | Between 3.0 to 1 and 3.5 to 1 |  |  |  |  |

## 22-4 APPLICATION PROBLEM, p. 663

**Journalizing adjusting, closing, and reversing entries for a corporation**

**1.**

GENERAL JOURNAL                                    PAGE 15

| | DATE | | ACCOUNT TITLE | DOC. NO. | POST. REF. | DEBIT | CREDIT | |
|---|---|---|---|---|---|---|---|---|
| 1 | | | | | | | | 1 |
| 2 | | | | | | | | 2 |
| 3 | | | | | | | | 3 |
| 4 | | | | | | | | 4 |
| 5 | | | | | | | | 5 |
| 6 | | | | | | | | 6 |
| 7 | | | | | | | | 7 |
| 8 | | | | | | | | 8 |
| 9 | | | | | | | | 9 |
| 10 | | | | | | | | 10 |
| 11 | | | | | | | | 11 |
| 12 | | | | | | | | 12 |
| 13 | | | | | | | | 13 |
| 14 | | | | | | | | 14 |
| 15 | | | | | | | | 15 |
| 16 | | | | | | | | 16 |
| 17 | | | | | | | | 17 |
| 18 | | | | | | | | 18 |
| 19 | | | | | | | | 19 |
| 20 | | | | | | | | 20 |
| 21 | | | | | | | | 21 |
| 22 | | | | | | | | 22 |
| 23 | | | | | | | | 23 |
| 24 | | | | | | | | 24 |
| 25 | | | | | | | | 25 |
| 26 | | | | | | | | 26 |
| 27 | | | | | | | | 27 |
| 28 | | | | | | | | 28 |
| 29 | | | | | | | | 29 |
| 30 | | | | | | | | 30 |
| 31 | | | | | | | | 31 |
| 32 | | | | | | | | 32 |

**2.**

GENERAL JOURNAL PAGE 16

| | DATE | ACCOUNT TITLE | DOC. NO. | POST. REF. | DEBIT | CREDIT | |
|---|---|---|---|---|---|---|---|
| 1 | | | | | | | 1 |
| 2 | | | | | | | 2 |
| 3 | | | | | | | 3 |
| 4 | | | | | | | 4 |
| 5 | | | | | | | 5 |
| 6 | | | | | | | 6 |
| 7 | | | | | | | 7 |
| 8 | | | | | | | 8 |
| 9 | | | | | | | 9 |
| 10 | | | | | | | 10 |
| 11 | | | | | | | 11 |
| 12 | | | | | | | 12 |
| 13 | | | | | | | 13 |
| 14 | | | | | | | 14 |
| 15 | | | | | | | 15 |
| 16 | | | | | | | 16 |
| 17 | | | | | | | 17 |
| 18 | | | | | | | 18 |
| 19 | | | | | | | 19 |
| 20 | | | | | | | 20 |
| 21 | | | | | | | 21 |
| 22 | | | | | | | 22 |
| 23 | | | | | | | 23 |
| 24 | | | | | | | 24 |
| 25 | | | | | | | 25 |
| 26 | | | | | | | 26 |
| 27 | | | | | | | 27 |
| 28 | | | | | | | 28 |
| 29 | | | | | | | 29 |
| 30 | | | | | | | 30 |
| 31 | | | | | | | 31 |
| 32 | | | | | | | 32 |
| 33 | | | | | | | 33 |

## 22-4 APPLICATION PROBLEM (concluded)

**3.**

GENERAL JOURNAL                                          PAGE 17

| | DATE | ACCOUNT TITLE | DOC. NO. | POST. REF. | DEBIT | CREDIT | |
|---|---|---|---|---|---|---|---|
| 1 | | | | | | | 1 |
| 2 | | | | | | | 2 |
| 3 | | | | | | | 3 |
| 4 | | | | | | | 4 |
| 5 | | | | | | | 5 |
| 6 | | | | | | | 6 |
| 7 | | | | | | | 7 |
| 8 | | | | | | | 8 |
| 9 | | | | | | | 9 |
| 10 | | | | | | | 10 |
| 11 | | | | | | | 11 |
| 12 | | | | | | | 12 |
| 13 | | | | | | | 13 |
| 14 | | | | | | | 14 |
| 15 | | | | | | | 15 |
| 16 | | | | | | | 16 |
| 17 | | | | | | | 17 |
| 18 | | | | | | | 18 |
| 19 | | | | | | | 19 |
| 20 | | | | | | | 20 |
| 21 | | | | | | | 21 |
| 22 | | | | | | | 22 |
| 23 | | | | | | | 23 |
| 24 | | | | | | | 24 |
| 25 | | | | | | | 25 |
| 26 | | | | | | | 26 |
| 27 | | | | | | | 27 |
| 28 | | | | | | | 28 |
| 29 | | | | | | | 29 |
| 30 | | | | | | | 30 |
| 31 | | | | | | | 31 |
| 32 | | | | | | | 32 |
| 33 | | | | | | | 33 |

**Preparing a work sheet, financial statement, and end-of-fiscal-period entries for a corporation**

**1.**

Benford Corporation

Work Sheet

For Year Ended December 31, 20 - -

| ACCOUNT TITLE | TRIAL BALANCE DEBIT | TRIAL BALANCE CREDIT | ADJUSTMENTS DEBIT | ADJUSTMENTS CREDIT | INCOME STATEMENT DEBIT | INCOME STATEMENT CREDIT | BALANCE SHEET DEBIT | BALANCE SHEET CREDIT |
|---|---|---|---|---|---|---|---|---|
| 1 Cash | 2 5 1 8 25 | | | | | | | |
| 2 Petty Cash | 5 0 0 00 | | | | | | | |
| 3 Notes Receivable | 4 0 0 0 00 | | | | | | | |
| 4 Interest Receivable | | | | | | | | |
| 5 Accounts Receivable | 125 8 4 8 25 | | | | | | | |
| 6 Allowance for Uncoll. Accts. | 1 6 0 00 | | | | | | | |
| 7 Merchandise Inventory | 288 3 1 8 08 | | | | | | | |
| 8 Supplies | 6 4 8 1 28 | | | | | | | |
| 9 Prepaid Insurance | 14 0 0 0 00 | | | | | | | |
| 10 Office Equipment | 29 1 4 8 22 | | | | | | | |
| 11 Accum. Depr.—Office Equip. | | 8 7 1 0 00 | | | | | | |
| 12 Store Equipment | 27 1 5 8 00 | | | | | | | |
| 13 Accum. Depr.—Store Equip. | | 18 1 6 0 00 | | | | | | |
| 14 Notes Payable | | 25 0 0 0 00 | | | | | | |
| 15 Interest Payable | | | | | | | | |
| 16 Accounts Payable | | 32 1 5 8 29 | | | | | | |
| 17 Employee Inc. Tax Payable | | 2 4 5 8 80 | | | | | | |
| 18 Federal Inc. Tax Payable | | | | | | | | |
| 19 Social Security Tax Payable | | 2 1 2 1 31 | | | | | | |
| 20 Medicare Tax Payable | | 5 1 2 69 | | | | | | |
| 21 Sales Tax Payable | | 2 5 1 8 66 | | | | | | |
| 22 Unemploy. Tax Pay.—Fed. | | 4 5 60 | | | | | | |
| 23 Unemploy. Tax Pay.—State | | 2 9 2 80 | | | | | | |
| 24 Health Ins. Premiums Pay. | | 6 7 2 00 | | | | | | |
| 25 Dividends Payable | | 8 0 0 0 00 | | | | | | |
| 26 Capital Stock | | 150 0 0 0 00 | | | | | | |
| 27 Retained Earnings | | 149 1 8 3 00 | | | | | | |
| 28 Dividends | 32 0 0 0 00 | | | | | | | |
| 29 Income Summary | | | | | | | | |
| 30 Sales | | 2251 8 9 3 17 | | | | | | |
| 31 Sales Discount | 5 8 9 4 36 | | | | | | | |
| 32 Sales Ret. and Allowances | 15 4 8 7 39 | | | | | | | |

Total of Income Statement Credit column  _____

*Less* total of Income Statement Debit column

before federal income tax  _____

*Equals* Net Income before Federal Income Tax  _____

**22-5** **MASTERY PROBLEM (continued)**

Benford Corporation
Work Sheet (continued)
For Year Ended December 31, 20 --- ---

| | ACCOUNT TITLE | TRIAL BALANCE DEBIT (1) | TRIAL BALANCE CREDIT (2) | ADJUSTMENTS DEBIT (3) | ADJUSTMENTS CREDIT (4) | INCOME STATEMENT DEBIT (5) | INCOME STATEMENT CREDIT (6) | BALANCE SHEET DEBIT (7) | BALANCE SHEET CREDIT (8) | |
|---|---|---|---|---|---|---|---|---|---|---|
| 33 | Purchases | 1498183 08 | | | | | | | | 33 |
| 34 | Purchases Discount | | 13118 02 | | | | | | | 34 |
| 35 | Purchases Ret. and Allow. | | 6184 16 | | | | | | | 35 |
| 36 | Advertising Expense | 16486 90 | | | | | | | | 36 |
| 37 | Cash Short and Over | 16 88 | | | | | | | | 37 |
| 38 | Credit Card Fee Expense | 8489 33 | | | | | | | | 38 |
| 39 | Depr. Exp.—Office Equip. | | | | | | | | | 39 |
| 40 | Depr. Exp.—Store Equip. | | | | | | | | | 40 |
| 41 | Insurance Expense | | | | | | | | | 41 |
| 42 | Miscellaneous Expense | 42186 30 | | | | | | | | 42 |
| 43 | Payroll Taxes Expense | 32184 02 | | | | | | | | 43 |
| 44 | Rent Expense | 45000 00 | | | | | | | | 44 |
| 45 | Repair Expense | 6154 99 | | | | | | | | 45 |
| 46 | Salary Expense | 421548 36 | | | | | | | | 46 |
| 47 | Supplies Expense | | | | | | | | | 47 |
| 48 | Uncollectible Accounts Exp. | | | | | | | | | 48 |
| 49 | Utilities Expense | 20445 61 | | | | | | | | 49 |
| 50 | Gain on Plant Assets | | 1548 00 | | | | | | | 50 |
| 51 | Interest Income | | 648 00 | | | | | | | 51 |
| 52 | Interest Expense | 3600 00 | | | | | | | | 52 |
| 53 | Loss on Plant Assets | 2415 20 | | | | | | | | 53 |
| 54 | Federal Income Tax Expense | 25000 00 | | | | | | | | 54 |
| 55 | | 2673224 50 | 2673224 50 | | | | | | | 55 |
| 56 | Net Inc. after Fed. Inc. Tax | | | | | | | | | 56 |
| 57 | | | | | | | | | | 57 |

| Net Income before Taxes | × | Tax Rate | = | Federal Income Tax Amount |
|---|---|---|---|---|
| $50,000.00 | × | 15% | = | |
| Plus 25,000.00 | × | 25% | = | |
| Plus 25,000.00 | × | 34% | = | |
| Plus | × | 39% | = | |
| Total | | | | |

2.

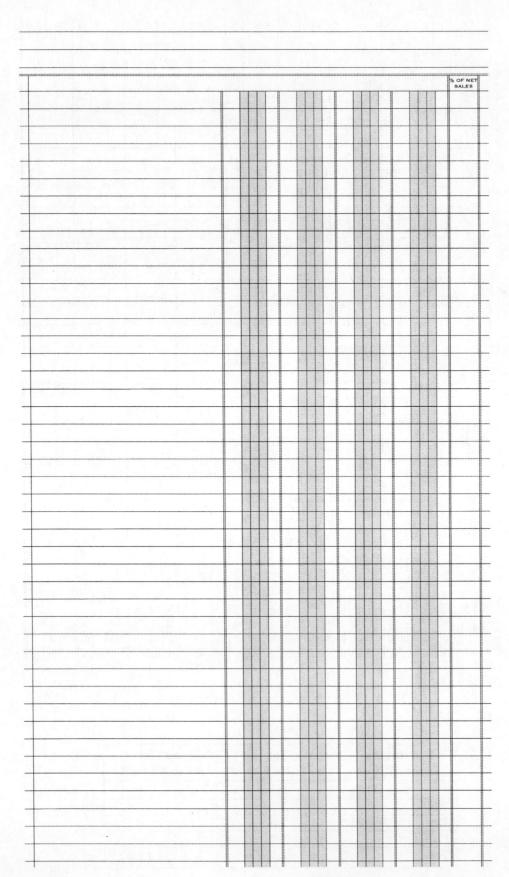

## 22-5 MASTERY PROBLEM (continued)

### 3. Income Statement Analysis

| | Acceptable % | Actual % | Positive Result | | Recommended Action If Needed |
|---|---|---|---|---|---|
| | | | Yes | No | |
| Cost of merchandise sold | Not more than 70.0% | | | | |
| Gross profit on operations | Not less than 30.0% | | | | |
| Total operating expenses | Not more than 25.0% | | | | |
| Income from operations | Not less than 5.0% | | | | |
| Net deduction from other revenue and expenses | Not more than 0.1% | | | | |
| Net income before federal income tax | Not less than 4.9% | | | | |

**4.**

5.

## 22-5 MASTERY PROBLEM (continued)

### 6. Balance Sheet Analysis

| | Acceptable | Actual | Positive Result | | Recommended Action If Needed |
|---|---|---|---|---|---|
| | | | Yes | No | |
| Working capital | Not less than $150,000 | | | | |
| Current ratio | Between 3.0 to 1 and 4.0 to 1 | | | | |

### 7.

GENERAL JOURNAL                                    PAGE 15

| | DATE | ACCOUNT TITLE | DOC. NO. | POST. REF. | DEBIT | CREDIT | |
|---|---|---|---|---|---|---|---|
| 1 | | | | | | | 1 |
| 2 | | | | | | | 2 |
| 3 | | | | | | | 3 |
| 4 | | | | | | | 4 |
| 5 | | | | | | | 5 |
| 6 | | | | | | | 6 |
| 7 | | | | | | | 7 |
| 8 | | | | | | | 8 |
| 9 | | | | | | | 9 |
| 10 | | | | | | | 10 |
| 11 | | | | | | | 11 |
| 12 | | | | | | | 12 |
| 13 | | | | | | | 13 |
| 14 | | | | | | | 14 |
| 15 | | | | | | | 15 |
| 16 | | | | | | | 16 |
| 17 | | | | | | | 17 |
| 18 | | | | | | | 18 |
| 19 | | | | | | | 19 |
| 20 | | | | | | | 20 |
| 21 | | | | | | | 21 |

**8.**

GENERAL JOURNAL

| | DATE | ACCOUNT TITLE | DOC. NO. | POST. REF. | DEBIT | CREDIT | |
|---|---|---|---|---|---|---|---|
| 1 | | | | | | | 1 |
| 2 | | | | | | | 2 |
| 3 | | | | | | | 3 |
| 4 | | | | | | | 4 |
| 5 | | | | | | | 5 |
| 6 | | | | | | | 6 |
| 7 | | | | | | | 7 |
| 8 | | | | | | | 8 |
| 9 | | | | | | | 9 |
| 10 | | | | | | | 10 |
| 11 | | | | | | | 11 |
| 12 | | | | | | | 12 |
| 13 | | | | | | | 13 |
| 14 | | | | | | | 14 |
| 15 | | | | | | | 15 |
| 16 | | | | | | | 16 |
| 17 | | | | | | | 17 |
| 18 | | | | | | | 18 |
| 19 | | | | | | | 19 |
| 20 | | | | | | | 20 |
| 21 | | | | | | | 21 |
| 22 | | | | | | | 22 |
| 23 | | | | | | | 23 |
| 24 | | | | | | | 24 |
| 25 | | | | | | | 25 |
| 26 | | | | | | | 26 |
| 27 | | | | | | | 27 |
| 28 | | | | | | | 28 |
| 29 | | | | | | | 29 |
| 30 | | | | | | | 30 |
| 31 | | | | | | | 31 |
| 32 | | | | | | | 32 |
| 33 | | | | | | | 33 |

**22-5** **MASTERY PROBLEM (concluded)**

9.

GENERAL JOURNAL

| | DATE | ACCOUNT TITLE | DOC. NO. | POST. REF. | DEBIT | CREDIT | |
|---|---|---|---|---|---|---|---|
| 1 | | | | | | | 1 |
| 2 | | | | | | | 2 |
| 3 | | | | | | | 3 |
| 4 | | | | | | | 4 |
| 5 | | | | | | | 5 |
| 6 | | | | | | | 6 |
| 7 | | | | | | | 7 |
| 8 | | | | | | | 8 |
| 9 | | | | | | | 9 |
| 10 | | | | | | | 10 |
| 11 | | | | | | | 11 |
| 12 | | | | | | | 12 |
| 13 | | | | | | | 13 |
| 14 | | | | | | | 14 |
| 15 | | | | | | | 15 |
| 16 | | | | | | | 16 |
| 17 | | | | | | | 17 |
| 18 | | | | | | | 18 |
| 19 | | | | | | | 19 |
| 20 | | | | | | | 20 |
| 21 | | | | | | | 21 |
| 22 | | | | | | | 22 |
| 23 | | | | | | | 23 |
| 24 | | | | | | | 24 |
| 25 | | | | | | | 25 |
| 26 | | | | | | | 26 |
| 27 | | | | | | | 27 |
| 28 | | | | | | | 28 |
| 29 | | | | | | | 29 |
| 30 | | | | | | | 30 |
| 31 | | | | | | | 31 |
| 32 | | | | | | | 32 |
| 33 | | | | | | | 33 |
| 34 | | | | | | | 34 |

**Analyzing financial strength**

**1.**

| Name of Corporation | Working Capital | Current Ratio |
|---|---|---|
| 1. | | |
| 2. | | |

**Calculations:**

**2.**

_____

_____

_____

_____

_____

_____

_____

_____

_____

_____

_____

_____

_____

_____

**22-6** **CHALLENGE PROBLEM (concluded)**

3.

An accounting cycle for a corporation: end-of-fiscal-period work

10., 11., 12.

Sparkle, Inc.

Work Sheet

For Year Ended December 31, 20X4

| | ACCOUNT TITLE | TRIAL BALANCE DEBIT | TRIAL BALANCE CREDIT | ADJUSTMENTS DEBIT | ADJUSTMENTS CREDIT | INCOME STATEMENT DEBIT | INCOME STATEMENT CREDIT | BALANCE SHEET DEBIT | BALANCE SHEET CREDIT | |
|---|---|---|---|---|---|---|---|---|---|---|
| 1 | Cash | 8 1 0 0 70 | | | | | | | | 1 |
| 2 | Petty Cash | 2 0 0 00 | | | | | | | | 2 |
| 3 | Notes Receivable | 3 6 0 0 00 | | | | | | | | 3 |
| 4 | Interest Receivable | | | | | | | | | 4 |
| 5 | Accounts Receivable | 7 8 9 4 60 | | | | | | | | 5 |
| 6 | Allowance for Uncoll. Accts. | 1 4 6 9 40 | | | | | | | | 6 |
| 7 | Merchandise Inventory | 74 1 7 6 95 | | | | | | | | 7 |
| 8 | Supplies | 3 0 9 9 05 | | | | | | | | 8 |
| 9 | Prepaid Insurance | 8 6 0 0 00 | | | | | | | | 9 |
| 10 | Office Equipment | 23 8 3 0 00 | | | | | | | | 10 |
| 11 | Accum. Depr.—Office Equip. | | 7 1 6 0 00 | | | | | | | 11 |
| 12 | Warehouse Equipment | 26 1 1 0 00 | | | | | | | | 12 |
| 13 | Accum. Depr.—Warehouse Equip. | | 7 0 4 0 00 | | | | | | | 13 |
| 14 | Notes Payable | | 16 0 0 0 00 | | | | | | | 14 |
| 15 | Interest Payable | | | | | | | | | 15 |
| 16 | Accounts Payable | | 14 1 1 2 65 | | | | | | | 16 |
| 17 | Federal Income Tax Pay. | | | | | | | | | 17 |
| 18 | Employee Income Tax Pay. | | 3 1 0 00 | | | | | | | 18 |
| 19 | Social Security Tax Pay. | | 6 9 1 92 | | | | | | | 19 |
| 20 | Medicare Tax Payable | | 1 6 1 82 | | | | | | | 20 |
| 21 | Sales Tax Payable | | 6 2 1 0 66 | | | | | | | 21 |
| 22 | Unemploy. Tax Pay.—Fed. | | 2 1 53 | | | | | | | 22 |
| 23 | Unemploy. Tax Pay.—State | | 1 4 5 29 | | | | | | | 23 |
| 24 | Health Ins. Premiums Pay. | | 1 1 0 5 00 | | | | | | | 24 |
| 25 | Dividends Payable | | 5 0 0 0 00 | | | | | | | 25 |
| 26 | Capital Stock | | 30 0 0 0 00 | | | | | | | 26 |
| 27 | Retained Earnings | | 23 8 8 9 20 | | | | | | | 27 |
| 28 | Dividends | 20 0 0 0 00 | | | | | | | | 28 |
| 29 | Income Summary | | | | | | | | | 29 |
| 30 | Sales | | 779 2 1 0 90 | | | | | | | 30 |
| 31 | Sales Discount | 1 8 8 9 20 | | | | | | | | 31 |

# REINFORCEMENT ACTIVITY 3 PART B (continued)

**Sparkle, Inc.**

**Work Sheet (continued)**

**For Year Ended December 31, 20X4**

| | ACCOUNT TITLE | TRIAL BALANCE DEBIT | TRIAL BALANCE CREDIT | ADJUSTMENTS DEBIT | ADJUSTMENTS CREDIT | INCOME STATEMENT DEBIT | INCOME STATEMENT CREDIT | BALANCE SHEET DEBIT | BALANCE SHEET CREDIT |
|---|---|---|---|---|---|---|---|---|---|
| 32 | Sales Returns and Allow. | 6 1 7 4 80 | | | | | | | |
| 33 | Purchases | 529 0 2 2 40 | | | | | | | |
| 34 | Purchases Discount | | 3 5 9 6 08 | | | | | | |
| 35 | Purchases Returns and Allow. | | 3 2 3 6 00 | | | | | | |
| 36 | Advertising Expense | 9 6 0 6 70 | | | | | | | |
| 37 | Cash Short and Over | 2 0 09 | | | | | | | |
| 38 | Credit Card Fee Expense | 14 5 2 9 40 | | | | | | | |
| 39 | Depr. Expense—Office Equip. | 2 4 0 0 00 | | | | | | | |
| 40 | Depr. Expense—Ware. Equip. | 4 4 0 0 00 | | | | | | | |
| 41 | Insurance Expense | | | | | | | | |
| 42 | Miscellaneous Expense | 5 8 2 8 32 | | | | | | | |
| 43 | Payroll Taxes Expense | 10 6 6 9 44 | | | | | | | |
| 44 | Rent Expense | 21 0 0 0 00 | | | | | | | |
| 45 | Repairs Expense | 1 3 9 4 80 | | | | | | | |
| 46 | Salary Expense | 104 8 7 8 00 | | | | | | | |
| 47 | Supplies Expense | | | | | | | | |
| 48 | Uncollectible Accounts Exp. | | | | | | | | |
| 49 | Utilities Expense | 7 2 3 6 20 | | | | | | | |
| 50 | Gain on Plant Assets | | 7 4 5 00 | | | | | | |
| 51 | Interest Income | | 4 1 4 00 | | | | | | |
| 52 | Interest Expense | 2 7 5 0 00 | | | | | | | |
| 53 | Loss on Plant Assets | 2 9 0 00 | | | | | | | |
| 54 | Federal Income Tax Expense | 6 0 0 0 00 | | | | | | | |
| 55 | | 899 0 5 0 05 | 899 0 5 0 05 | | | | | | |
| 56 | Net Income after Fed. In. Tax | | | | | | | | |
| 57 | | | | | | | | | |

Total of Income Statement Credit column _____

*Less* total of Income Statement Debit column
before federal income tax _____

*Equals* Net Income before Federal Income Tax _____

| | | Tax Rate | | | Federal Income Tax Amount |
|---|---|---|---|---|---|
| Net Income before Taxes | | 15% | × | = | _____ |
| $50,000.00 | | 25% | × | = | _____ |

**13.**

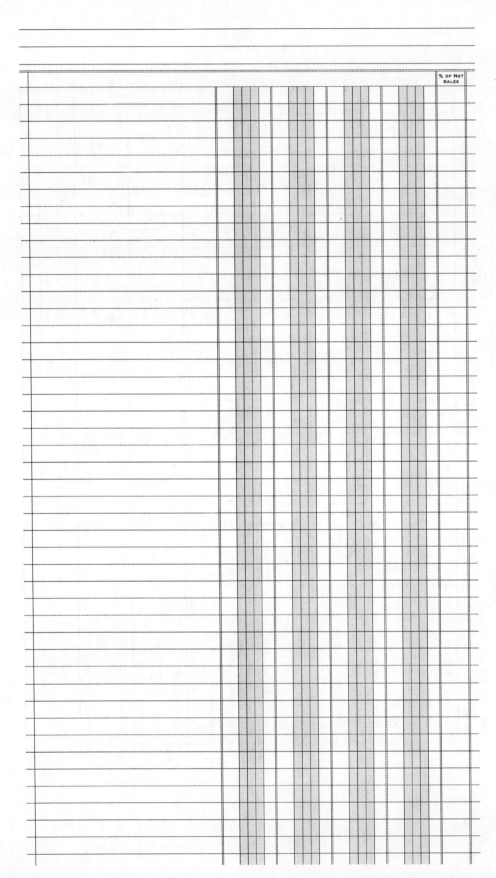

# REINFORCEMENT ACTIVITY 3 PART B (continued)

**14.**

| | Acceptable % | Actual % | Positive Result | | Recommended Action If Needed |
|---|---|---|---|---|---|
| | | | Yes | No | |
| Cost of merchandise sold | Not more than 62.0% | | | | |
| Gross profit on operations | Not less than 38.0% | | | | |
| Total operating expenses | Not more than 28.0% | | | | |
| Income from operations | Not less than 10.0% | | | | |
| Net deductions from other revenue and expenses | Not more than 0.5% | | | | |
| Net income before federal income tax | Not less than 9.5% | | | | |

**15.**

| Net Income after Federal Income Tax | ÷ | Number of Shares Outstanding | = | Earnings per Share |
|---|---|---|---|---|
| $ | ÷ | | = | $ |

| Market Price per Share | ÷ | Earnings per Share | = | Price-Earnings Ratio |
|---|---|---|---|---|
| $ | ÷ | $ | = | |

16.

**REINFORCEMENT ACTIVITY 3 PART B (continued)**

17.

**18.**

GENERAL JOURNAL                                    PAGE 13

| | DATE | ACCOUNT TITLE | DOC. NO. | POST. REF. | DEBIT | CREDIT | |
|---|---|---|---|---|---|---|---|
| 1 | | | | | | | 1 |
| 2 | | | | | | | 2 |
| 3 | | | | | | | 3 |
| 4 | | | | | | | 4 |
| 5 | | | | | | | 5 |
| 6 | | | | | | | 6 |
| 7 | | | | | | | 7 |
| 8 | | | | | | | 8 |
| 9 | | | | | | | 9 |
| 10 | | | | | | | 10 |
| 11 | | | | | | | 11 |
| 12 | | | | | | | 12 |
| 13 | | | | | | | 13 |
| 14 | | | | | | | 14 |
| 15 | | | | | | | 15 |
| 16 | | | | | | | 16 |
| 17 | | | | | | | 17 |
| 18 | | | | | | | 18 |
| 19 | | | | | | | 19 |
| 20 | | | | | | | 20 |
| 21 | | | | | | | 21 |
| 22 | | | | | | | 22 |
| 23 | | | | | | | 23 |
| 24 | | | | | | | 24 |
| 25 | | | | | | | 25 |
| 26 | | | | | | | 26 |
| 27 | | | | | | | 27 |
| 28 | | | | | | | 28 |
| 29 | | | | | | | 29 |
| 30 | | | | | | | 30 |
| 31 | | | | | | | 31 |
| 32 | | | | | | | 32 |
| 33 | | | | | | | 33 |

## REINFORCEMENT ACTIVITY 3 PART B (continued)

**19.**

### GENERAL JOURNAL

| | DATE | ACCOUNT TITLE | DOC. NO. | POST. REF. | DEBIT | CREDIT | |
|---|---|---|---|---|---|---|---|
| 1 | | | | | | | 1 |
| 2 | | | | | | | 2 |
| 3 | | | | | | | 3 |
| 4 | | | | | | | 4 |
| 5 | | | | | | | 5 |
| 6 | | | | | | | 6 |
| 7 | | | | | | | 7 |
| 8 | | | | | | | 8 |
| 9 | | | | | | | 9 |
| 10 | | | | | | | 10 |
| 11 | | | | | | | 11 |
| 12 | | | | | | | 12 |
| 13 | | | | | | | 13 |
| 14 | | | | | | | 14 |
| 15 | | | | | | | 15 |
| 16 | | | | | | | 16 |
| 17 | | | | | | | 17 |
| 18 | | | | | | | 18 |
| 19 | | | | | | | 19 |
| 20 | | | | | | | 20 |
| 21 | | | | | | | 21 |
| 22 | | | | | | | 22 |
| 23 | | | | | | | 23 |
| 24 | | | | | | | 24 |
| 25 | | | | | | | 25 |
| 26 | | | | | | | 26 |
| 27 | | | | | | | 27 |
| 28 | | | | | | | 28 |
| 29 | | | | | | | 29 |
| 30 | | | | | | | 30 |
| 31 | | | | | | | 31 |
| 32 | | | | | | | 32 |
| 33 | | | | | | | 33 |

**20.**

| ACCOUNT TITLE | DEBIT | CREDIT |
|---|---|---|
| | | |
| | | |
| | | |
| | | |
| | | |
| | | |
| | | |
| | | |
| | | |
| | | |
| | | |
| | | |
| | | |
| | | |
| | | |
| | | |
| | | |
| | | |
| | | |
| | | |
| | | |
| | | |
| | | |
| | | |
| | | |

**REINFORCEMENT ACTIVITY 3 PART B (concluded)**

21.

GENERAL JOURNAL

| | DATE | ACCOUNT TITLE | DOC. NO. | POST. REF. | DEBIT | CREDIT | |
|---|---|---|---|---|---|---|---|
| 1 | | | | | | | 1 |
| 2 | | | | | | | 2 |
| 3 | | | | | | | 3 |
| 4 | | | | | | | 4 |
| 5 | | | | | | | 5 |
| 6 | | | | | | | 6 |
| 7 | | | | | | | 7 |
| 8 | | | | | | | 8 |
| 9 | | | | | | | 9 |
| 10 | | | | | | | 10 |
| 11 | | | | | | | 11 |
| 12 | | | | | | | 12 |
| 13 | | | | | | | 13 |
| 14 | | | | | | | 14 |
| 15 | | | | | | | 15 |
| 16 | | | | | | | 16 |
| 17 | | | | | | | 17 |
| 18 | | | | | | | 18 |
| 19 | | | | | | | 19 |
| 20 | | | | | | | 20 |
| 21 | | | | | | | 21 |
| 22 | | | | | | | 22 |
| 23 | | | | | | | 23 |
| 24 | | | | | | | 24 |
| 25 | | | | | | | 25 |
| 26 | | | | | | | 26 |
| 27 | | | | | | | 27 |
| 28 | | | | | | | 28 |
| 29 | | | | | | | 29 |
| 30 | | | | | | | 30 |
| 31 | | | | | | | 31 |
| 32 | | | | | | | 32 |
| 33 | | | | | | | 33 |

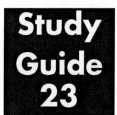

**Study Guide 23**

| Name | Perfect Score | Your Score |
|---|---|---|
| Identifying Accounting Terms | 8 Pts. | |
| Identifying Accounting Concepts and Practices | 12 Pts. | |
| Analyzing Partnership Transactions | 27 Pts. | |
| **Total** | 47 Pts. | |

## Part One—Identifying Accounting Terms

**Directions:** Select the one term in Column I that best fits each definition in Column II. Print the letter identifying your choice in the Answers column.

| Column I | Column II | Answers |
|---|---|---|
| A. distribution of net income statement | 1. A business in which two or more persons combine their assets and skills. (p. 674) | 1. _____ |
| B. owners' equity statement | 2. Each member of a partnership. (p. 674) | 2. _____ |
| C. partner | 3. A written agreement setting forth the conditions under which a partnership is to operate. (p. 675) | 3. _____ |
| D. partnership | 4. A partnership financial statement showing net income or loss distribution to partners. (p. 680) | 4. _____ |
| E. partnership agreement | 5. A financial statement that summarizes the changes in owners' equity during a fiscal period. (p. 682) | 5. _____ |
| F. liquidation of a partnership | 6. The process of paying a partnership's liabilities and distributing remaining assets to the partners. (p. 686) | 6. _____ |
| G. limited liability partnership (LLP) | 7. Cash received from the sale of assets during liquidation of a partnership. (p. 686) | 7. _____ |
| H. realization | 8. A partnership that combines the advantages of the partnership and the corporation, while avoiding their disadvantages. (p. 688) | 8. _____ |

## Part Two—Identifying Accounting Concepts and Practices

**Directions:** Place a *T* for True or an *F* for False in the Answers column to show whether each of the following statements is true or false.

1. In a partnership, it is not necessary to separate reports and financial records of the business from the personal records of the partners. (p. 674)

   1. _____

2. During a fiscal period, partners may take assets out of the partnership in anticipation of the net income for the period. (p. 677)

   2. _____

3. Withdrawals reduce the amount of a business's capital. (p. 677)

   3. _____

4. The drawing accounts have normal credit balances. (p. 677)

   4. _____

5. Withdrawals are normally recorded in separate accounts so that the total amounts are easily determined for each accounting period. (p. 677)

   5. _____

6. A partnership's net income or net loss must be divided equally between the partners. (p. 680)

   6. _____

7. The owners' equity statement enables business owners to determine if owners' equity is increasing or decreasing and what is causing the change. (p. 682)

   7. _____

8. When a partnership goes out of business, any remaining cash is distributed to the partners according to each partner's total equity. (p. 686)

   8. _____

9. Noncash assets cannot be sold for more than the recorded book value. (p. 687)

   9. _____

10. A credit balance in the Loss and Gain on Realization account indicates a gain on realization. (p. 689)

    10. _____

11. The distribution for loss or gain on realization is based on the method of distributing net income or net loss as stated in the partnership agreement. (p. 689)

    11. _____

12. If there is a loss on realization, each partner's capital account is debited for the partner's share of the loss. (p. 689)

    12. _____

Name _____ Date _____ Class _____

## Part Two—Analyzing Partnership Transactions

**Directions:** Analyze each of the following transactions into debit and credit parts. Print the letter identifying your choices in the proper Answers column. Determine in which journal each of the transactions is to be recorded.

G—General Journal   CP—Cash Payments Journal   CR—Cash Receipts Journal

| Account Titles | Transactions | Journal | Answers Debit | Credit |
|---|---|---|---|---|
| **A.** Accounts Payable | **1–2–3.** Partners Katrina Welsh and Bruce Collinson each contribute cash and office equipment to the partnership. (p. 676) | 1. _____ | 2. _____ | 3. _____ |
| **B.** Accumulated Depreciation— Office Equipment | **4–5–6.** Bruce Collinson withdraws cash from the business for personal use. (p. 677) | 4. _____ | 5. _____ | 6. _____ |
| **C.** Bruce Collinson, Capital | **7–8–9.** Katrina Welsh withdraws office equipment for personal use. (p. 678) | 7. _____ | 8. _____ | 9. _____ |
| **D.** Bruce Collinson, Drawing | **10–11–12.** The partnership is liquidated, and the office equipment, costing $32,000 and having a book value of $20,000, is sold for $22,500. (p. 686) | 10. _____ | 11. _____ | 12. _____ |
| **E.** Cash | **13–14–15.** The partnership is liquidated, and the supplies valued at $800 are sold for $650. (p. 687) | 13. _____ | 14. _____ | 15. _____ |
| **F.** Katrina Welsh, Capital | **16–17–18.** The partnership is liquidated, and cash is paid to all creditors for the amounts owed. (p. 688) | 16. _____ | 17. _____ | 18. _____ |
| **G.** Katrina Welsh, Drawing | **19–20–21.** A gain on realization is distributed to the partners. (p. 689) | 19. _____ | 20. _____ | 21. _____ |
| **H.** Loss and Gain on Realization | **22–23–24.** A loss on realization is distributed to the partners. (p. 689) | 22. _____ | 23. _____ | 24. _____ |
| **I.** Office Equipment | **25–26–27.** After liquidation, the remaining cash is distributed to the partners. (p. 689) | 25. _____ | 26. _____ | 27. _____ |
| **J.** Purchases | | | | |
| **K.** Supplies | | | | |

# 23-1 WORK TOGETHER, p. 679

## Journalizing partners' investments and withdrawals

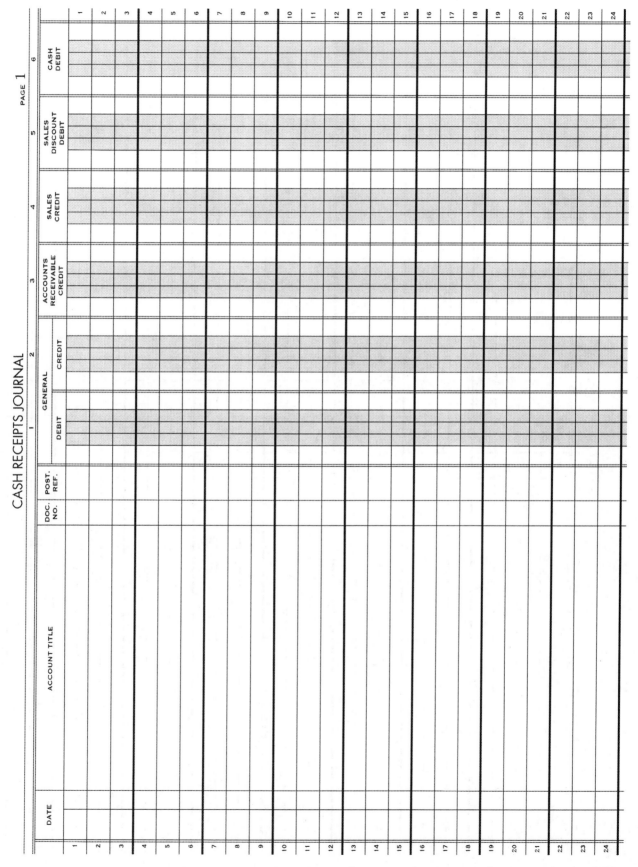

1.

CASH RECEIPTS JOURNAL

PAGE 1

| | | | | | | | GENERAL | | ACCOUNTS RECEIVABLE CREDIT | SALES CREDIT | SALES DISCOUNT DEBIT | CASH DEBIT |
|---|---|---|---|---|---|---|---|---|---|---|---|---|
| DATE | ACCOUNT TITLE | DOC. NO. | POST. REF. | | DEBIT | CREDIT | | 3 | 4 | 5 | 6 |
| | | | | 1 | 2 | | | | | | |

**2.**

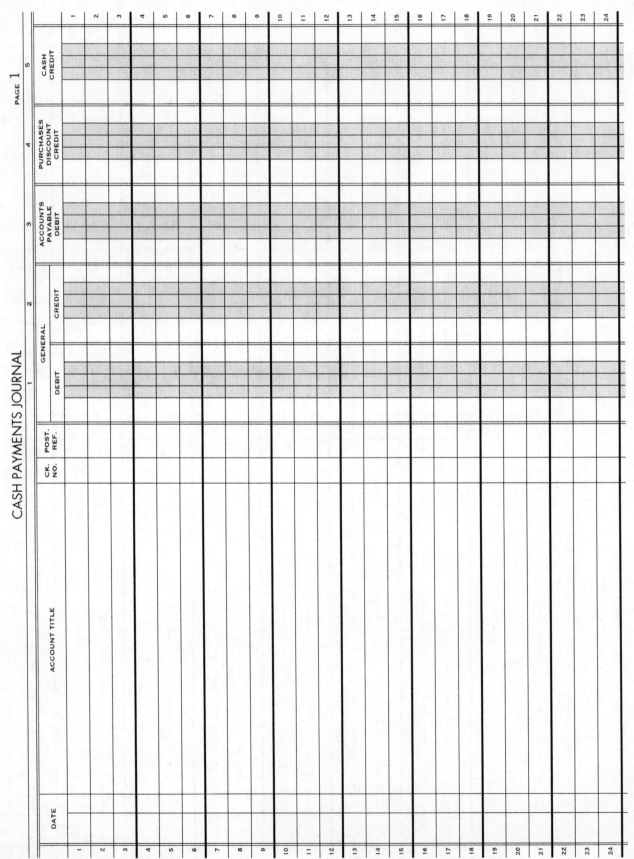

CASH PAYMENTS JOURNAL

PAGE 1

| | DATE | ACCOUNT TITLE | CK. NO. | POST. REF. | GENERAL DEBIT | GENERAL CREDIT | ACCOUNTS PAYABLE DEBIT | PURCHASES DISCOUNT CREDIT | CASH CREDIT | |
|---|---|---|---|---|---|---|---|---|---|---|
| 1 | | | | | | | | | | 1 |
| 2 | | | | | | | | | | 2 |
| 3 | | | | | | | | | | 3 |
| 4 | | | | | | | | | | 4 |
| 5 | | | | | | | | | | 5 |
| 6 | | | | | | | | | | 6 |
| 7 | | | | | | | | | | 7 |
| 8 | | | | | | | | | | 8 |
| 9 | | | | | | | | | | 9 |
| 10 | | | | | | | | | | 10 |
| 11 | | | | | | | | | | 11 |
| 12 | | | | | | | | | | 12 |
| 13 | | | | | | | | | | 13 |
| 14 | | | | | | | | | | 14 |
| 15 | | | | | | | | | | 15 |
| 16 | | | | | | | | | | 16 |
| 17 | | | | | | | | | | 17 |
| 18 | | | | | | | | | | 18 |
| 19 | | | | | | | | | | 19 |
| 20 | | | | | | | | | | 20 |
| 21 | | | | | | | | | | 21 |
| 22 | | | | | | | | | | 22 |
| 23 | | | | | | | | | | 23 |
| 24 | | | | | | | | | | 24 |

## 23-1 WORK TOGETHER (concluded)

**2.**

| | | GENERAL JOURNAL | | | | PAGE 3 | |
|---|---|---|---|---|---|---|---|

| | DATE | ACCOUNT TITLE | DOC. NO. | POST. REF. | DEBIT | CREDIT | |
|---|---|---|---|---|---|---|---|
| 1 | | | | | | | 1 |
| 2 | | | | | | | 2 |
| 3 | | | | | | | 3 |
| 4 | | | | | | | 4 |
| 5 | | | | | | | 5 |
| 6 | | | | | | | 6 |
| 7 | | | | | | | 7 |
| 8 | | | | | | | 8 |
| 9 | | | | | | | 9 |
| 10 | | | | | | | 10 |
| 11 | | | | | | | 11 |
| 12 | | | | | | | 12 |
| 13 | | | | | | | 13 |
| 14 | | | | | | | 14 |
| 15 | | | | | | | 15 |
| 16 | | | | | | | 16 |
| 17 | | | | | | | 17 |
| 18 | | | | | | | 18 |
| 19 | | | | | | | 19 |
| 20 | | | | | | | 20 |
| 21 | | | | | | | 21 |
| 22 | | | | | | | 22 |
| 23 | | | | | | | 23 |
| 24 | | | | | | | 24 |
| 25 | | | | | | | 25 |
| 26 | | | | | | | 26 |
| 27 | | | | | | | 27 |
| 28 | | | | | | | 28 |
| 29 | | | | | | | 29 |
| 30 | | | | | | | 30 |
| 31 | | | | | | | 31 |
| 32 | | | | | | | 32 |
| 33 | | | | | | | 33 |

**Journalizing partners' investments and withdrawals**

1.

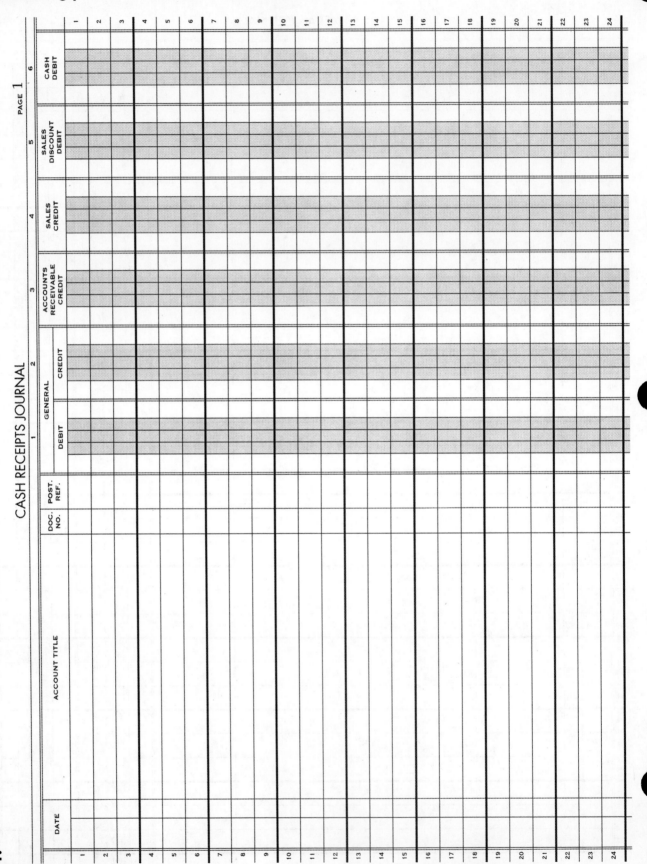

CASH RECEIPTS JOURNAL

PAGE 1

| | | | GENERAL | | ACCOUNTS RECEIVABLE CREDIT | SALES CREDIT | SALES DISCOUNT DEBIT | CASH DEBIT |
|---|---|---|---|---|---|---|---|---|
| DATE | ACCOUNT TITLE | DOC. NO. | POST. REF. | DEBIT | CREDIT | | | | |

**23-1** ON YOUR OWN (continued)

CASH PAYMENTS JOURNAL

PAGE 1

2.

2.

GENERAL JOURNAL

PAGE 9

| | DATE | | ACCOUNT TITLE | DOC. NO. | POST. REF. | DEBIT | CREDIT | |
|---|---|---|---|---|---|---|---|---|
| 1 | | | | | | | | 1 |
| 2 | | | | | | | | 2 |
| 3 | | | | | | | | 3 |
| 4 | | | | | | | | 4 |
| 5 | | | | | | | | 5 |
| 6 | | | | | | | | 6 |
| 7 | | | | | | | | 7 |
| 8 | | | | | | | | 8 |
| 9 | | | | | | | | 9 |
| 10 | | | | | | | | 10 |
| 11 | | | | | | | | 11 |
| 12 | | | | | | | | 12 |
| 13 | | | | | | | | 13 |
| 14 | | | | | | | | 14 |
| 15 | | | | | | | | 15 |
| 16 | | | | | | | | 16 |
| 17 | | | | | | | | 17 |
| 18 | | | | | | | | 18 |
| 19 | | | | | | | | 19 |
| 20 | | | | | | | | 20 |
| 21 | | | | | | | | 21 |
| 22 | | | | | | | | 22 |
| 23 | | | | | | | | 23 |
| 24 | | | | | | | | 24 |
| 25 | | | | | | | | 25 |
| 26 | | | | | | | | 26 |
| 27 | | | | | | | | 27 |
| 28 | | | | | | | | 28 |
| 29 | | | | | | | | 29 |
| 30 | | | | | | | | 30 |
| 31 | | | | | | | | 31 |
| 32 | | | | | | | | 32 |
| 33 | | | | | | | | 33 |

## 23-2 WORK TOGETHER, p. 685

**Preparing distribution of net income and owners' equity statements**

**1.**

| | | |
|---|---|---|
| | | |
| | | |
| | | |
| | | |
| | | |
| | | |
| | | |
| | | |

**2.**

| | | | | |
|---|---|---|---|---|
| | | | | |
| | | | | |
| | | | | |
| | | | | |
| | | | | |
| | | | | |
| | | | | |
| | | | | |
| | | | | |
| | | | | |
| | | | | |

**23-2** ON YOUR OWN, p. 685

**Preparing distribution of net income and owners' equity statements**

**1.**

**2.**

## 23-3 WORK TOGETHER, p. 690

**Liquidation of a partnership**

| | |
|---|---:|
| Cash | $12,500.00 |
| Supplies | 1,250.00 |
| Office Equipment | 15,000.00 |
| Accumulated Depreciation—Office Equipment | 8,250.00 |
| Truck | 25,500.00 |
| Accumulated Depreciation—Truck | 18,300.00 |
| Accounts Payable | 1,250.00 |
| Jason Edson, Capital | 13,450.00 |
| Peggy Karam, Capital | 13,000.00 |

**1.**

### GENERAL JOURNAL

PAGE 4

| | DATE | ACCOUNT TITLE | DOC. NO. | POST. REF. | DEBIT | CREDIT | |
|---|---|---|---|---|---|---|---|
| 1 | | | | | | | 1 |
| 2 | | | | | | | 2 |
| 3 | | | | | | | 3 |
| 4 | | | | | | | 4 |
| 5 | | | | | | | 5 |
| 6 | | | | | | | 6 |
| 7 | | | | | | | 7 |
| 8 | | | | | | | 8 |
| 9 | | | | | | | 9 |
| 10 | | | | | | | 10 |
| 11 | | | | | | | 11 |
| 12 | | | | | | | 12 |
| 13 | | | | | | | 13 |
| 14 | | | | | | | 14 |
| 15 | | | | | | | 15 |
| 16 | | | | | | | 16 |
| 17 | | | | | | | 17 |
| 18 | | | | | | | 18 |
| 19 | | | | | | | 19 |
| 20 | | | | | | | 20 |

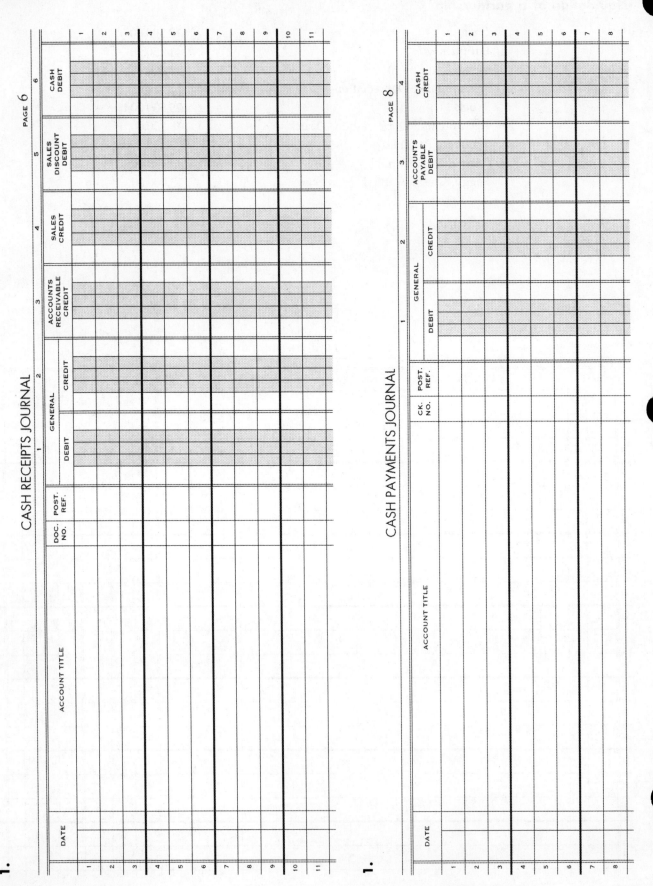

**1.**

CASH RECEIPTS JOURNAL

PAGE 6

| | DATE | ACCOUNT TITLE | DOC. NO. | POST. REF. | GENERAL | | ACCOUNTS RECEIVABLE CREDIT | SALES CREDIT | SALES DISCOUNT DEBIT | CASH DEBIT | |
| --- | --- | --- | --- | --- | --- | --- | --- | --- | --- | --- | --- |
| | | | | | DEBIT | CREDIT | | | | | |
| 1 | | | | | | | | | | | 1 |
| 2 | | | | | | | | | | | 2 |
| 3 | | | | | | | | | | | 3 |
| 4 | | | | | | | | | | | 4 |
| 5 | | | | | | | | | | | 5 |
| 6 | | | | | | | | | | | 6 |
| 7 | | | | | | | | | | | 7 |
| 8 | | | | | | | | | | | 8 |
| 9 | | | | | | | | | | | 9 |
| 10 | | | | | | | | | | | 10 |
| 11 | | | | | | | | | | | 11 |

**1.**

CASH PAYMENTS JOURNAL

PAGE 8

| | DATE | ACCOUNT TITLE | CK. NO. | POST. REF. | GENERAL | | ACCOUNTS PAYABLE DEBIT | CASH CREDIT | |
| --- | --- | --- | --- | --- | --- | --- | --- | --- | --- |
| | | | | | DEBIT | CREDIT | | | |
| 1 | | | | | | | | | 1 |
| 2 | | | | | | | | | 2 |
| 3 | | | | | | | | | 3 |
| 4 | | | | | | | | | 4 |
| 5 | | | | | | | | | 5 |
| 6 | | | | | | | | | 6 |
| 7 | | | | | | | | | 7 |
| 8 | | | | | | | | | 8 |

## 23-3 ON YOUR OWN, p. 690

**Liquidation of a partnership**

| | |
|---|---:|
| Cash | $17,500.00 |
| Supplies | 1,500.00 |
| Office Equipment | 10,000.00 |
| Accumulated Depreciation—Office Equipment | 8,000.00 |
| Truck | 35,000.00 |
| Accumulated Depreciation—Truck | 30,000.00 |
| Accounts Payable | 8,000.00 |
| Daska Madura, Capital | 13,000.00 |
| Lawrence Neary, Capital | 5,000.00 |

**1.**

GENERAL JOURNAL                                          PAGE 5

| | DATE | ACCOUNT TITLE | DOC. NO. | POST. REF. | DEBIT | CREDIT | |
|---|---|---|---|---|---|---|---|
| 1 | | | | | | | 1 |
| 2 | | | | | | | 2 |
| 3 | | | | | | | 3 |
| 4 | | | | | | | 4 |
| 5 | | | | | | | 5 |
| 6 | | | | | | | 6 |
| 7 | | | | | | | 7 |
| 8 | | | | | | | 8 |
| 9 | | | | | | | 9 |
| 10 | | | | | | | 10 |
| 11 | | | | | | | 11 |
| 12 | | | | | | | 12 |
| 13 | | | | | | | 13 |
| 14 | | | | | | | 14 |
| 15 | | | | | | | 15 |
| 16 | | | | | | | 16 |
| 17 | | | | | | | 17 |
| 18 | | | | | | | 18 |
| 19 | | | | | | | 19 |
| 20 | | | | | | | 20 |

**1.**

CASH RECEIPTS JOURNAL

PAGE 8

| | | | | | | 1 GENERAL | | 3 ACCOUNTS RECEIVABLE | 4 SALES | 5 SALES DISCOUNT | 6 CASH |
| DATE | ACCOUNT TITLE | DOC. NO. | POST. REF. | | | DEBIT | CREDIT | CREDIT | CREDIT | DEBIT | DEBIT |
|---|---|---|---|---|---|---|---|---|---|---|---|

**1.**

CASH PAYMENTS JOURNAL

PAGE 10

| | | | | 1 GENERAL | 2 | 3 ACCOUNTS PAYABLE | 4 CASH |
| DATE | ACCOUNT TITLE | CK. NO. | POST. REF. | DEBIT | CREDIT | DEBIT | CREDIT |
|---|---|---|---|---|---|---|---|

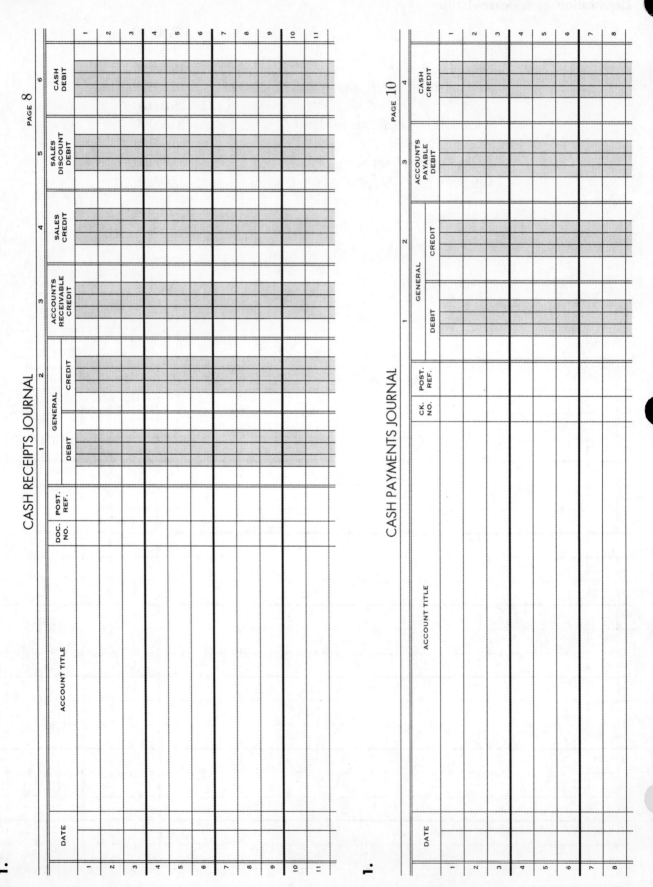

## 23-1 APPLICATION PROBLEM, p. 692

**Journalizing partners' investments and withdrawals**

**1.**

CASH RECEIPTS JOURNAL

PAGE 1

| DATE | ACCOUNT TITLE | DOC. NO. | POST. REF. | GENERAL DEBIT | GENERAL CREDIT | ACCOUNTS RECEIVABLE CREDIT | SALES CREDIT | SALES DISCOUNT DEBIT | CASH DEBIT |
|------|---------------|----------|------------|---------------|----------------|----------------------------|--------------|----------------------|------------|
| | | | | | | | | | |
| | | | | | | | | | |
| | | | | | | | | | |
| | | | | | | | | | |
| | | | | | | | | | |
| | | | | | | | | | |
| | | | | | | | | | |
| | | | | | | | | | |
| | | | | | | | | | |
| | | | | | | | | | |
| | | | | | | | | | |
| | | | | | | | | | |
| | | | | | | | | | |
| | | | | | | | | | |
| | | | | | | | | | |
| | | | | | | | | | |
| | | | | | | | | | |
| | | | | | | | | | |
| | | | | | | | | | |
| | | | | | | | | | |
| | | | | | | | | | |
| | | | | | | | | | |
| | | | | | | | | | |
| | | | | | | | | | |

**2.**

CASH PAYMENTS JOURNAL

PAGE 5

| | DATE | ACCOUNT TITLE | CK. NO. | POST. REF. | GENERAL | | ACCOUNTS PAYABLE DEBIT | PURCHASES DISCOUNT CREDIT | CASH CREDIT | |
|---|---|---|---|---|---|---|---|---|---|---|
| | | | | | DEBIT | CREDIT | | | | |
| 1 | | | | | | | | | | 1 |
| 2 | | | | | | | | | | 2 |
| 3 | | | | | | | | | | 3 |
| 4 | | | | | | | | | | 4 |
| 5 | | | | | | | | | | 5 |
| 6 | | | | | | | | | | 6 |
| 7 | | | | | | | | | | 7 |
| 8 | | | | | | | | | | 8 |
| 9 | | | | | | | | | | 9 |
| 10 | | | | | | | | | | 10 |
| 11 | | | | | | | | | | 11 |
| 12 | | | | | | | | | | 12 |
| 13 | | | | | | | | | | 13 |
| 14 | | | | | | | | | | 14 |
| 15 | | | | | | | | | | 15 |
| 16 | | | | | | | | | | 16 |
| 17 | | | | | | | | | | 17 |
| 18 | | | | | | | | | | 18 |
| 19 | | | | | | | | | | 19 |
| 20 | | | | | | | | | | 20 |
| 21 | | | | | | | | | | 21 |
| 22 | | | | | | | | | | 22 |
| 23 | | | | | | | | | | 23 |
| 24 | | | | | | | | | | 24 |

**23-1** **APPLICATION PROBLEM (concluded)**

**2.**

GENERAL JOURNAL

| | DATE | ACCOUNT TITLE | DOC. NO. | POST. REF. | DEBIT | CREDIT | |
|---|---|---|---|---|---|---|---|
| 1 | | | | | | | 1 |
| 2 | | | | | | | 2 |
| 3 | | | | | | | 3 |
| 4 | | | | | | | 4 |
| 5 | | | | | | | 5 |
| 6 | | | | | | | 6 |
| 7 | | | | | | | 7 |
| 8 | | | | | | | 8 |
| 9 | | | | | | | 9 |
| 10 | | | | | | | 10 |
| 11 | | | | | | | 11 |
| 12 | | | | | | | 12 |
| 13 | | | | | | | 13 |
| 14 | | | | | | | 14 |
| 15 | | | | | | | 15 |
| 16 | | | | | | | 16 |
| 17 | | | | | | | 17 |
| 18 | | | | | | | 18 |
| 19 | | | | | | | 19 |
| 20 | | | | | | | 20 |
| 21 | | | | | | | 21 |
| 22 | | | | | | | 22 |
| 23 | | | | | | | 23 |
| 24 | | | | | | | 24 |
| 25 | | | | | | | 25 |
| 26 | | | | | | | 26 |
| 27 | | | | | | | 27 |
| 28 | | | | | | | 28 |
| 29 | | | | | | | 29 |
| 30 | | | | | | | 30 |
| 31 | | | | | | | 31 |
| 32 | | | | | | | 32 |
| 33 | | | | | | | 33 |

**Preparing distribution of net income and owners' equity statements (net income)**

**1.**

## 23-2 APPLICATION PROBLEM (concluded)

**2.**

**Preparing an owners' equity statement (net loss)**

1.

## 23-4 APPLICATION PROBLEM, p. 693

**Liquidating a partnership**

**1.**

| | GENERAL JOURNAL | | | PAGE 7 | |
|---|---|---|---|---|---|

GENERAL JOURNAL                                                    PAGE 7

| | DATE | ACCOUNT TITLE | DOC. NO. | POST. REF. | DEBIT | CREDIT | |
|---|---|---|---|---|---|---|---|
| 1 | | | | | | | 1 |
| 2 | | | | | | | 2 |
| 3 | | | | | | | 3 |
| 4 | | | | | | | 4 |
| 5 | | | | | | | 5 |
| 6 | | | | | | | 6 |
| 7 | | | | | | | 7 |
| 8 | | | | | | | 8 |
| 9 | | | | | | | 9 |
| 10 | | | | | | | 10 |
| 11 | | | | | | | 11 |
| 12 | | | | | | | 12 |
| 13 | | | | | | | 13 |
| 14 | | | | | | | 14 |
| 15 | | | | | | | 15 |
| 16 | | | | | | | 16 |
| 17 | | | | | | | 17 |
| 18 | | | | | | | 18 |
| 19 | | | | | | | 19 |
| 20 | | | | | | | 20 |
| 21 | | | | | | | 21 |
| 22 | | | | | | | 22 |
| 23 | | | | | | | 23 |
| 24 | | | | | | | 24 |
| 25 | | | | | | | 25 |
| 26 | | | | | | | 26 |
| 27 | | | | | | | 27 |
| 28 | | | | | | | 28 |
| 29 | | | | | | | 29 |
| 30 | | | | | | | 30 |
| 31 | | | | | | | 31 |
| 32 | | | | | | | 32 |

**1.**

CASH RECEIPTS JOURNAL

PAGE 13

| | | | | | GENERAL | | ACCOUNTS RECEIVABLE CREDIT | SALES CREDIT | SALES DISCOUNT DEBIT | CASH DEBIT |
|---|---|---|---|---|---|---|---|---|---|---|
| DATE | ACCOUNT TITLE | DOC. NO. | POST. REF. | | DEBIT | CREDIT | | | | |
| | | | | | 1 | 2 | 3 | 4 | 5 | 6 |

**1.**

CASH PAYMENTS JOURNAL

PAGE 13

| | | | | GENERAL | | ACCOUNTS PAYABLE DEBIT | PURCHASES DISCOUNT CREDIT | CASH CREDIT |
|---|---|---|---|---|---|---|---|---|
| DATE | ACCOUNT TITLE | CK. NO. | POST. REF. | DEBIT | CREDIT | | | |
| | | | | 1 | 2 | 3 | 4 | 5 |

## 23-5    MASTERY PROBLEM, pp. 694, 695

**Recording partners' investments and withdrawals, preparing financial statements, and liquidating a partnership**

**1., 5.**

CASH RECEIPTS JOURNAL

PAGE 13

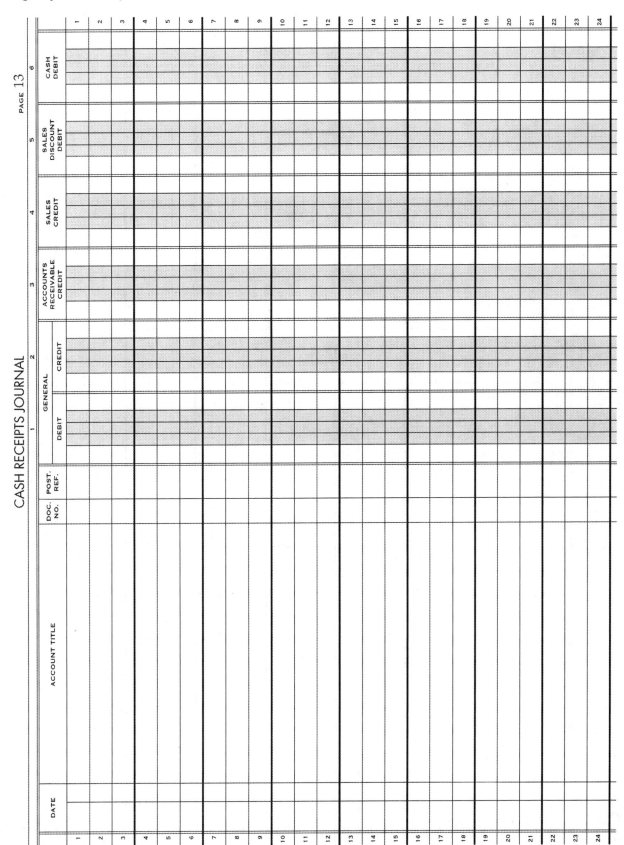

| DATE | ACCOUNT TITLE | DOC. NO. | POST. REF. | GENERAL DEBIT | GENERAL CREDIT | ACCOUNTS RECEIVABLE CREDIT | SALES CREDIT | SALES DISCOUNT DEBIT | CASH DEBIT |
|------|---------------|----------|-----------|---------------|----------------|---------------------------|--------------|---------------------|-----------|
| | | | | | | | | | |

**2., 5.**

CASH PAYMENTS JOURNAL

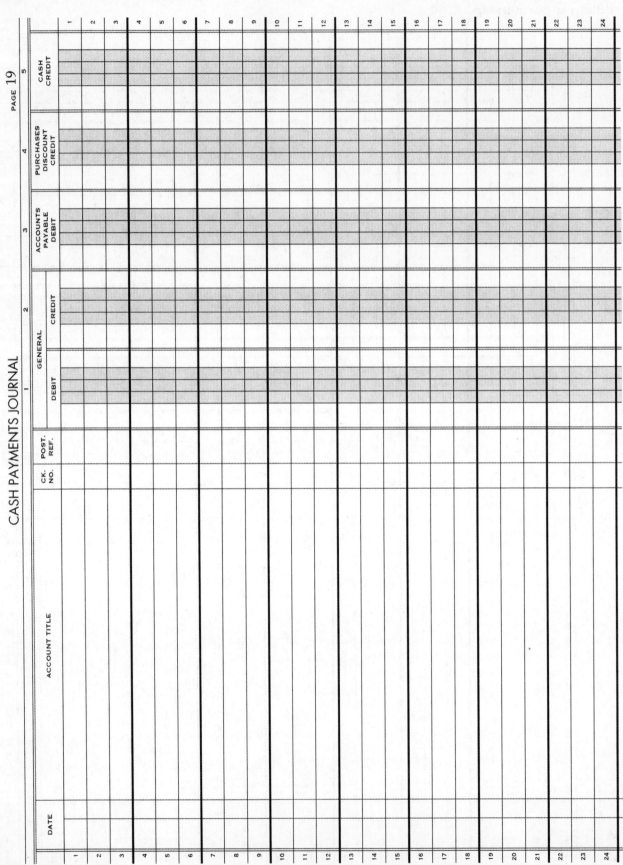

## 23-5 MASTERY PROBLEM (continued)

**2., 5.**

GENERAL JOURNAL

| | DATE | ACCOUNT TITLE | DOC. NO. | POST. REF. | DEBIT | CREDIT | |
|---|---|---|---|---|---|---|---|
| 1 | | | | | | | 1 |
| 2 | | | | | | | 2 |
| 3 | | | | | | | 3 |
| 4 | | | | | | | 4 |
| 5 | | | | | | | 5 |
| 6 | | | | | | | 6 |
| 7 | | | | | | | 7 |
| 8 | | | | | | | 8 |
| 9 | | | | | | | 9 |
| 10 | | | | | | | 10 |
| 11 | | | | | | | 11 |
| 12 | | | | | | | 12 |
| 13 | | | | | | | 13 |
| 14 | | | | | | | 14 |
| 15 | | | | | | | 15 |
| 16 | | | | | | | 16 |
| 17 | | | | | | | 17 |
| 18 | | | | | | | 18 |
| 19 | | | | | | | 19 |
| 20 | | | | | | | 20 |
| 21 | | | | | | | 21 |
| 22 | | | | | | | 22 |
| 23 | | | | | | | 23 |
| 24 | | | | | | | 24 |
| 25 | | | | | | | 25 |
| 26 | | | | | | | 26 |
| 27 | | | | | | | 27 |
| 28 | | | | | | | 28 |
| 29 | | | | | | | 29 |
| 30 | | | | | | | 30 |
| 31 | | | | | | | 31 |
| 32 | | | | | | | 32 |
| 33 | | | | | | | 33 |

3.

**23-5** **MASTERY PROBLEM (concluded)**

**4.**

**Preparing a distribution of net income statement and owners' equity statement (unequal distribution of net loss; additional investment)**

1.

## 23-6 CHALLENGE PROBLEM (concluded)

2.

| Name | Perfect Score | Your Score |
|---|---|---|
| Identifying Accounting Terms | 10 Pts. | |
| Analyzing International and Internet Sales | 10 Pts. | |
| Analyzing Accounts Affected by International and Internet Transactions | 12 Pts. | |
| **Total** | 32 Pts. | |

## Part One—Identifying Accounting Terms

**Directions:** Select the one term in Column I that best fits each definition in Column II. Print the letter identifying your choice in the Answers column.

**Column I**

A. bill of lading

B. commercial invoice

C. contract of sale

D. draft

E. exports

F. imports

G. letter of credit

H. sight draft

I. time draft

J. trade acceptance

**Column II**

1. Goods or services shipped out of a seller's home country to a foreign country. (p. 702)

2. Goods or services bought from a foreign country and brought into a buyer's home country. (p. 702)

3. A document that details all the terms agreed to by seller and buyer for a sales transaction. (p. 703)

4. A letter issued by a bank guaranteeing that a named individual or business will be paid a specified amount provided stated conditions are met. (p. 703)

5. A receipt signed by the authorized agent of a transportation company for merchandise received that also serves as a contract for the delivery of the merchandise. (p. 704)

6. A statement prepared by the seller of merchandise addressed to the buyer showing a detailed listing and description of merchandise sold, including price and terms. (p. 704)

7. A written, signed, and dated order from one party ordering another party, usually a bank, to pay money to a third party. (p. 704)

8. A draft payable on sight when the holder presents it for payment. (p. 704)

9. A draft that is payable at a fixed or determinable future time after it is accepted. (p. 707)

10. A form signed by a buyer at the time of a sale of merchandise in which the buyer promises to pay the seller a specified sum of money, usually at a stated time in the future. (p. 708)

**Answers**

1. _____

2. _____

3. _____

4. _____

5. _____

6. _____

7. _____

8. _____

9. _____

10. _____

## Part Two—Analyzing International and Internet Sales

**Directions:** Place a *T* for True or an *F* for False in the Answers column to show whether each of the following statements is true or false.

**Answers**

1. International sales are just as simple as domestic sales. (p. 702)    1. _____

2. All transactions in the United States are covered by the same universal commercial laws and the same accounting standards. (p. 703)    2. _____

3. The risk of uncollected amounts is increased with international sales. (p. 703)    3. _____

4. A draft is sometimes referred to as a bank exchange. (p. 704)    4. _____

5. Sales taxes are normally paid only on sales to the final consumer. (p. 706)    5. _____

6. A seller generally has much more assurance of receiving payment from a buyer than from a bank. (p. 708)    6. _____

7. Most businesses use trade acceptances in international sales. (p. 708)    7. _____

8. Companies that sell on the Internet must be able to accept credit card sales. (p. 710)    8. _____

9. The terminal summary is used as the source document for Internet sales. (p. 710)    9. _____

10. Credit card sales are not considered to be cash sales. (p. 711)    10. _____

**240** • Working Papers

CENTURY 21 ACCOUNTING, 9TH EDITION

## Part Three—Analyzing Accounts Affected by International and Internet Transactions

**Directions:** Analyze each of the following transactions into debit and credit parts. Print the letter identifying your choices in the proper Answers column. Determine in which journal each of the transactions is to be recorded.

G—General Journal   CP—Cash Payments Journal   CR—Cash Receipts Journal

| Account Titles | Transactions | Journal | Answers Debit | Credit |
|---|---|---|---|---|
| A. Cash | 1–2–3. Recorded an international cash sale. (p. 706) | 1. _____ | 2. _____ | 3. _____ |
| B. Sales | 4–5–6. Received a time draft for an international sale. (p. 707) | 4. _____ | 5. _____ | 6. _____ |
| C. Time Drafts Receivable | 7–8–9. Received cash for the value of a time draft. (p. 708) | 7. _____ | 8. _____ | 9. _____ |
| | 10–11–12. Recorded Internet credit card sales. (p. 711) | 10. _____ | 11. _____ | 12. _____ |

# Preparing for Examinations

Some students seem to make poor grades anytime they take an examination. They say, "Taking an exam has always been impossible for me. I am not able to work well when there is any pressure." What they often actually mean is that they are unprepared for the exam.

Because you will take so many examinations in the future, you should do anything you can to become proficient in taking them. It is just good insurance for your future success.

## Prepare Every Day

The best way to prepare for an exam is to complete every day's assignment on time. If you do, reviewing for an exam will be easy. You can review material the day before an exam, but you cannot make up for a term of neglect.

Find out when your next exam will be and pace your study so that you will have all work completed well before the exam. If there are review questions at the end of the chapters in your text, read them to determine if you know the answers. In this way, you will know if you understand the material.

## Prepare Personally

You should make every effort to be prepared personally for an exam. Getting proper rest before the exam is essential. A student who arrives at the exam room sleepy and tired will not be able to do good work. Do not stay up late the evening before an exam even if you feel you need the time to study. To do well on an exam, you must be well rested and alert.

You should try to keep personal problems from interfering with your study or with your preparation for an exam. If you are concerned about a personal problem, it is difficult to concentrate your efforts on preparing for an exam.

## Necessary Supplies

On the day of the exam, be sure that you have all the necessary supplies. You will likely need pens, pencils, and paper. Sometimes a special exam notebook is required.

It is a very good idea to take a watch with you to the exam so that you will be able to check the time regularly. In this way, you will not spend too much time on one part of the exam and fail to finish the entire exam.

## Be Confident

If you are properly prepared, you can actually look forward to exams. Good preparation will help you to present your ideas and knowledge in the best possible way. Plan for exams and face them with confidence. You will be proud of yourself, and you will very likely make much better grades.

Name _____ Date _____ Class _____

**24-1** **WORK TOGETHER, p. 709**

**Journalizing international sales transactions**

**1., 2.**

CASH RECEIPTS JOURNAL

PAGE 9

| | | | | | GENERAL | | ACCOUNTS RECEIVABLE CREDIT | SALES CREDIT | SALES DISCOUNT DEBIT | CASH DEBIT | |
|---|---|---|---|---|---|---|---|---|---|---|---|
| DATE | ACCOUNT TITLE | DOC. NO. | POST. REF. | DEBIT | CREDIT | | | | | | |
| | | | | | | | | | | | 1 |
| | | | | | | | | | | | 2 |
| | | | | | | | | | | | 3 |
| | | | | | | | | | | | 4 |
| | | | | | | | | | | | 5 |
| | | | | | | | | | | | 6 |
| | | | | | | | | | | | 7 |
| | | | | | | | | | | | 8 |
| | | | | | | | | | | | 9 |
| | | | | | | | | | | | 10 |

**1.**

GENERAL JOURNAL

PAGE 5

| DATE | ACCOUNT TITLE | DOC. NO. | POST. REF. | DEBIT | CREDIT | |
|---|---|---|---|---|---|---|
| | | | | | | 1 |
| | | | | | | 2 |
| | | | | | | 3 |
| | | | | | | 4 |
| | | | | | | 5 |
| | | | | | | 6 |

**Journalizing international sales transactions**

**1., 2.**

CASH RECEIPTS JOURNAL

PAGE 17

| | DATE | ACCOUNT TITLE | DOC. NO. | POST. REF. | GENERAL DEBIT | GENERAL CREDIT | ACCOUNTS RECEIVABLE CREDIT | SALES CREDIT | SALES DISCOUNT DEBIT | CASH DEBIT | |
|---|---|---|---|---|---|---|---|---|---|---|---|
| | | | | | 1 | 2 | 3 | 4 | 5 | 6 | |
| 1 | | | | | | | | | | | 1 |
| 2 | | | | | | | | | | | 2 |
| 3 | | | | | | | | | | | 3 |
| 4 | | | | | | | | | | | 4 |
| 5 | | | | | | | | | | | 5 |
| 6 | | | | | | | | | | | 6 |
| 7 | | | | | | | | | | | 7 |
| 8 | | | | | | | | | | | 8 |
| 9 | | | | | | | | | | | 9 |
| 10 | | | | | | | | | | | 10 |

**1.**

GENERAL JOURNAL

PAGE 9

| | DATE | ACCOUNT TITLE | DOC. NO. | POST. REF. | DEBIT | CREDIT | |
|---|---|---|---|---|---|---|---|
| | | | | | 1 | 2 | |
| 1 | | | | | | | 1 |
| 2 | | | | | | | 2 |
| 3 | | | | | | | 3 |
| 4 | | | | | | | 4 |
| 5 | | | | | | | 5 |
| 6 | | | | | | | 6 |

**24-2 WORK TOGETHER p. 712**

**Journalizing Internet sales transactions**

**1.**

CASH RECEIPTS JOURNAL

| DATE | ACCOUNT TITLE | DOC. NO. | POST. REF. | GENERAL DEBIT | GENERAL CREDIT | ACCOUNTS RECEIVABLE CREDIT | SALES CREDIT | SALES DISCOUNT DEBIT | CASH DEBIT |
|---|---|---|---|---|---|---|---|---|---|
| | | | | | | | | | |

**Journalizing Internet sales transactions**

**1.**

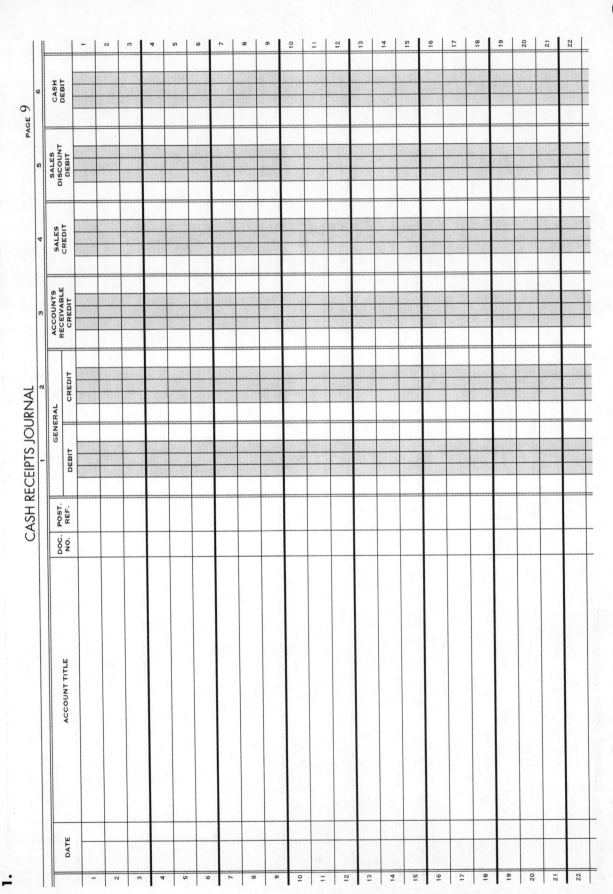

CASH RECEIPTS JOURNAL

PAGE 9

| DATE | ACCOUNT TITLE | DOC. NO. | POST. REF. | GENERAL | | ACCOUNTS RECEIVABLE CREDIT | SALES CREDIT | SALES DISCOUNT DEBIT | CASH DEBIT |
|---|---|---|---|---|---|---|---|---|---|
| | | | | DEBIT | CREDIT | | | | |
| 1 | | | | | | | | | |
| 2 | | | | | | | | | |
| 3 | | | | | | | | | |
| 4 | | | | | | | | | |
| 5 | | | | | | | | | |
| 6 | | | | | | | | | |
| 7 | | | | | | | | | |
| 8 | | | | | | | | | |
| 9 | | | | | | | | | |
| 10 | | | | | | | | | |
| 11 | | | | | | | | | |
| 12 | | | | | | | | | |
| 13 | | | | | | | | | |
| 14 | | | | | | | | | |
| 15 | | | | | | | | | |
| 16 | | | | | | | | | |
| 17 | | | | | | | | | |
| 18 | | | | | | | | | |
| 19 | | | | | | | | | |
| 20 | | | | | | | | | |
| 21 | | | | | | | | | |
| 22 | | | | | | | | | |

**24-1** **APPLICATION PROBLEM, p. 714**

**Journalizing international sales transactions**

**1., 2.**

CASH RECEIPTS JOURNAL

PAGE 10

| | DATE | ACCOUNT TITLE | DOC. NO. | POST. REF. | GENERAL DEBIT | GENERAL CREDIT | ACCOUNTS RECEIVABLE CREDIT | SALES CREDIT | SALES DISCOUNT DEBIT | CASH DEBIT | |
|---|---|---|---|---|---|---|---|---|---|---|---|
| | | | | | 1 | 2 | 3 | 4 | 5 | 6 | |
| 1 | | | | | | | | | | | 1 |
| 2 | | | | | | | | | | | 2 |
| 3 | | | | | | | | | | | 3 |
| 4 | | | | | | | | | | | 4 |
| 5 | | | | | | | | | | | 5 |
| 6 | | | | | | | | | | | 6 |
| 7 | | | | | | | | | | | 7 |
| 8 | | | | | | | | | | | 8 |
| 9 | | | | | | | | | | | 9 |
| 10 | | | | | | | | | | | 10 |
| 11 | | | | | | | | | | | 11 |
| 12 | | | | | | | | | | | 12 |
| 13 | | | | | | | | | | | 13 |
| 14 | | | | | | | | | | | 14 |
| 15 | | | | | | | | | | | 15 |
| 16 | | | | | | | | | | | 16 |
| 17 | | | | | | | | | | | 17 |
| 18 | | | | | | | | | | | 18 |
| 19 | | | | | | | | | | | 19 |
| 20 | | | | | | | | | | | 20 |
| 21 | | | | | | | | | | | 21 |
| 22 | | | | | | | | | | | 22 |

1.

GENERAL JOURNAL

PAGE 6

| | DATE | | ACCOUNT TITLE | DOC. NO. | POST. REF. | DEBIT | CREDIT | |
|---|---|---|---|---|---|---|---|---|
| 1 | | | | | | | | 1 |
| 2 | | | | | | | | 2 |
| 3 | | | | | | | | 3 |
| 4 | | | | | | | | 4 |
| 5 | | | | | | | | 5 |
| 6 | | | | | | | | 6 |
| 7 | | | | | | | | 7 |
| 8 | | | | | | | | 8 |
| 9 | | | | | | | | 9 |
| 10 | | | | | | | | 10 |
| 11 | | | | | | | | 11 |
| 12 | | | | | | | | 12 |
| 13 | | | | | | | | 13 |
| 14 | | | | | | | | 14 |
| 15 | | | | | | | | 15 |
| 16 | | | | | | | | 16 |
| 17 | | | | | | | | 17 |
| 18 | | | | | | | | 18 |
| 19 | | | | | | | | 19 |
| 20 | | | | | | | | 20 |
| 21 | | | | | | | | 21 |
| 22 | | | | | | | | 22 |
| 23 | | | | | | | | 23 |
| 24 | | | | | | | | 24 |
| 25 | | | | | | | | 25 |
| 26 | | | | | | | | 26 |
| 27 | | | | | | | | 27 |
| 28 | | | | | | | | 28 |
| 29 | | | | | | | | 29 |
| 30 | | | | | | | | 30 |
| 31 | | | | | | | | 31 |
| 32 | | | | | | | | 32 |
| 33 | | | | | | | | 33 |

**24-2** APPLICATION PROBLEM, p. 714

**Journalizing Internet sales transactions**

**1., 2.**

CASH RECEIPTS JOURNAL

PAGE 15

| DATE | ACCOUNT TITLE | DOC. NO. | POST. REF. | GENERAL DEBIT | GENERAL CREDIT | ACCOUNTS RECEIVABLE CREDIT | SALES CREDIT | SALES DISCOUNT DEBIT | CASH DEBIT |
|------|---------------|----------|------------|---------------|----------------|----------------------------|--------------|----------------------|------------|
| 1 | | | | | | | | | |
| 2 | | | | | | | | | |
| 3 | | | | | | | | | |
| 4 | | | | | | | | | |
| 5 | | | | | | | | | |
| 6 | | | | | | | | | |
| 7 | | | | | | | | | |
| 8 | | | | | | | | | |
| 9 | | | | | | | | | |
| 10 | | | | | | | | | |
| 11 | | | | | | | | | |
| 12 | | | | | | | | | |
| 13 | | | | | | | | | |
| 14 | | | | | | | | | |
| 15 | | | | | | | | | |
| 16 | | | | | | | | | |
| 17 | | | | | | | | | |
| 18 | | | | | | | | | |
| 19 | | | | | | | | | |
| 20 | | | | | | | | | |
| 21 | | | | | | | | | |
| 22 | | | | | | | | | |

**Recording international and Internet sales**

**1., 2.**

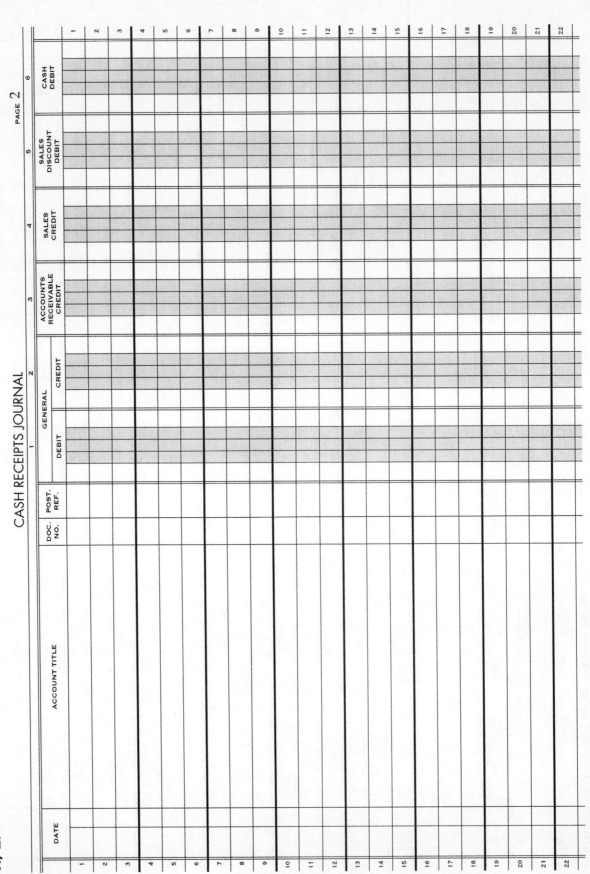

CASH RECEIPTS JOURNAL

PAGE 2

**24-3** **MASTERY PROBLEM (concluded)**

**1.**

GENERAL JOURNAL                                                    PAGE 2

| | DATE | ACCOUNT TITLE | DOC. NO. | POST. REF. | DEBIT | CREDIT | |
|---|---|---|---|---|---|---|---|
| 1 | | | | | | | 1 |
| 2 | | | | | | | 2 |
| 3 | | | | | | | 3 |
| 4 | | | | | | | 4 |
| 5 | | | | | | | 5 |
| 6 | | | | | | | 6 |
| 7 | | | | | | | 7 |
| 8 | | | | | | | 8 |
| 9 | | | | | | | 9 |
| 10 | | | | | | | 10 |
| 11 | | | | | | | 11 |
| 12 | | | | | | | 12 |
| 13 | | | | | | | 13 |
| 14 | | | | | | | 14 |
| 15 | | | | | | | 15 |
| 16 | | | | | | | 16 |
| 17 | | | | | | | 17 |
| 18 | | | | | | | 18 |
| 19 | | | | | | | 19 |
| 20 | | | | | | | 20 |
| 21 | | | | | | | 21 |
| 22 | | | | | | | 22 |
| 23 | | | | | | | 23 |
| 24 | | | | | | | 24 |
| 25 | | | | | | | 25 |
| 26 | | | | | | | 26 |
| 27 | | | | | | | 27 |
| 28 | | | | | | | 28 |
| 29 | | | | | | | 29 |
| 30 | | | | | | | 30 |
| 31 | | | | | | | 31 |
| 32 | | | | | | | 32 |
| 33 | | | | | | | 33 |

**Recording international sales and converting foreign currency**

**1., 2.**

CASH RECEIPTS JOURNAL

PAGE 11

| | | | | | GENERAL | | ACCOUNTS RECEIVABLE CREDIT | SALES CREDIT | SALES DISCOUNT DEBIT | CASH DEBIT |
|---|---|---|---|---|---|---|---|---|---|---|
| DATE | ACCOUNT TITLE | DOC. NO. | POST. REF. | DEBIT | CREDIT | | | | | |
| 1 | | | | | | | | | | 1 |
| 2 | | | | | | | | | | 2 |
| 3 | | | | | | | | | | 3 |
| 4 | | | | | | | | | | 4 |
| 5 | | | | | | | | | | 5 |
| 6 | | | | | | | | | | 6 |
| 7 | | | | | | | | | | 7 |
| 8 | | | | | | | | | | 8 |
| 9 | | | | | | | | | | 9 |
| 10 | | | | | | | | | | 10 |
| 11 | | | | | | | | | | 11 |
| 12 | | | | | | | | | | 12 |

## PRACTICE PROBLEM A-1, p. A-6

**Preparing a statement of cash flows**

# PRACTICE PROBLEM A-2, p. A-6

**Preparing a statement of cash flows**